REVIEW COPY

# *See It Now* Confronts McCarthyism

STUDIES IN RHETORIC AND COMMUNICATION
*General Editors:*
E. Culpepper Clark
Raymie E. McKerrow
David Zarefsky

Thomas Rosteck

# *See It Now* Confronts McCarthyism
Television Documentary and the
Politics of Representation

The University of Alabama Press   Tuscaloosa and London

∞

The paper on which this book is printed meets the minimum requirements of American National Standard for Information Science-Permanence of Paper for Printed Library Materials, ANSI Z39.48-1984.

**Library of Congress Cataloging-in-Publication Data**

Rosteck, Thomas, 1951–
 See it now confronts McCarthyism : television documentary and the politics of representation / Thomas Rosteck.
  p. cm—(Studies in rhetoric and communication)
 Includes bibliographical references and index.
 ISBN 0-8173-0705-2 (alk. paper)
 1. Internal security—United States—History—20th century.
2. See it now (Television program) 3. McCarthy, Joseph, 1908–1957.
4. Documentary television programs—United States. 5. Television broadcasting of news—United States. 6. Subversive activities—United States—History—20th century. 7. Anti-communist movements—United States—History—20th century. I. Title. II. Series.
E743.5.R717 1994
791.45'72—dc20            93-4780

British Library Cataloguing-in-Publication Data available

To Kathleen,
Christopher, and William
  because . . .

"No journalistic age was ever given a weapon for truth with quite the same scope of this fledgling television."
—Edward R. Murrow

"Documentary seeks to inform but, above all, it seeks to influence."
—A. William Bluem

"Some of the complaint about 'the confusion between reality and fiction' is naive or disingenuous. . . . It depends on the convention that 'factual' television simply shows, neutrally, what is happening."
—Raymond Williams

# Contents

# Acknowledgments

Some portions of this book originally appeared, usually in very different form, in periodicals, and some were first presented as lectures. A version of chapter 4 was presented at the 1987 meeting of the Speech Communication Association. Part of the middle section of chapter 5 was delivered as a lecture in the Temple University School of Communication Colloquium series. An abbreviated version of chapter 6 first appeared under the title "Irony, Argument, and Reportage in Television Documentary: *See It Now* versus Senator McCarthy" in the *Quarterly Journal of Speech* 75 (1989): 277–98, copyright by the Speech Communication Association, and reprinted by permission of the publisher. Portions of chapter 4, entitled "Synecdoche and Audience in *See It Now*'s 'Case of Milo Radulovich,'" were published in the *Southern Communication Journal* 57 (1992): 229–40, and are reprinted by permission. I am indebted to the editors of these journals. I also thank Hastings House Publishers for permission to quote from A. William Bluem, *Documentary in American Television* (New York, 1970).

This book began its evolutionary journey in 1987 when, with a different design, it originated as a thesis presented for the doctoral degree at the University of Wisconsin—Madison. Many people have contributed along the way, and some of them deserve special mention. My analyses of these *See It Now* programs would not have been possible without access to the transcripts and to video copies of the original broadcasts. Transcripts of "The Case Against Lt. Milo

Radulovich, October 20, 1953," "An Argument in Indianapolis, November 24, 1953," "Murrow's Report on Senator Joseph R. McCarthy, March 9, 1954," and "Annie Lee Moss Before the McCarthy Committee, March 16, 1954," originally broadcast on the CBS Television Network, are in the Edward R. Murrow Papers, Edwin Ginn Library, Fletcher School of Law and Diplomacy, Tufts University, Medford, Massachusetts, and have been used by permission. These papers have been microfilmed and are available from the Microfilming Corporation of America. I am indebted to Barbara Boyce, the archivist at the Fletcher School, and especially the Murrow estate, for permission to work with the transcripts and to reproduce portions of them here.

My use of the Murrow Papers scripts was supplemented by repeated viewings of video copies of the programs available in the public holdings collection of the Museum of Broadcasting, New York City, New York. Without the unfailing cooperation of the staff there and the facilities available for scholars to access material, my endlessly repeated visits would have been a waste of time. I thank the University of Wisconsin Alumni Research Foundation and the Temple University Summer Fellows Program for grants and fellowships that helped to make the book, in its present configuration, possible.

The contributions of some individuals run throughout these pages in ways to which scholarly citations and footnotes could never do justice: Mike Leff, Vance Kepley, Ed Black, Tom Benson, Herb Simons, Mark Pollock, Anita Pomerantz, Janice Rushing, Tom Frentz, Bob Ivie, Nicole Mitchell at The University of Alabama Press, and Marcia Brubeck. You all contributed in ways you both know and do not know; I thank you. I am grateful to H. and E. J. who always thought it was great when I learned new stuff; to Kathee, Kit, and Will for patience, peace, and a willing suspension of disbelief; and especially to the big brother who asked, expecting an answer, "See *what* now?"

I had hoped to include photographs from the four *See It Now* programs in my book but was unable to do so. The costs of reproducing crucial frames of the filmed programs far, far exceed the funds available in the publishing budget for a purely scholarly book. It is unfortunate that the Columbia Broadcasting System felt unable to waive or reduce its reproduction fees in light of the value that these stills would have had for students of the television documentary.

*See It Now* Confronts McCarthyism

# Introduction

See It Now, Edward R. Murrow and Fred W. Friendly's early documentary television program, has come to be recognized as the exemplar of nonfiction television. One important element in its reputation is a series of four telecasts directly dealing with abuses of McCarthyism and the Red Scare. This book is about those programs, but it is also about the early 1950s in America, the troubled era in which these programs were broadcast. This book is, then, both cultural history and media analysis.

As media analysis, this book seeks to understand the symbolic form, the aesthetic construction, and the subsequent experience that these four programs offered viewers. This sort of critical analysis is a development of recent vintage in American media studies. Whereas a decade ago television and the media were studied largely through an empiricist social scientific paradigm, now humanistic approaches to media discourses engage the interest of scholars in history, rhetoric and communication, political science, anthropology, and American studies. As case study, then, this book bridges classical humanist and contemporary mass media approaches, and as we go, I shall essay the utility of humanistic methods for the understanding and explication of mass media that is primarily visual in nature.

As cultural history, this book seeks to illuminate a unique era in the recent American past. My aim is to understand the programs as articulations of public "common sense" and as artifacts that help convey this common sense. Thus, a second theme of this book will be to locate—through the analysis of public discourse cast in the television documentary form—an American ideology: a set of "templates" that both ground the programs and reveal the cultural assumptions of the historical period.

In addition, from a slightly different historical perspective, our increased understanding of these *See It Now* broadcasts gains us an appreciation of the development of the television industry and the genre of television documentary. Coming at a time when few Americans had television sets, these *See It Now* programs coincided with an exponential increase in television ownership and popularity. As an elaborate defense of free speech for the medium, these documentaries may have helped to establish autonomy and a direction for a nascent broadcasting industry. More specifically, as the paradigm for the television documentary and as the first regularly scheduled documentary series, these *See It Now* programs shaped expectations and set the benchmark to which all nonfiction television, from *Twentieth Century* to *White Paper* to *Sixty Minutes*, has been compared. Thus, a third theme will be the implications of these seminal programs for media institutions and for the genre of television news documentary.

In sum, the multilayered approach of this book seeks evidence from the media artifacts themselves to reveal aesthetic, cultural, ideological, generic, and historical dimensions of these classic television broadcasts. I consider the four *See It Now* McCarthyism programs as institutional, formal, and social texts that expose a crucial era in American political life and materially represent cultural themes and ideological assumptions of that era within the form of the television documentary. It is my contention that the culture of this peculiar era, and a paradigmatic moment of American ideological conflict, may be illuminated by a close analysis of a product of that moment—the television documentary.

## Ideology and Form

In late October 1953, unheralded at the moment of its telecast, the Columbia Broadcasting System's *See It Now* television program aired the story of an obscure Air Force Reserve lieutenant who faced dismissal from the service as a "security risk." As Murrow and *See It Now* told it, "The Case of Milo Radulovich" became a story of "McCarthyism"—a case of "guilt by association." Over the next six months *See It Now* programs focused ever more directly on the fears and attitudes that seized the public mind in the era of Mc-

Carthyism. In short order, *See It Now* followed "The Case of Milo Radulovich" with "An Argument in Indianapolis," then "A Report on Senator McCarthy," and finally, "Annie Lee Moss Before the McCarthy Committee."

These four broadcasts make up a striking set of discourses that have been rather routinely discussed by media historians and critics since the date of their production. Most writers have approached *See It Now* with a mind to consider local historical effect; that is, the impact of the broadcasts on the immediate audience in 1953–1954 or upon Sen. Joseph R. McCarthy himself. Indeed, to some scholars these programs appear actually to have changed the minds of viewers who were neutral or even those favorably disposed toward Senator McCarthy and his tactics.[1] But such questions of direct and immediate effect are paradoxically too simple and too difficult to advance our understanding very far. Too difficult because *See It Now* was neither the first nor the only source of criticism of McCarthyism in those years. Any determination and quantification of such historical "effects" on the audience or the movement becomes difficult to verify because of these multiple messages and because of the impossibility of isolating the message and meaning of these programs from the net of news and public discourse within which they participate.

The question is too simplistic, not because we would disavow the notion of effect altogether, but rather because in its traditional sense, this consideration takes only an amputated sense of "effect." Such tradition ignores the programs' effects on removed audiences, its effects on the producers of the program, on the conventions of television broadcasting or the genre of documentary, even on the long-term effects on culture—what has been called the "ideological effect." These two latter senses—the relationship to convention and to culture—are especially important. On the one hand, these *See It Now* broadcasts define and describe an ideological counterweight to McCarthyism. On the other, they enact cultural values, attitudes, and assumptions in the process of telling the story of that movement.

More seriously, however, I believe that focusing analysis upon the "effect on McCarthyism" perhaps sidesteps more important questions we might ask about these artifacts—questions to which only a critical perspective can afford an answer. The central query here is not, as Todd Gitlin has put it, "What is the impact of these programs?" but rather two prior ones, "What do these programs mean?" and "How do they mean?" For only after thinking through the programs' possible meanings as cultural objects and as signs of cultural interactions between producers and audiences may we begin intelligibly to ask about their "effects."[2] I will try to show how cultural assumptions are relayed through various forms of the *See It Now* documentaries and how the programs register ideological structures and conflicts. I am convinced that the public argument over McCarthyism and its alternative, as it was represented in these *See It Now* programs has special salience in light of what we know today about the interaction of ideology and argument and the power of symbols to elicit social action.

But because the term "ideology" is itself contested, I am obliged, I think, at this stage to clarify my working definitions. In general, ideologies are frameworks of feeling, thinking, and calculation about the world—the ideas that people use to analyze the workings of the social world, their place in it, and their proper courses of action.[3] These frameworks are composed of concepts, myths, or images through which we express the world to ourselves and to one another. Functioning as patterns or models, these frameworks—whether political, religious, philosophical, aesthetic, or scientific systems—provide a template or blueprint for the organization of social processes, much as genetic systems provide a template for the organization of organic processes.[4]

From this perspective, however, ideologies cannot be reduced to their social or cultural moorings. Ideologies are not just a reflection of social settings or psychological predispositions; they are also articulations and producers of meanings. Ideologies attempt to render otherwise incomprehensible social situations meaningful and to construe them in such a way as to make it possible to act purposefully within them. Thus ideology is a symbolic and imaginative "work" that struggles to encompass and explain the exigencies of a specific historical time.

But in explicating this ideological struggle, it is a problem to assume that one might ever "know" ideology or identify its workings: it seems impossible to analyze ideology from a vantage point beyond it. An alternative way to gain perspective on ideology, however, is to study how it is embodied as a set of symbolic strategies within a particular text, and ideology thus considered is materially situated and exemplified in social practice. Viewed in this perspective, communication texts are reflections and embodiments of culture and ideology while at the same time being artifacts that construct and convey this ideology. In part ideology is spoken through the text in the way that the text is structured and in what is taken for granted—what is "naturalized" within it.[5]

One other point seems especially important: because they offer explanation and guidance, these ideological templates come most crucially into play in situations where stress is apparent—where, in other words, the particular kind of information they contain is lacking. Where such institutionalized guides for behavior, thought, or feeling are weak or absent, ideological patterns compete for dominance. As Clifford Geertz has forcefully argued, ideology, in any explicit sense, is marginal in politics as usual. But when accepted opinions and rules of life are questioned, the search for systematic ideological formulations, either to reinforce them or to replace them, flourishes.[6] This struggle for dominance takes place in the public communication texts of the specific historical period. Turning the question the other way round, conflicts over competing ideologies are found in the clash over representations within texts. In short, a conflict over symbols is also a conflict over ideologies.[7]

It seems likely, then, that in examining the public discourse of television news documentary in the pivotal and turbulent era of McCarthyism, we might discover the textual struggle over the meaning and the relevance of competing ideology especially prominent and revealing. Perhaps, in this way, by considering the texts as both embodying ideology and constructing it, we may explicate the "ideological effects" of this set of *See It Now* documentaries and begin to understand what and how these programs "mean."

## Rhetoric and Documentary

My approach to the *See It Now* McCarthy broadcasts reflects, broadly speaking, a rhetorical perspective. These days, the rhetorical approach is understood to be a perspective on communication focused on the art of using symbols. It considers how people use symbols to alter perception, to explain, to change, to reinforce and channel belief, to initiate and maintain action—to foster or to undermine a competing ideology. It has thus come to mean the study of the way that we humans use symbols to confer significance upon the world.

In ancient Athens and Rome, rhetoric had to do with the preparation of the orator and with the theory and practice of public argument. Concentrating upon the invention and arrangement of oral modes of persuasion, rhetoricians were also keenly interested in the way that orators used social truths, that is, the kinds of truths that are created and tested by people in groups, truths that influence social and political decisions. And thus, rhetoricians have been historically concerned with the production of texts, with their aesthetic or stylistic arrangement, and with the social issues that such texts engage.

Such a perspective would seem to fit hand in glove with the

analysis of the documentary form. Since its inception, the documentary form has been acknowledged as suasive in nature, and the appeal of documentary has always been its ability to make us see the world. Documentary puts before us social issues and cultural values, current problems and possible solutions, actual situations and specific ways of representing them. This link between the documentary text and the historical world it represents raises salient questions about interpretations of historical issues, processes, and events. Bill Nichols makes this point succinctly when he compares the status of the documentary as "evidence from" the world with its status as "discourse about" the world. Documentaries, Nichols writes, "offer pleasure and appeal while their own structure remains virtually invisible, their own rhetorical strategies and stylistic choices largely unnoticed."[8]

Given its historical grounding, then, rhetorical analysis has a special potential for adding to our understanding of the documentary form. Rhetorical analysis, as practiced today, more than other critical approaches, has the potential to explicate the technical dimensions of production, the aesthetic dimensions of textuality, and social dimensions of referentiality, context, and ideology in the documentary form without granting to any of those dimensions a necessary determinacy.

Of course, every interpretation begins with assumptions; one of mine is that television documentaries are artful fabrications. Another is that documentary is not reality frozen in the amber of the photographic image but a system that generates meaning from the selection and combination of features on both the visual level and the verbal. Moreover, I have assumed that the documentary's subject matter addresses central social concerns and provides a way of working out political conflict through the medium of a mass communication form.

But aside from its examination of four early 1950s television news documentaries, the present book also sets out to test the ability of rhetorical analysis to address such contemporary visual communication texts. This inquiry entails an experiment of more than passing interest, for in our contemporary mass-media society ever greater importance is given to visually mediated forms of communication, while the critical tools we have for understanding are, at this stage, brand new, fragile, and tentative. In the end, these four case studies are submitted as a proof of sorts that rhetoric, which accounts precisely for the time-bound, linear process of verbal inference, can offer a way to interpret the dynamics of televisual discourses.

The assertion that rhetoric can do so and does is an important affirmation. For television is more than mere entertainment: television communicates something—ideas, attitudes, values, content with implications and consequences for human action. Television is more than a "vast wasteland." It is, instead, the prime form of public discourse of our time, and it exists at the intersection of rhetoric and mass communication.

But rhetoricians, traditional students of public discourse, have spent too much time ignoring television and too little time thinking about it. I believe that principles of rhetoric and methods of rhetorical analysis can aid the growing study of television by contributing a systematic examination of its style and technique, its messages and implicit ideologies. In this way, the discipline may foster not only an increased understanding of one medium of public address but also an abiding appreciation of its own strengths and abilities.

## A Preview

This book has two parts. Chapter 1 develops the historical context for the *See It Now* telecasts dealing with McCarthyism. Our understanding of the programs involves finding the correct context, and I argue that one useful context is the setting of the perceived threat of McCarthyism on the fledgling television industry. The chapter opens with an overview of the era and discusses McCarthyism and the psychological condition of the Decade of Fear. Refocusing slightly, it traces the history of Murrow and *See It Now* with special attention to the development of the television industry. It concludes with consideration of the conflict between the senator and the industry.

In chapter 2, I situate the *See It Now* programs within the genre of the television news documentary form. As a complement to the historical perspective of the first chapter, this generic context helps us to develop the likely expectations of typical viewers of the programs. From these assumptions we can begin to formulate the critical topics that will provide the analytic openings for study. Of special significance, I argue that the television news documentary is a bifurcated form—torn by an inherent tension between fact and argument. The second chapter explores the structure of the television documentary in order to pose the problems of reading and interpretation that motivate one aspect of our investigation.

Chapter 3 makes explicit the connection that I suggest between the forms of the programs and the ideology that sponsors them. I argue that we can best understand these programs by considering the crucial relationship between the verbal and the visual discourses within the texts. When this sort of close analysis is supplemented with what we may know about the genre of the programs, we are in a position to understand the ideological dimension of the programs. Finally, in this chapter, I present a short case analysis of the opening title credit sequence used in all the *See It Now* broadcasts.

The second part of the book consists of four chapters each of which comprises a distinct case study of one of the *See It Now* programs. Although each chapter deals with a specific text, the method of approaching each text remains constant across all studies. Moreover, some concepts developed in the earlier studies and cultured for their interpretive potency are carried over to subsequent chapters, so that the development of the critiques is, in a sense, cumulative. In chapter 4, I analyze "The Case of Milo Radulovich" and address the documentary as a form of representation. Chapter 5 is devoted to "An Argument in Indianapolis," the program that was broadcast only one month after "Radulovich." This *See It Now* program highlights the issue of depiction and suggests how this issue necessarily interacts with the recurring problem of impartiality and bias in the documentary form. In chapter 6, attention focuses on the most famous of the *See It Now* broadcasts, "A Report on Senator McCarthy." There I continue to consider objectivity and argument and ideological opposition to McCarthyism as revealed by the program. Chapter 7 is devoted to "Annie Lee Moss Before the McCarthy Committee," a program broadcast scarcely a week later. In style, "Annie Lee Moss" is quite different from the ones that preceded it and, because it is reminiscent of cinema verité, addresses questions of naturalism in documentary argument as well as the relationship between documentary and fictional forms. This concentration upon rhetorical performance returns us to theory and questions of ideology in the end, and the book concludes with a summary.

# Part I

# 1

# McCarthyism, the Red Scare, and the Television Industry

Count Leo Tolstoy once observed that happy families resemble one another. But of more interest, he said, are troubled families—for they are at once unique and rich with potential revelations about our identity and the basis for our relations with one another.

With a slight twist, Tolstoy's point—that crisis has a way of illuminating basic principles and beliefs—applies equally well to those larger "families," to whole cultures and to social formations. Indeed, in the study of history, "crisis" periods in the life cycle of cultures have special interest. A period of strife, when a social organization is under stress either from within or from outside, has rich potential for revealing social values, cultural assumptions—ideology. The observation of organisms under stress, as novelists and scientists alike seem to understand, can expose hidden assumptions and overlooked beliefs.

One such period of crisis in American society was the ten years following the end of the Second World War. The decade 1945–1955 has come to be known by a cluster of descriptive yet synonymous epithets: the "Decade of Fear," "Nightmare Decade," "Second Red Scare," and so forth. By whatever name, historians and sociologists seem to agree that America clearly faced this decade with diminishing confidence in its own strength and integrity. As Communism expanded worldwide and consolidated its grip on Eastern Europe and the Middle and Far East, as it came to be perceived as monolithic and intent upon the obliteration of the West, American self-assurance, won so dearly through the world war, languished.

The "Red-baiters" or "Red-hunters" of the era sought an explanation for Communism's seeming triumphs by looking within, and their diagnosis—that of an insidious Communist "cancer" destroying the American will, weakening American values, and undoing American power by stealth and subversion—necessarily called for extreme remedies and for radical surgery upon society. Paranoia about the hidden enemy led to distrust, suspicion, accusation, and to the blacklist, to ever stricter bonds upon free expression, free assembly, and free press.

Without doubt, the personification of the era's excesses was the junior senator from Wisconsin, Joseph R. McCarthy. Beginning in 1950 and for the next four years, Senator McCarthy was rarely out of the news. Seen by his supporters as an "indefatigable hunter" of Communist conspiracies and by his enemies as a "totalitarian evil," McCarthy amassed controversial power so great that he even came to challenge the claim to headlines and influence of a president who belonged to his own political party.

McCarthy's ominous presence also had a chilling effect upon the American media. Many times content simply to report the senator's accusations and little inclined to confirm them, the media of the day—newspapers, radio, and the fledgling television industry—contributed to McCarthy's favored tactics the "smear" and the "unsupported rumor."

In this chapter, we shall look at the history and context of the years of McCarthyism. To do so is to begin to locate *See It Now* within its historical, institutional, and generic matrix, as we must to understand the social and material setting of these programs.

## The "Nightmare Decade"

For many Americans, the world had simply gone crazy. As a new decade began in 1950, the American mood was unsettled and uncertain. To perhaps a majority, the situation both at home and abroad seemed grim, forbidding, and sinister. Communism was a threat—an "evil shadow" hanging over the world, an implacable enemy threatening and powerful. Worldwide communism seemed to gain strength after the end of the Second World War and, no longer confined to Soviet Russia, proclaimed its public dedication to the annihilation of Western democracies.

In foreign affairs, the Communists, or "Reds," seemed voracious aggressors. Immediately after the war, to America's dismay, the Soviet Union consolidated its hold on the nations of Eastern Europe, establishing Socialist regimes apparently directed from Moscow.

More disturbing still, nuclear war seemed somehow inevitable after 1949. When the Soviet Union successfully detonated an atomic bomb, and a few years later exploded a hydrogen device, America ceased to be the only nation with the fearsome nuclear weapon. In response, Truman, and later the Eisenhower administration, through the foreign aid program took an increasingly hard line against Communist aggression in Western Europe, in Greece, and in Turkey.

But these actions seemed less important to most Americans than the shocking fall of China to communism. Despite American aid and support in early 1950, the Nationalist Chinese forces of Chiang Kai-shek withdrew to the island of Taiwan, leaving mainland China to the Communist forces of Mao Tse-Tung. Only a few short months later, a public weary of war saw American men again in battle. This time, combat came in support of United Nations forces in Korea—a "police action" against a North Korean Communist invasion of the South. The undeclared war would drag on—influencing the public mood and domestic politics—for three and a half years.

During this era, many Americans sensed danger not only from the outside but also from within. "Spies" were exposed and arrested in many of the Western democracies, with results that fed fears, suspicions, and the perception that America was a beleaguered society under constant "attack" from traitors and turncoats. In England, a prominent scientist confessed that he had passed American atomic information to the Russians, and in the United States, J. Edgar Hoover branded the American Communist party a "fifth column" dedicated to the undermining of democracy. Throughout the postwar years, the House Committee on Un-American Activities made headlines with sensational charges of Communist infiltration—eventually launching a series of well-publicized hearings on subversive activities in the motion picture and entertainment industries.

The shocks continued. In October 1949, eleven leaders of the American Communist party, after a notorious and lengthy trial, were found guilty of conspiring to teach the necessity of overthrowing the American government by force and violence. Then, in January 1950, Alger Hiss, a U.S. diplomat, was found guilty of lying when he denied passing secret government documents to Whittaker Chambers, a former Communist agent. Only a year later, Ethel and Julius Rosenberg were sentenced to death for wartime espionage in a sensational trial. And it came to seem that anyone might be subjected to rumor or innuendo, if not to actual charges. Not even former presidents were exempt, as Harry Truman found when he was forced to defend himself against accusations of harboring and then promoting one Harry Dexter White, supposedly a known Communist, in the inner circles of his administration.

In the decade after the war, it seemed to many in America that "Reds," "fellow travelers," and "sympathizers" sought to undermine American democracy and institutions at every turn. The press and media fueled the national paranoia with stories that trumpeted the exposure, the dismissal, and the trials of suspected Communists. As newspapers featured ever more sensational revelations about Communist infiltration of institutions, about plots and cabals to weaken American resolve, concern mounted. In the presidential election of 1948, and even more in the congressional and state races two years later, both major political parties played upon the public's fear, trading accusations that seemed to "prove" that the opposition "coddled Communists" in government or was "soft" toward the Soviet Union or the Chinese Communists. Distrust became the dominant motivation of the era. As one historian put it: the times were "troubled times; times when traditional American values and rights were sacrificed on the altar of political madness; times when American public life seemed to be dominated by betrayal, bullying, ignorance, and—above all—fear."[1]

On February 9, 1950, with no advance notice, speaking before a dinner of about 250 guests sponsored by the County Women's Republican Club in the city of Wheeling, West Virginia, a heretofore unremarkable senator from Wisconsin waved aloft a sheet of paper. "I have here in my hand," said Joseph R. McCarthy, "a list of 205 people who were known to the Secretary of State as being members of the Communist party and who, nevertheless, are still working and shaping policy in the State Department."[2]

Beginning there and continuing for the next four years, the senator and his varying charges dominated national attention and became the focus of the national "fear." So significant was his presence that McCarthy gave his name to this entire era. Since then, "McCarthyism" has come to signify the complex of postwar attitudes and the dark national mood of the decade.

In an oft-quoted statement, Harry Truman defined McCarthyism as "the corruption of the truth, abandonment of our historical devotion to fair play and of due process of law. It is the use of the Big Lie and the unfounded accusation against any citizen, in the name of Americanism and security. It is the rise to power of a demagogue who lives on untruth; it is the spread of fear and the destruction of faith at every level of our society."[3] But Joseph R. McCarthy neither "caused" the era nor invented its dominant attitudes. Blacklisting, the distrust of anything "liberal," the fear of so-called subversive groups, even the bullying of witnesses before congressional committees, predated Joseph McCarthy's election to public office.[4] Indeed, the ethos of the era seems rather to reflect certain specific traumas of conservative Republican activists of the postwar decade. Central among them were the fear of internal Communist subversion, distrust of anything from Franklin D. Roosevelt's New Deal, and a profound suspicion of centralized government, left-wing intellectuals, and the corrupting influences of a cosmopolitan society. Given these circumstances, it is fair to conclude that Joseph McCarthy was as much shaped by his times and its psychology as he was their author, and after a fashion, Joseph McCarthy came to embody both his times and its fears.[5]

Nevertheless, the senator has a well-deserved notoriety as the era's most ruthless and thorough "anti-Communist." Though the tactics he made famous were shared with other "Communist-hunters" of the time, it was McCarthy who honed them to fine perfection. And in the process, Joseph McCarthy himself became one of the "issues" of McCarthyism. For, in a word, it was the senator who represented, in rarefied form, the essence of his decade—the ideology of McCarthyism.

## McCarthyism and the Media

Within this era of fear, the trajectories of the junior senator from Wisconsin and the so-called McCarthyism movement, of the new-born television industry, and of the *See It Now* television series intersected at several junctions long before the telecast of the *See It Now* programs on McCarthyism. In fact, the long and complex curve of their relationship reveals the pressures and counterpressures of the age. For it is more than coincidence that the early, formative years of the television industry coincided with the purge years at the height of McCarthyism. As the witch-hunt atmosphere grew unabated in the years 1948 through 1954, the fledgling medium was unavoidably shaped by it, and the effects of this era of McCarthyism upon the industry may be traced directly.

Blacklisting in the broadcast industry began with the first appearance of a broadside entitled *Counterattack: The Newsletter of Facts on Communism*. Appearing late in 1947, it was published by three former FBI agents: Theodore C. Kirkpatrick, Kenneth M. Bierly, and John G. Keenan—who called themselves American Business Consultants. The trio assembled back files of the *Daily Worker*, *New Masses*, and other publications, along with the programs of rallies, fund-raising appeals, organization letterheads, and other documents from "subversive" groups. From these sources, they compiled names of those mentioned and listed these people alongside "citations" of their "front" activities. Three years later, the Consultants produced another list, this one focusing only upon the infant broadcasting industry.

*Red Channels: The Report of Communist Influence in Radio and Television* appeared in June 1950. In its preface, the pamphlet claimed that Communists relied on television and radio as their chief transmission "belts" to give pro-Sovietism to the American people. The book assigned "citations" to 151 people in the broadcasting media. The list included some of the most talented and admired people in the industry—mostly writers, directors, and performers.[6]

Although its influence may seem difficult to understand today, *Red Channels* had enormous impact. Once it had been widely distributed, it was used as a reference before anyone was hired by any network, any producer, or any advertising agency for any job, even as a consultant. Scores of artists were denied employment by cautious network executives eager to avoid the semblance of impropriety, which might, they reasoned, invite increased political interference in the new "business" of television. Among the networks, the Columbia Broadcasting System (CBS) was especially zealous in institutionalizing blacklisting and established, in 1950, a sort of loyalty oath, followed in 1951 by the appointment of an executive specializing in security. At the National Broadcasting Corporation (NBC) the legal department assumed similar duties.[7]

But these problems for the broadcasters were exacerbated by Senator McCarthy. From the very beginning of his rise, McCarthy seemed to understand the media and how they worked—and the senator demonstrated a talent for generating and sustaining publicity unmatched by any other politician of his era.[8] McCarthy and his followers were especially dependent upon the press, notably the news organizations outside the District of Columbia and the large eastern cities, to carry their message to the people. Edwin Bayley notes that by the height of McCarthy's power, the senator or his activities were featured in daily coverage, usually on page 1 and often in several stories in a single day, reaching a peak in 1954, when it was not unusual for a paper to carry fifteen to twenty stories a day in which McCarthy was the central figure.[9] A like proportion of McCarthy stories figured in radio and television news.

Because they recognized the advantages of the media in reaching their constituencies, as broadcasting increased in reach and influence, the McCarthyites made sporadic forays into issues of the industry. For instance, there was widespread speculation before Dwight Eisenhower's inauguration that there would be a purge of officials at the Federal Communications Commission (FCC) and that Senator McCarthy might well conduct a probe of its affairs. Anxieties within the industry increased when in May 1952, McCarthy announced, "We have a vast number of communists in the press and radio," and he demanded lists of State Department contracts with radio-TV newsmen.[10] Four months later, he introduced legislation to ban television showing of films written by supporters of "communists and communist fronts."

Beyond threats and posturing, McCarthy was never reluctant to bully the newly licensed stations that operated under the tenuous protection of the "equal time provision." In October 1952, McCarthy threatened to ask the FCC to revoke the license of KING-TV, Seattle, Washington, after he had demanded "time" to rebut a criticism of his activities and after the station refused to broadcast the senator's prepared speech unless he deleted statements that the station's attorneys considered libelous. In 1953, McCarthy pressured the FCC over the assignment of licenses to new stations in his home state of Wisconsin.[11]

As McCarthy made tentative moves against the new industry, rumor, speculation, and suspicion made those inside the business even more wary. Typical of this mood was one especially potent report according to which a "loyal underground" of McCarthy followers in government agencies and in the broadcasting industry were feeding him dossiers with tidbits on anyone who might be one of "them." To many in the industry, rumors of McCarthy's interest in overseeing and controlling the broadcasters were already supported in fact. For example, upon taking office, President Eisenhower had an immediate chance to fill a vacancy on the FCC, and he appointed a McCarthy protégé, John C. Doerfer, to the position. Soon after, when the senator charged that some stations had refused to carry McCarthy campaign speeches (he called this "a communist symptom"), Doerfer set out, under the guise of regulatory investigation, to substantiate this charge.[12] Even more ominously to some, late in 1953 another FCC vacancy was filled by Robert E. Lee, also considered a member of McCarthy's inner circle, and this was taken as a sure sign of the senator's influence over the administration.

At the same time, McCarthy began to turn the powerful new medium of television to his own direct advantage. The senator's first appearance on national television occurred in February 1950, during a Senate investigation of his charges of Communist subversion of the State Department—the same charges that had thrust him into the national spotlight. While the so-called Tydings subcommittee investigation of McCarthy's charges reached no conclusions largely because the senator shifted and reshifted the various charges and names of those involved, exposure on the national medium apparently persuaded the senator that television appeals could move public opinion, and McCarthy soon began appearing with some regularity on television in those days. He would demand "equal time" to answer supposed "attacks" on him, and he was careful to schedule the hearings of his own investigative subcommittee to take advantage of live television coverage. One such milestone in McCarthy's career and use of television occurred in November 1952. On the eve of the presidential election, the senator appeared in a prime-time speech attacking Adlai Stevenson, the Democratic nominee, and claiming that Stevenson had ties to "Red fronts." McCarthy's speech was subsequently denounced by Democrats and disavowed by Republicans. But the Senator won enormous publicity as a result—an outcome that must once and for all have confirmed for the McCarthyites the value of television as a way of reaching the public with their message by going "over the heads" of the established political parties.[13]

Another milestone in the senator's rise and his exploitation of television broadcasting occurred in February 1953. As a more or less direct warning to those in the broadcast industry, McCarthy announced an investigation of the Voice of America for the purpose of eliminating "mismanagement and subversion" in the agency. The charges of subversion were the most interesting and quickly became an argument about how to make propaganda, with McCarthy and his accusatory witnesses taking the position that anything less than complete denunciation of Communists and enthusiastic praise for anti-Communists was subversion. The hearings were carried intermittently on one or another of the networks and quickly became a national sensation, "with McCarthy bullying a series of defiant or cringing bureaucrats, mocking their protestations of innocence and sneering at their declarations of hatred for communism."[14] Even when McCarthy turned to other, still more sensational matters, the Voice of America investigation had a disheartening effect upon industry insiders, who found themselves growing ever more wary of the increasing interest taken by the senator and his followers in the industry's access to the public.

Clearly, the situation for the broadcast industry was a difficult one. On the one hand, as a thoroughly "modern" politician, the senator and his followers had quickly grasped the value of the electronic mass media and sought to take advantage of the "free time" provision, the freeze on FCC licenses, and the scheduling of "live" coverage of hearings to gain publicity and as a means to explain their case to an audience. Such immediate pressure, subtle or otherwise, that McCarthyism exerted was difficult for the broadcasting industry to resist. As Edwin Bayley explains it, the networks were subject to strict government regulation, and executives in the industry reasoned that the McCarthyites had influence among the regulators and regulatory commissions. Moreover, Bayley adds, the tradition of the sponsor system, under which at the time an advertiser was held responsible for the content of programs, further weakened the industry's resolve. Extreme pressure was mounted in many cases by advertisers who were fearful of negative publicity and subsequent market problems should any of their sponsored programs or associated celebrities be "exposed" as suspect.[15]

But more serious than these relatively short-range exploitations of the medium by the McCarthyites is the underlying question of control over the mass communication medium of television. Indeed, the most important facet of McCarthyism's relationship with the media is the longer-range conflict "about" who would control this new television industry.[16] One area of controversy is the relationship of the industry to government institutions, and the appropriate exercise of governmental influence in such communication. This controversy was fought out over a medium thought, in the early years of the 1950s, to possess enormous yet untested persuasive potential. In line with the then prevailing view of mass society, the mass media in general and television in particular were considered capable of directing and forcing men to do things or believe things they were otherwise incapable of doing or believing.[17] For the McCarthyites, this subversive "power" precisely matched the tactics of the Communists, and thus confirmed that the broadcast industry was too influential to be left alone. It is likely that the McCarthyites felt an added desire to see such a potent weapon used not to "brainwash" an unsuspecting public, but rather to "expose" subversives seeking to undermine a patriotic and moral society.[18]

Another controversy in what may be called the argument over control is the more abstract constitutional question of free speech—of the rights and freedoms of a public communication medium to express diversity and a plurality of viewpoints. Because the television networks were new and their policies unformed, because they were considered to use the "public" airwaves as a means of transmission and thus were subject to license application and oversight committees, they lacked the tradition of autonomy and free speech that helped sustain newspapers in seeking to avoid McCarthyism's domination.[19] The new medium found itself pulled simultaneously in two opposite directions: one way was the mandate to offer "equal time" for all sides, the other was to avoid any appearance of endorsing communism or even "liberal" ideas. Caught between openness and suspicion, between secrecy and disclosure, the television industry was born and came of age. It was this matrix of long- and short-range forces that made at this time for a medium tentative in taking on "sensitive" issues, fearful of "controversy," and eager for accommodation with extremists of any stripe. And it is this argument over control that animates *See It Now*'s confrontation with McCarthyism.

## "For the first time in history": *See It Now*

As the McCarthyites' interest in television was intensifying, a new "documentary" program, one that was to shape future perception of the role of news and public affairs television, quietly began. On Sunday afternoon, November 18, 1951, at 3:30 eastern standard time (EST) with little fanfare, CBS introduced *See It Now.* The result of a collaboration between a young producer, Fred W. Friendly, and Edward R. Murrow, the hero of World War II's Battle of Britain and one of the most respected news commentators of the day, *See It Now* evolved from Friendly's original inspiration of covering a variety of different news stories or features over the radio, an idea that was eventually transplanted to the new medium of television. With Murrow before the camera, the first episode opened with simultaneous views of the Golden Gate Bridge in San Francisco and New York's Brooklyn Bridge. As this image appeared, Murrow said: "For the first time in the history of man we are able to look out at both the Atlantic and Pacific coasts of this great country at the same time." And then he continued, "no journalistic age was ever given a weapon for truth with quite the same scope as this fledgling television."[20] The debut was applauded by television critics: *Variety* said of the premiere, "There was careful planning, editing and a maximum flair for showmanship."[21] Soon relocated to Sunday evenings, *See It Now* during its first year comprised various feature news items—some live, some on film.[22]

It is difficult to overstate or to exaggerate the appraisal that media historians give to *See It Now* and to its contribution to the development of television and television documentary coverage. Indeed much of the writing about the series verges on hagiography. In part, the reason was the state of American commercial television programming in the years after World War II and prior to *See It Now.* "Banal, meretricious," "mediocre," and "a vast wasteland" were some of the negative judgments pronounced on the medium in those years.[23] But the judgment of *See It Now* is very different, both in its day and since then. For example, one current survey of American nonfiction television calls it "the prototype of the in-depth quality television documentary."[24] Others have claimed that Murrow and Friendly did nothing less than "create the television documentary . . . prior to *See It Now,* it did not exist in any coherent form"; "[they] invented the TV documentary."[25] Some have argued that the program established the style and the standards for "the 'prestige' documentaries which drew their inspiration from *See It Now*"; and pioneer television producer Fred Freed asserted that "*See It Now* was the real beginning for all network news documentary."[26]

The series innovated with respect to both the way that television news documentary was produced and expectations regarding subject matter. Its production techniques were unique for the time, and *See It Now* was the first to shoot its own film for its own specific purposes rather than use film that had already been shot for the newsreels or the daily news programs or had been taken from archives. And unlike any other documentary of the time, *See It Now* sent its cameras out without a prepared script. According to its producers, the program always filmed with a sound track, never dubbed, never used actors, and never rehearsed an interview.[27]

But more important, *See It Now* was innovative in the way that it handled controversy. In the tense days of McCarthyism, the series was novel for engaging controversial subject matter. In its day, *See It Now* was "the dominant if not the only news documentary series dealing with the sensitive topics and issues."[28] Contemporary historians have said that Murrow and Friendly "endowed TV news with a sense of substance."[29] Perhaps as a result, it is often held up as the most "courageous instance of broadcast journalism during the history of television."[30] *See It Now* seemed able, as Friendly observed later, to "do controversy and get away with it."[31] The program supplied to network television what Friendly called "conviction, controversy, and a point of view."[32]

But the evolution of *See It Now* from the "gimmick" of showing both coasts "at the same time" to a program considered both courageous and innovative occurred during a period of several years on the air. The 1952–1953 season brought not only a change in time for *See It Now* (to Tuesday evenings at 10:30 P.M. EST) but a change in format as well. On the first program of the season, September 22, the entire half hour was devoted to a report on Berlin—the first of a number of shows that season to concentrate on one subject. Thus, from its original plan of handling several stories in the half hour, the program gradually moved to doing only one major story in each show.[33] But even then, in the first years, not many episodes of *See It Now* addressed controversial subjects.[34] On the contrary, most broadcasts were benign, and a typical program of the first seasons might show how a symphony orchestra prepares for a concert or might interview an aerial stunt woman. Murrow and Friendly dealt and quite well (winning various prestigious awards) with a potpourri of topics—including current events, speeches of national significance, disasters, and international happenings.[35] But paradoxically, this too seemed to help build the prestige of the program. Each week it accumulated more respect, not only for its interest and skill, but precisely for its balance and its impartiality.[36] Also, significantly, during its first years, while *See It Now* examined a number of issues, it did not investigate the issues of McCarthyism. Some have reported that it troubled many people that Murrow, a symbol of courage during World War II, should ignore what they considered such a vital and troubling subject.[37]

But one program, presented on November 23, 1952, revealed the direction in which Murrow and Friendly wished to move the television documentary. In this program, *See It Now*'s cameras covered the refusal of a high school in Harrison, New York, to permit the use of its auditorium for a public meeting without a loyalty oath. As part of the "national malaise in microcosm . . . for the first time, *See It Now* took sides, making small pretense at evenhandedness in filming the debate between the two sides."[38] The first foray by Murrow and Friendly into the issues surrounding McCarthyism—the division over the use of the public meeting hall—was a "small picture" of the national debate over the movement.

The paths of Senator McCarthy and the *See It Now* series had first crossed directly when *See It Now* featured the senator in a four-minute segment broadcast in mid-December of 1951, its first month on the air. In format, the segment presaged the later "Report on Senator McCarthy" by presenting a contrasting series of McCarthy public statements. But the telecast received little notice at the time.[39] A few months later, Murrow interviewed McCarthy live on the March 16, 1952, edition. The senator aroused Murrow's ire by ignoring his questions and instead attacking colleagues in the Congress for questioning his actions and his motives.[40]

By the beginning of the 1953–1954 season the *See It Now* team had developed its techniques, approach, and style and began both to treat a wider range of subjects and to cover them in greater depth.[41] Now consistently dealing with only one story in each thirty-minute episode, a typical telecast moved swiftly between filmed segments, Murrow's interviews with involved parties live on the air, and "follow-ups" on previous reports, to the concluding Murrow "tailpieces" that were frequently calls to citizen action or evidence of problems and their causes and possible solutions. Thus *See It Now* began to focus on controversial issues and provocative subjects such as health care and costs, the defense industry, and the relationship between smoking and lung cancer in a way that made the program influential with opinion leaders and helped television in those early years to become an indispensable medium.[42]

It was inevitable, of course, that Murrow and Friendly would eventually address McCarthyism on a telecast of the program. On March 8, 1953, *See It Now* made its third and most direct pass at Senator McCarthy. This broadcast was devoted to McCarthy's questioning of Reed Harris, the director of the Voice of America, during the sensational hearings that the senator was at that time conducting. Presented without interruption, Murrow summed it up, dryly, as "an example of investigatory technique." This footage, shown here in its entirety, would become a portion of the program "A Report on Senator McCarthy" that was broadcast one year later. Finally, in late October 1953, the *See It Now* team took on the question of the political and social phenomenon of McCarthyism directly. They broadcast "The Case of Milo Radulovich," a program that centered on the story of a young lieutenant in the Air Force Reserve. For Murrow and Friendly, "Milo Radulovich" was a story representative of the effects of "McCarthyism" and the question of the blacklist and guilt by association. "The Case of Milo Radulovich" was followed one month later by "An Argument in Indianapolis," which examined the suspicion and fear attendant on anything "controversial." Then, in four months "A Report on Senator McCarthy," which focused on the man at the center of the movement, and finally "Annie Lee Moss Before the McCarthy Committee," a program that scrutinized the typical abuses of the congressional investigations that fueled McCarthyism's most sensational publicity coups. "Annie Lee Moss" followed only one week after "Report." These programs—this direct assault on McCarthyism, including the blacklist, the fear of groups labeled "subversive," the tactics of the senator himself, and the abuse of the congressional investigation—consolidated *See It Now*'s position as one of the most heroic moments in the history of journalism and of television broadcasting.

Certainly, it is significant that Joseph McCarthy's rise to national prominence and *See It Now*'s rising influence coincided with an explosive growth of television in the United States. Where in 1947 only roughly 1 in 100 homes had television receivers, by 1955 nearly 80 in 100 owned at least one receiver.[43] Erik Barnouw has discussed the importance of *See It Now*.

> The sequence of *See It Now* programs on McCarthyism had extraordinary impact. They placed Murrow in the forefront of the documentary film movement; he was hailed as its television pioneer. . . . coming at the same

time as the finest of the anthology programs, the Murrow documentaries helped to make television an indispensable medium. Few people now dared to be without a television set, and few major advertisers dared to be unrepresented on the home screen. . . . Murrow and the others popularized the medium.[44]

The *See It Now* telecasts, we should keep in mind, are situated at the locus of intersecting historical forces. One vector is, as we have seen, the familiar one of the era of the Red Scare with its blacklists, its guilt-by-association, its sensational spy stories. But another equally significant vector, as we have also seen, involves a more specific threat to the freedoms of the new media institutions. Born in the midst of the era of McCarthyism, the television industry was necessarily shaped by the intimidation associated with that era. Thus, in one way, the *See It Now* series on McCarthyism represents a second and parallel context: the television industry moving against the increasing threat of McCarthyism's domination. As is evident from the particular historical circumstances that surround the *See It Now* programs, each in some way responded to the senator's direct or implied threats; each can be understood as a counter or limit to McCarthyism's circumscription of the topic and treatment of current events.

Such a political motive, however, is not unique to the *See It Now* documentary series. As we will see, the documentary genre has long been occupied with social or political subject matter. The history of the form is itself interesting and illuminates *See It Now*'s assumption of the burden of opposing McCarthyism. Moreover, this question of genre and the generic antecedents of *See It Now* constitutes the third and final vector of the situational context and is vital to our developing understanding of the ideological conflict at the heart of *See It Now* versus McCarthyism.

2

# Documentary Television and *See It Now*

During the controversy over the 1971 television documentary "The Selling of the Pentagon," one viewer wrote *Harper's Magazine* to ask: "What is 'documentary'? Is it an honest and reasonably objective report or is it a case for the prosecution?"[1] In asking this question, the viewer framed a central issue in television documentary and one that even today animates much of the discussion about the form. For the word "documentary," as in "documentary television," is both complex and contradictory, having both of the senses suggested in the viewer's letter. Documentary's identity as both a "record" of an experienced world and an "advocate" for a position or an "argument" about the world complicates the task of understanding the documentary form and *See It Now*. In part, "documentary" may have two meanings because, more than most other media forms, it developed as a hybrid. Its progenitors include nonfiction "travelogues," wartime propaganda films, newsreels, and the radio news report. Each in its own way contributed to the development of the meaning of the term "television documentary"; each contributed to the television documentary as it appeared in nascent form in the *See It Now* series on McCarthyism in 1953–1954.

## Documentary as Persuasion

In one sense, "documentary" draws upon the idea of fairness and impartiality. This sense of "documentary" grows from the word "document," and this meaning appears in the dictionary definition of "documentary" as "presenting facts objectively and without editorializing and inserting fictional matter, as in a book, newspaper account or film."[2] Used in this way, "documentary" often appears as "documentary facts" or "documentary evidence" with the sense of "legal documents" and "historical documents." In this meaning, the status of the documentary as *evidence from* the world predominates, and the documentary is thus perceived to "show us situations and events that are recognizably part of a realm of shared experience: the historical world as we know and encounter it, or as we believe others to encounter it."[3]

In its parallel and "shadow" sense, however, documentary is framed as a discourse of advocacy, a constructed case that marshals evidence in support of a predetermined conclusion. In this meaning, the documentary confounds accepted and traditional concepts of objectivity, reportage, and argument. In this "shadow sense," the status of documentary as *discourse about* the world predominates. From this perspective, documentary seemingly hides its intention, and documentaries so conceived are seen to appeal and argue while their own rhetorical structure seeks to remain invisible.[4]

Yet despite this discreet division at the heart of the documentary project, this shadow sense of documentary—documentary as advocate—has been bound up in documentary practice since its earliest days. So, for instance, while the concept of the nonfiction film originally sprang from the French word *documentaire,* which referred to "travel films" in the early part of the century, the suasive potential seemed always to be recognized, if not explicitly acknowledged, by documentary filmmakers. Russian filmmakers of the 1920s, to mention one clear example, used the informational as well as the persuasive dimensions of nonfiction film in support of the Soviet revolution and of social programs in the Soviet Union thereafter.[5]

But the emergence of documentary film as a genre that explicitly acknowledged its rhetorical potential and celebrated its status as discourse about the world is in large part due to the influence of one man, the Scot, John Grierson. While working on an advanced degree in moral philosophy, Grierson was taken by the idea that popular media and film in particular had acquired a leverage over ideas and actions that had once been exercised by church and school.[6] First, as a filmmaker for the Empire Marketing Board, Grierson explored his ideas about the potential of nonfiction film in his own documentaries, *Drifters* (1929) and *Night Mail* (1934). Later, as director of the British General Post Office film unit and then of the National Film Board of Canada, he sponsored and encouraged the work of two generations of documentary makers.[7] But Grierson's writings, which defined and explained the "documentary idea," were without doubt more important for the development of the documentary form.

In a series of provocative essays, Grierson enunciated the first documentary aesthetics—an aesthetics that should be, to Grierson's mind, always in the service of a greater social and political purpose. The essays envisioned a grand promise for the documentary: it could take over where traditional forms of culture and socialization left off and offered nothing less than a means for social education. Nonfiction film could "teach," Grierson said, and most of all, this "teaching" could forge a national identity and unity. The documentary could be a form of "social persuasion," what he called "gear for action and decision."[8] To these ends, Grierson urged the documentarist to move away from the mere accumulation of fact and toward what he termed the "arrangement, the rearrangement, and the reshaping of the natural material of the world" in order to present an "interpretation of the world" to an audience (146). Thus, in advocating the documentary film as a means of civic education and social construction, as providing the impetus for decision and action, as suggesting the structuring of "evidence" into a form "about" the world, Grierson also defined documentary, from its modern origins, as discourse that reconstructs and represents the world, rather than a piece of evidence that reflects it. Quite clearly, in articulating a documentary aesthetics, Grierson also formulated a documentary pragmatics and politics—that is, he described a documentary rhetoric.

The American Pare Lorentz created films illustrating Grierson's conclusion that the nonfiction film could serve the larger interests of a society and could function as a medium leading implicitly or explicitly to social action.[9] As one of the leading filmmakers of the Government Film Unit, Lorentz was charged with giving the American public a firm and sympathetic understanding of Franklin Roosevelt's New Deal and the liberalizing change of these reforms. In his works *The Plow That Broke the Plains* in 1936 and *The River* one year later, Lorentz promoted social action and promised social improvement. These documents were a combination of what one critic has described as "brilliant photography, self-conscious cinema and verbal explanation—both art and social document."[10] In his study of these depression-era social documentaries, William Stott characterized Lorentz's work as clearly and inherently designed for suasive purpose: "To right wrongs, to promote social action, [such] documentary tries to influence its audience's intellect and feelings."[11]

Grierson's sense of the social purpose of the documentary was easily extended and adapted to the presentation of news as well. In line with this purpose, the film newsreel, a staple of movie houses, went through a dramatic transformation. Whereas the newsreel had at first typically covered several discrete events, often of a sensational nature—disasters, floods, train wrecks, fires, and so forth—the format changed radically during the depression. In 1935, Time, Inc., introduced a new concept in screen journalism, a series of short nonfiction films called the *March of Time*. Developed by Louis de Rochemont, the *March of Time* presented more lengthy and in-depth reports than the newsreel. But more significantly, the *March of Time* combined actual news footage with staged scenes featuring actors and recreations of certain events that had taken place when no cameras were present. These innovations had a direct impact on later television documentaries in two distinct ways. First, the *March of Time* contrasted with newsreels and set a precedent in its use of actors to dramatize the scripted, directed, and edited recreated scenes. Blurring the status of documentary as nonfiction, the *March of Time* consciously sought to reveal the "meaning" behind the events, as its producers said, to "use fakery in allegiance to the truth."[12] Second, in its content, the *March of Time* revealed how much attention could be gained by controversy. Setting out to be deliberately provocative, it taught later documentarists how controversial topics could gain and hold an audience.[13]

But Grierson's sense of documentary as social education was perhaps best illustrated by the use of the film medium to support nationalistic goals during the 1930s and 1940s. As prewar tensions rose in Europe, interest in the nonfiction film as a propaganda tool and as an instrument of direct persuasion likewise began to grow. In Nazi Germany, the Ministry of Propaganda began using all communications media for the benefit of the Party. The extent to which documentary could be used to shape and to lead public opinion was epitomized by the work of Leni Reifenstahl (*Triumph of the Will*, 1934), who transmitted to the world the emotional fervor of the hard Nazi core.[14] With the outbreak of the war, America's documentary and fiction filmmakers were brought into service. The most famous, and indeed perhaps the most impressive, of the work flowing from the early years of the war was Frank Capra's *Why We Fight*. This series of seven films defined American war objectives for military and civilian audiences throughout the world. And these films revealed how effective a weapon the documentary film could be, provided that the natural power of the visual image was given a "point of view" or a clear persuasive "intent."[15] These explicitly persuasive wartime documentaries clearly demonstrated the potential of visual argument to change attitudes and to influence subsequent action.

But television documentary as we have come to know it was also directly inspired by national radio, a medium whose own power and influence was likewise discovered in the war years. As the conflict continued, Americans turned increasingly to radio, which soon became the most trusted medium for news. With its "instantaneous" and "on-the-spot" reporting, radio news quickly supplemented the daily newspaper and the newsreel. In large measure, as David Culbert suggests, the nation developed its sense of the war through the moving descriptions furnished by the "news commentator," a combination of reporter and analyst, and a figure unique to radio.[16] But radio also cultivated the documentary tradition. Throughout the war on the nationwide radio networks, programs such as "Report to the Nation" and "Dateline" adopted the earlier traditions and techniques of the *March of Time* and presented informational and inspirational news-feature programs that featured "dramatizations" of current events.[17]

But within radio news, the pull between the two meanings of documentary is reflected in its subsequent history as well. At war's end, the Columbia Broadcasting System's News Division established the first radio documentary unit in 1946. Spurred by the inherent power of actuality reports—what many at the network considered to be radio's peculiar strength—the CBS documentary unit moved away from the dramatic recreations that had been so influential during the war years and focused instead upon actual people speaking in their own voices, recorded in their own locales. One significant and short-lived radio documentary series of this species was CBS's *Hear It Now,* produced by Edward R. Murrow and Fred W. Friendly. Renamed and moved to television in 1951, it became *See It Now.* But the techniques used in most of these CBS programs—the unrehearsed man-on-the-street interviews, the on-the-scene report, the unrehearsed narrative—all became a standard feature in radio of the late 1940s and early 1950s. And indeed, this format for radio documentary seemed to return the documentary idea, full circle, to the world—to the presentation of "facts" about the world.

The documentary thus has two aspects, that of "record" and that of "argument." A history of the broadcast documentary could be written as a story of the tension between these two senses of the "documentary idea." In their dual role as evidence from the world and discourse about the world, propaganda films, newsreels, and radio reports each in turn found a specific manner of giving people some idea of the situation around them. Each in turn negotiated the senses of "documentary" in ways that may be understood in terms of the dialectic of the documentary idea and its shadow theme.

## Modes of Television Documentary

The two meanings of the term "documentary," as evidence or record and as advocate or argument, also reveal themselves in a specific tension within the television documentary, a tension that defines the genre of television news documentary. As we shall see, this also creates a contradiction that challenges the form itself.

It has become commonplace to say that before Murrow and Friendly produced *See It Now*, television news documentary did not exist in any coherent form. These two men created the prototype for a new type of program that explored how techniques of television could present current affairs in an exciting way. As television historian William Bluem has observed, "the approaches developed here were borrowed by all subsequent series of this type, and its influence spread throughout the entire field of 'depth' documentary news reporting. . . . [Murrow and Friendly] found television's form for documentary journalism."[18]

Bluem argues that the television documentary, like its predecessors in film and radio, found its purpose in "the presentation of socially useful information." Sounding distinctly Griersonian, Bluem argues that, for the makers of television documentary, the presentation of such information was designed to lead directly to action. "Documentary communication seeks to initiate a process which culminates in public action by presenting information, and to complete the process by making this presentation persuasive."[19] William Stott agreed and suggested that what he terms the "social documentary" uses tactics designed to make the world "vivid" to its audience while at the same moment to "encourage social improvement."[20]

In spite of this unity of purpose, however, Bluem found when he studied the history of television documentary, that it soon developed a bifurcation of form, and he puts forward an interesting distinction between subgenres of television documentary based on "whether [a subgenre] is controlled in approach and technique by its subject or by its theme."[21] In Bluem's descriptive terminology, the former yields the "television news documentary" and the latter, the "television theme documentary."

Television documentary divides into the "journalistic" . . . and the "poetic." . . . The first allows for the precision and impartiality of description, with emphasis upon the detached and dispassionate in techniques of presentation; the other frees its techniques and approaches to advance the subjective purpose of the poet in his presentation of those universal themes of life and humanity which he senses in the documents themselves. The journalistic is controlled by subject, the poetic by theme.[22]

Part of what Bluem has located in his historical survey of the television documentary is, as we have seen earlier, perhaps a reflection of the dual sense of documentary, and the "bifurcation" he argues for within the genre is part and parcel of the split sense of documentary as report or as argument. For Bluem, this distinction between the journalistic, or news, and the poetic, or theme, documentaries draws upon the divided meaning of the word "documentary," but as will soon be clear, this distinction cannot hold when we turn to an examination of the actual practice of television news documentary.

In Bluem's argument, the theme documentary places control of the interpretive process in the hands of the poet, who seeks the expression of a universal theme and so creates a form in which all elements serve the chosen theme. Typically, the theme documentary is a compilation of preexisting film footage chosen from libraries or film archives. To this edited footage is often added an orchestral score and dramatic narration. These documentary materials are fashioned, Bluem says, in such a way as to move an audience emotionally, using many of the same techniques found in feature-length fiction films.[23] From this perspective, *Victory at Sea*, *The Twentieth Century*, and *The Real West* serve as prototypical examples of the television theme documentary.

### The News Documentary

*See It Now* is Bluem's prototype of the television news documentary—it is a factual, timely report in depth on issues of concern and, as such, differs significantly from the theme documentary. In the news form, control of the interpretive process shifts from the poet to the journalist or reporter, so that standards of news practice take precedence over techniques that aim for poetic effect. Bluem argues that those who work in news documentary "are not so free to engage in flights of imagination, to use emotion-arousing devices." Instead, they are governed by "objectivity."[24] In short, the news documentary seeks first of all to "reconstruct the essential framework of an event," and the maker of the news documentary strives for an "objective" presentation. "In the news documentary," Bluem says, "life must always be in control of art" (91).

Bluem identifies some of the characteristics that define the genre and that will become important for a consideration of the documentary programs on McCarthyism. First of all, the news documentary has a characteristic subject matter that usually deals with current and contemporary crises of national or international import—sometimes of a controversial nature. Because this often involves "issues" in the public domain, the news documentary typically entails a social or political emphasis.

Moreover, news documentary, since it is controlled by its subject, often highlights verbal content. Although it uses the camera to reveal events and situations, for Bluem, the television news documentary uses "word logic" (123). By this comment, Bluem seems to suggest that the patterns of reasoning and association in the news documentary remain propositional and sequential, much as in print journalism, which relies upon the written word. Pictures, when they are used, merely illustrate the verbal argument. This word logic may heighten the presence of the "reporter" in the typical news documentary, which typically features a correspondent/narrator who addresses the audience directly.

Finally, Bluem observes that the television documentary often relies on "a relentless reduction of issues" to antithetical positions. Usually, he says, the television documentary presents only two opposing viewpoints on an issue.[25] This dialectic is then used to dramatize conflicting positions.

In sum, historically, we may be warranted in concluding that the television news documentary adheres to Bluem's distinctions. Also, we may infer that audiences for *See It Now,* while having a more local response to the documentary, in all likelihood approached the programs with a set of expectations that broadly resembled those described by Bluem. Conditioned by television news broadcasts of the time, by the movie newsreel (especially *March of Time*), by radio news with its prominent news commentator or analyst, and by previous *See It Now* episodes, audiences may well have expected *See It Now* to be a program guided by journalistic practice and by standards of "objectivity" rather than "poetic" or "thematic" ends. As news documentary, in other words, *See It Now* promises an "objective" view of a situation or event, and the program is built around "facts" that are appended to some kind of news lead, however controversial. Like other television news documentaries, it seeks to create in its audience the belief that it relies upon information or "fact" taken as the "way things are" and therefore is immune to question. In short, *See It Now* expects its viewers to assume that what they are indeed seeing is mere evidence from the world.

There is thus a paradox at the heart of the genre of television news documentary. As is clear, historically, the documentary genre in both its film and its television incarnations, has always been thought to have an essentially persuasive function—it has always consistently, even if covertly, maintained its status as discourse about the world, discourse that is, in the end, suasive. Moreover, this advocacy is invested with an intentional purpose: it asks its audience to feel, to ponder, and finally to take action and meet a need.

Yet, as Bluem describes the form's traditional double meaning, the genre of television news documentary is distinguished by its subject orientation. In contrast to the theme documentary, it is, in Bluem's view, controlled by journalistic "objectivity" and is characterized by "fairness" or "nonbias." So the form claims to be a transparent rendering of actuality, of "facts" that are verifiable in the world.

What may we make of this contradiction? One answer may be found in the "documentary idea," the phrase borrowed from John Grierson. This is the notion that the essence of documentary is the way in which "facts" or "documents" of life gain a meaningful significance.

> . . . the documentary idea is founded upon the conviction that the events and circumstances which shape life must not only be recorded and reported, but that such reporting must be made in as compelling a fashion as possible. The function of documentary communication is to make drama from life . . . , to make observation a little richer than it was by the creative interpretation of actuality.[26]

While this idea is not one that ends with Grierson, a review of its development within the history of television documentary suggests that, historically at least, the television documentary as a genre rests in "a gray area between art and journalism"[27] between "objectivity" on one side and "the larger truth" on the other.

This insight suggests a point of entry for our understanding of *See It Now:* programs that are both constructed artifacts and discourses that promote themselves as transparent referents to actuality; artifacts that are simultaneously records of the world beyond and arguments about that world. Next let us consider the way in which the programs "creatively shape reality"—that is, the way in which they use tactics and techniques drawn from other, even imaginative or fictional, discursive genres and apply these to achieve the presumed nonfictional "objectivity" of the news report.

# 3

# *See It Now,* Documentary Persuasion, and Rhetorical Analysis

Television news documentary, as we have seen, seeks to focus public attention on matters of concern made to seem vivid and pressing. In so doing, however, it is bound by journalistic constraints of objectivity and reportage. As a rhetorical construction, the form must use discursive strategies to move between and to reconcile these potentially antithetical ends and means. The tension inherent in the documentary form is plainly evident in the *See It Now* series. But before I describe the interrelationship of the programs' form with various social and ideological beliefs, however, I must acknowledge the assumptions that undergird my critical perspective.

The choice of a critical focus is a significant problem facing students of the communication media. This problem has been articulated recently in the literature of culture studies. The debate revolves, at least partially, around the question of the relationship between the constituents of the communication process—producers, texts, and audiences. Writing in 1990, David Morley and Roger Silverstone relate these three primary constituents by tracing the historical arc of the British culture studies movement.[1]

Initially, Morley and Silverstone argue, scholars working within assumptions of *auteur* criticism drawn from film theory were most interested in the producer of communication texts. Such studies took the intentions of the makers of such texts as uncomplicated statements of purpose and typically sought evidence in the programs for this intent or for this "preferred reading" (to use the terms of the original debate). In this stage, intentions were typically "read off" the texts themselves. In the second stage of development, partly in reaction to the prevailing producer emphasis, critics focused ever more closely upon texts themselves, seeking to locate ideological assumptions—marginalized and therefore problematic—within the dynamics of textual action. This view challenged the apparent surface meanings of messages with the aim of determining how ideologies and audiences (as "subjects") are constituted by the formal structures and/or "absences" of the text. A contemporary and final stage in the evolution of cultural studies has located its point of critical interest in the audiences of mass media texts. In some approaches, qualitative audience studies and ethnographic methods have taken the place of critical analysis altogether, but in all cases, the emphasis seems to be, in this third stage, upon the multiplicity of audiences within their historical, material circumstances and the multiplicity of meanings ("readings") that may be constructed by these active audiences from any single communication text. And yet, following their useful conceptualization of the relatively short history of culture studies, Morley and Silverstone lament the problems that these a priori and seemingly exclusionary decisions—producer or text or audience—force upon the analysis of media artifacts. These decisions result in critical analyses that often cannot "speak" to one another because they look at the various constituents of the text more or less in isolation from one another. In addition, and far worse, they produce analyses that neglect or "overlook" as much as they uncover about the workings of these objects. As corrective, Morley and Silverstone suggest a model of the communication process that "insists on an inquiry into the dynamics of production, textuality, and response without the need to grant . . . any one of the dimensions a necessary determinacy."[2]

I contend that rhetorical criticism provides just that "perception." In its present form, rhetorical criticism has been concerned with the political roots and implications of communication, with its social and historical context, with its persuasive powers, and with the societal values that communication is attempting to tap. Thus, rhetorical criticism balances attention to rhetor, to text, and to auditor, all the while recognizing that each is a necessary component of the rhetorical transaction. Furthermore, rhetoricians have long understood that "rhetoric" thus considered refers not only to strategies of textual presentation—techniques of symbolization—but also to the relationship between that text, its audience, and its historical context. This chapter, then, considers some ways of studying the *See It Now* documentary programs that will answer Morley and Silverstone's call for a more flexible and agile critique of communication transactions.

# The Promise of Rhetorical Criticism

In general, it seems that there are two broad means of arriving at an analytic perspective. One may either idealistically conceive of the art of rhetoric or persuasion and use that conception, modified and amended as necessary, to illuminate the texts, or one may descriptively derive certain emphases and critical topics used by other critics who interpret modern mediated and visual forms of public discourse. The first course would necessarily involve a certain selection of more or less theoretical decisions and a top-down set of determinations of what the critic should examine. For precisely these reasons, it is subject to the critical problems that Morley and Silverstone uncovered in their review of the culture studies project. The second course, however, "borrows" critical terms and perspectives from existing critiques and uses them not in the sense of a predictive set of topics but to explain the text under consideration. I will pursue this second course.

The work of Thomas W. Benson, taken as a whole, is a consistent and often brilliant set of critiques that illustrates by example one way in which rhetorical critics have analyzed documentary texts.[3] Concerned almost exclusively with the film documentaries of Frederick Wiseman, Benson redirects notions of "audience" and refocuses critical attention more upon the documentary construction itself than upon its subject matter or upon the "objectivity" or the "truth" of what is depicted. Furthermore, Benson accords to the visual plane a primary rather than secondary role in the text and goes on to argue that because of its essentially visual character, the documentary cannot be reduced to a series of propositions in the manner of traditional verbal, sequential, and "rational" argument.[4]

Benson's approach is illustrated in his case study and explication (coauthored with Martin Medhurst) of an archetypal 1930s social documentary, Steiner and Van Dyke's *The City*.[5] Benson emphasizes the image and considers the text as primarily visual rather than verbal. The critics draw upon film theory to explain how the rhythm of editing functions formally and rhetorically to create cinematic knowledge, and they suggest that these "stylistic identifications" invite an audience response. More specifically, Benson and Medhurst argue that a viewer's experience of film may in some way depend upon the interaction of the film's metrical and rhythmic construction with the referential aspects of its images. Hence, the viewer constructs the meaning of an image in the film not only from the "content" of the shot but also from the structural relations of shots to one another, to other dimensions of the film, and to the rhythm of the editing.[6] They argue that part of film's persuasive potency results from the "poetic expectation" it creates in the juxtaposition of shot composition and length. And they reason that as the viewer experiences the form, the viewer is invited to partake of the attitude inherent in the form and is prompted to transfer that sensibility to a historically material situation.[7]

Significantly, in his approach, Benson refocuses the problematic question of "effects." Instead of searching for evidence of the text's effects in history or other secondary texts, Benson studies the documentary text itself and tries to determine what an auditor is "induced" to believe on the basis of the symbolic structure of the film. For instance, Benson defines his study of Wiseman's film *High School* as "an inquiry into the states of thought and feeling an audience is invited to experience."[8] He then searches for the probable reactions of "an audience" and suggests that the documentary offers a "symbolic inducement" for audience response.[9] To Benson's mind, the symbolic structures of the film text engage the symbolic operations of the auditor's cognitive processes, and as a result, meanings in Wiseman's documentaries exceed their literal statement. Thus Benson is an example of a critic who attempts to deal with the question of "effects" by asking not what the audience does as a result of the discourse but rather what the audience is "invited" to do.

In developing his approach to the verité film documentary from a textual frame, Thomas Benson anticipates an approach to the news documentary.[10] From the work of Benson and his collaborators, we can derive three focal points for use in analysis of the *See It Now* television documentary. These are: (1) we may fruitfully apply the strategies of close textual analysis; (2) the audience is an active participant in making meaning from the documentary text; (3) the text permits us to identify the implied rhetor and the ideal audience. Let us consider each of these points.

## A Method for Study

In broad terms I will approach each of the four *See It Now* documentary texts through a close textual criticism governed by a shot-by-shot or sequence-by-sequence analysis. The approach will be descriptive and analytical rather than statistical or predictive. Because textual criticism, in refocusing critical attention upon rhetorical structure and texture, represents a radical shift in critical practice with respect to television documentary, it necessitates some methodological explanation.

## Textual Criticism

Textual criticism draws upon a rhetorical tradition extending back to the ancient teachers of oratory that resists any attempt to consider theory apart from practice. Concerned less with forms of argument and devices of style than with the rhetorical principles embodied in a particular case, this tradition assumes the inseparability of rhetorical performance from the particular circumstances that prompt its creation.[11] Textual analysis argues that rhetorical discourses are local phenomena and so are intimately bound within the circumstances of the individual case. As a result, textual criticism draws on the tradition in rhetoric that treats rhetorical precepts, indeed the whole body of rhetorical theory, as best studied through particular cases. This tradition necessarily emphasizes the connection of text and context, for texts can be read and understood only through the radical particularity of specific historical situation.

However, despite this weighting of the situational, critical attention focuses most tightly upon the text itself. And the critic begins with a rigorous "reading" and "rereading" of the text.[12] What attracts and sustains attention is the movement of idea and form across the discourse. Locating the significant features of the text, the critic seeks to account for the dynamics and transformation of these features as the discourse unfolds in time. The critic seeks an interpretation that both justifies the identification of significant features within the text and adjusts the interactions among these features.[13] Of course in the process of reading and interpretation, certain methodological assumptions are useful for the textual critic as ways to establish the dynamics of response, producer, and context within the confines of textuality. They include the active audience, the implied source, and the ideal viewer.

## The Active Audience

Textual reading begins with a recognition and celebration of the text as "read"—as "a sequenced experience." That is, interpretation of these programs will primarily view the text through its potential for interaction with its audience. Specifically, taking the perspective of the audience, *See It Now* is a temporal "experience" that unfolds in time and is not an "object." The text becomes an ongoing process in which particulars are made and rendered consequential by means of their structured interrelationship. Of course, this statement assumes the active engagement of an audience with a television text, a statement that, coincidentally, has been central to the development of humanistic studies of television.[14]

Because from an audience perspective, the text is an "experience" or an action—a developing rhetorical structure—rather than a static object, a part of the meaning of the text is found in the experiencing of it. Each element prepares its audience for the next; each sequence is conditioned by the sequence that preceded it. Moreover, a significant portion of the suasive potential of the *See It Now* text is found in the sequential pattern of formal structures that the text presents. Sometimes, as will become clear, the audience is prompted to react on the basis of this formal charge.

Furthermore, the meaning an audience is invited to attribute to the *See It Now* documentary is an interaction of features in the text and cognitive operations within the audience. The experience of *See It Now* is sequential, and we may say that, in a sense, the auditor is "trapped" by the visual documentary text.[15] The auditor strives to construct a coherent sense from the text, selecting and organizing its elements into consistent wholes.[16] That is, *See It Now*'s audience must reconstruct the work so as to render it internally consistent. And "the 'openness' of the work (the potential of readings it permits) is something to be gradually eliminated, as the auditor comes to construct a working hypothesis which can account for and render mutually coherent the greatest number of the text's elements."[17]

Such a redefinition of the experience of the *See It Now* text justifies a shift in critical approach. Like an auditor, the critic should begin assessment of the programs by reading, describing, and accounting for the texts, detail by detail, in a sequential mode. Such a conscious method of critical observation recognizes the dynamics of the text and focuses on the temporal aspect of the interaction of text and auditor as word and image succeed one another. In other words, this approach will be to read in "slow motion" to describe the cognitive acts that the reader is invited to undergo, and the critic's initial objective will be the description of a process by which the text invites its auditors' reactions. The critical act, then, becomes an act of recreation, of attempting to construct in slow motion what an auditor is invited to make of the text, and critical practice moves in tandem with the interpretive action of the auditor. Both, in the end, produce a hypothesis that accounts for the interaction of features in the *See It Now* program.

Without a doubt, this practice advocates a subjective process. To locate the action of a text and to describe what the rhetorical action does, in the last analysis, is to analyze the critic.[18] On the one hand, this is a recognition of the subjective nature of the audience experience and, likewise, of the critical experience. Still, a reading that describes response to the experience of the text is valid in part because responses to the *See It Now* texts are "generalizable," especially if the critic makes the conscious attempt to incorporate other possible responses and to repress what is personal and idiosyncratic. Yet, that being said, it must be noted that the interpretation reached is not wholly "subjective." Instead, it is grounded in the text. This enterprise of critical practice uncovers and makes explicit only one version of what is present already, implicit in the structures of the text.

## The Implied Rhetor and the Ideal Auditor

We may anticipate other gains as well from the practice of textual criticism of media discourses. As the paradigm of analysis described earlier in the work of Benson has suggested, watching the sequential transformation of theme and structure across the text places the critic in a position to sound the traditional notions of intention and audience in a new key. Edwin Black has demonstrated a compelling case for the sophisticated application of this textual method. In "The Second Persona," Black argues that, by attending closely to the features of a discourse, the perceptive critic is able to find traces of two personae within the text—the producer of the discourse and an implied audience.[19]

Discourses contain tokens of their authors. Discourses are, directly or in transmuted form, the external signs of internal states. In short, we accept it as true that a discourse implies an author, and we mean by that more than the tautology that an act entails an agent. We mean, more specifically, that certain features of a linguistic act entail certain characteristics of the language user. [110]

In this fashion, if sufficiently discerning, we can derive, within the features of style, structure, and appeal, the aims and the intentions of *See It Now*'s makers in a way that is more interesting and more illuminating than that associated with a historical perspective. But Black also specifies that the careful critic may find within stylistic tokens and the movement of appeal an indication of a "second persona"—the implied auditor of the text. In doing so, Black suggests that we may be able to consider *See It Now*'s audience apart from a traditional dependence upon demographics and empirical audience research data.

Students of literary discourses have long recognized that every work reflects a sense of its potential audience and includes an image of those for whom it is written. Every work "intimates in its every gesture the kind of 'addressee' it anticipates. Thus, all works of the mind contain within themselves the image of the reader for whom they are intended."[20] Black argues that because the text contains clues of the kind of beliefs and assumptions an auditor is asked to embrace quite apart from any statement of an overtly political nature, by a careful algorithm a critic may describe the nature of an ideology that a text asks its audience to assume. Thus, by careful attention to stylistic and thematic tokens in the text, the critic might be able to disclose the system of ideas implicit in the discourse and then identify the auditor for whom such appeal would most likely have resonance. In this way, we may characterize the "ideal audience" as it is defined within the text—the audience that a certain discourse is "designed for," or better, the audience that a certain discourse "creates" in the process of its being read.

Questions about "audience" have been pivotal ones in the rhetorical tradition. Indeed, the study of the relationship between audiences and texts has traditionally been delimited as the province of rhetorical studies. And in the modern era, rhetorical discourses were partly distinguished from other discursive forms by the effort of a rhetor to influence a well-defined, immediate audience on matters of immediate concern. But when questions of audience and effect are transferred to television texts, the problems increase. The television audience is not a localized one; indeed, each member of the audience is characterized by "separateness" in spatial, and often temporal, dimensions from other members of the audience. Likewise, the producer has no chance or opportunity for feedback from the audience—auditor and rhetor as separated from one another by the same medium that connects them.[21]

This audience in the text, the implied auditor, or what is known as the "implied reader," would seem therefore of great value to the perceptive critic.[22] By focusing on how an audience might respond to *See It Now* the perceptive critic may arrive at a sense not only of what appeals are made but also of the specific groups to whom the makers think they are appealing.[23] In other words, the critical project of analyzing television texts such as these will seek to paraphrase the "conversation" passing between the makers and their implied audience. We can then dramatize the social attitudes implicit in the text by reconstructing the understandings that the makers of the text and their audience reach quite apart from the manifest form and content of the program.[24] Moreover, in this fashion, we can define the ideological views that prompt the *See It Now* documentaries and are instantiated in the text as a response to a circumstance in the world.

Textual criticism when combined with these two analytic topoi—the active audience and the implied rhetor/ideal auditor—have a singular critical potential. But textual criticism, as it originally developed, was conceived as dealing with verbal discourse (chiefly platform oratory) in a particular way. We are proposing to shift radically from a verbal, sequential, linear form to one that is visual, simultaneous, diachronic. So while this proposed approach to the *See It Now* programs is based on textual criticism, it involves more than the simple transfer of the enterprise to the documentary. For in this book, textual criticism, though supplying an orientation, does not exhaust the critical practice that seeks to explain these programs. *See It Now* is a form quite different from verbal discourse, and in adapting textual criticism for visual texts, some tactics may be used directly, while others must be altered to make them fit the specifics of the visual form. As will become clearer in the course of the case studies, at certain points, the textual criticism of visual forms has no equivalent application in verbal discourse.

## Aspects of the *See It Now* Documentary

Like all critics, I draw certain conclusions from the nature of the rhetorical transaction and the generic features inscribed in these texts. Specifically, in seeking to explicate these programs and the ideology they articulate, I concentrate on two loci or moments of salient critical importance. First, the tension between the visual and verbal planes of *See It Now* demands special attention. Second, genre, and more directly the expectations attendant upon genre, potentially shape response; as a result, genre too is a crucial focus for interpretation. Both loci afford access to layers of meaning that would remain otherwise submerged in the discourse. Though in *See It Now* these moments of tension occur and move simultaneously across the text, for explanatory purposes, I will consider them one by one.

### The Verbal and the Visual

It is self-evident that the *See It Now* documentaries are visual texts, yet the visual aspect is emphasized in the discourses themselves. They self-consciously reference the visual throughout their structure—from their title to the way vision is celebrated within them as giving access to an unmediated "truth." As such, the programs are much more than illustrated essays and clearly work in a more complex fashion than by the simple use of the visual image as "evidence" in support of a "verbal" argument.[25] Instead, they bring a heightened importance to what has been called "depiction"—the use of "strategic pictures," "visualizations that linger in the collective memory of audiences as representative of their subjects."[26]

A sense of how the "visual" can contribute to argument has long been recognized in communication studies. Ancient rhetoricians understood that the sense of sight took precedence over all the other sensory modes, and as such, the visual had a considerable persuasive potency. The teachers of oratory recommended the use of depiction as a way to move an audience, and all ancient handbooks cite as most persuasive those orators who succeed in using the tropes and forms of language to "set before the eyes" of an audience some crucial scene of action. One means clearly recommended to the student of oratory was to force an auditor to "see" by giving a sense of "actuality" to the image, thereby imparting a "liveliness" to ideas.

In the visual text, however, "depiction" moves to center stage, and scenes or personae are presented to the auditor without the interposition of language. Michael Osborn has argued that precisely these visual images dominate media discourse. This "radically simplified hieroglyphics," Osborn says, is the means by which modern society carries on its most important public business, and consequently depiction, he argues, has even greater prominence in the "workaday rhetoric" of our world than it did to the ancients. Depiction and visualization drive the suasory appeal of the *See It Now* text. But what seems less clear is the manner in which depiction gains the potential to function as suasion within the programs and to invite a viewer to sustain an attitude toward situations in the world. The description of this "manner" is vital for an understanding of the telecasts. But this attention to depiction has other advantages. Sometimes, for instance, the way in which a scene or persona is depicted visually is more revealing than what is said. Indeed, it may be that attention to the way an image is presented has the potential to yield a sense of the intention of the makers from a perspective that would be obscured or flattened were we to attend solely to the verbal plane of the text.

But to bring visual depiction under scrutiny, we need a way of rethinking the image that allows us to find its various messages. Roland Barthes proposed a way of understanding the rhetorical power of visual depiction when he recognized that the visual had a great potential for meaning, especially when it is "anchored" by the linguistic or verbal structure of the text.[27] To explain how this power is achieved, Barthes proposed a distinction between levels of the photographic image in his important pair of essays, "The Photographic Message" and "The Rhetoric of the Image." Barthes uses a semiotic model of the sign to separate the photograph into what he calls the "denotated" and the "connotated" levels. On the first level is what Barthes terms the "denotated" image.[28] The photographic image gains a presumption because it is recognized as being a photograph "of" something, and a viewer cedes to the photograph a sort of "ontological power," given the unbreakable indexical link between the image on the film and some aspect of external reality.[29] Except in the case of obviously altered or "doctored" photographs, it is a commonplace that we "believe" what we "see." This union of image and reality is central to the denotative aspect of the photograph.

The second level of potential meaning in the photographic image is what Barthes calls the symbolic level. This second level may be called the "connotated" image. In Barthes's model, the connotative message is "written" upon the indexical or denoted message through the "interventions" of the makers of the text. This "inflecting" of the denotative and "uncoded" image is what Barthes calls the "rhetoric" of the photograph.[30] The connotated message is a set of associations that are largely arbitrary, unmotivated, and as such dependent upon cultural knowledge and convention.[31] Such rhetoric is found in the way the photographic image is presented—upon the plane of expression. All of the rhetors' interventions—from the way the photograph is taken to how it is developed or put in context—take place between the natural image and its second-level connotations.

To bring this insight to bear upon the *See It Now* telecasts, we must make two inquiries. First, we must compare the message carried in the linguistic, verbal plane of the text with the message drawn from the connotated visual image. Often the rhetoric of the image and the rhetoric of the linguistic will coincide. But this coincidence need not be complete or totalizing; at times, it may not coincide at all. A second query involves locating the strategies of the *See It Now* texts in the way the makers go about structuring the visual and verbal planes and how they might seek to encode connotated meaning upon the natural and denotated photograph. Attention to those moments of tension when they arise between the articulation of the visual and the verbal planes should illuminate implicit meanings in *See It Now.* Also, in line with Barthes's insight, it may be that elements that are not marked as partisan verbally come to have a strong connotative and suasive effect as they are expressed in images.

Explicating the depictive and visual mode of these programs, the study will rely first upon a descriptive vocabulary suggested by contemporary film analysts. One such approach, described by David

Bordwell, is a functional one.[32] He argues that every technique of the film medium has a formal function; that is, in this case, the elements of film style (mise-en-scène, the cinematographic qualities of the image, the editing, and sound) are continually interacting with film form (in this case, argumentative) to define a particular film. For instance, a careful marking of the strategies of camera placement might reveal where and how the text seeks to direct our sympathies and might disclose a subtle attempt to guide our responses.

Thus, this moment of analytic access to the *See It Now* text hinges upon the myth of photographic naturalness. That is, the *See It Now* text wields this myth of the uncoded image in a paradoxical fashion: the denoted image "certifies" the "facticity" of what we see and also "naturalizes" the connotated message, soliciting our assent to a second level of meaning, without our being aware of its status as constructed meaning.[33] When and how this process may occur provides one critical locus in our investigation.

*Genre*

We reach a second locus or moment of critical tension by bracketing the expectations that potentially direct our response to the documentary news genre. That is, as auditors and critics, we encounter the programs through the terminology and expectations of its ostensible generic type. Our understanding of these programs is partly a matter of our tacit knowledge of the conventions of the genre of discourse. As we become familiar with "codes" of the news documentary—the rules that systematically govern the ways that these sorts of programs create meanings, we bring to the *See It Now* texts certain "preunderstandings," that is, a context of beliefs and expectations within which the work's various features are assessed.

The importance of genre and the advantages of approaching texts generically have been well rehearsed in the literature of speech communication and need not be argued here. But certain assumptions of the generic perspective will be central to our analysis of these programs—specifically the constraints imposed by the expectations of genre. Kathleen Jamieson has argued quite persuasively that expectations are created both in the rhetor and in the audience when genres are employed and that these color perception of the object as well as evaluation of it.[34] Moreover, these same generic expectations constrain rhetorical response, and "the proper response to a rhetorical situation grows not merely from the situation but also from antecedent rhetorical forms."[35]

One element in the implied contract between rhetor and audience is a clause stipulating that the rhetor fulfill rather than frustrate the expectations created for the audience by previous rhetoric generated in response to similar situations. Indeed, to Jamieson's mind, antecedent genres are capable of imposing almost monolithic constraints, and audiences react negatively when the genre chosen is not what they expect.[36]

Certainly, it may be reasonable to suppose that an audience will approach these *See It Now* programs "expecting" a news documentary—an expository report distinguished by its journalistic objectivity. So far as the text satisfies a viewer's learned conventions with respect to news documentary, the text is likely ceded a measure of assent—that is, as a "document" that "objectively" presents some exigence. But one earmark of the rhetoric of *See It Now* to which we must incline is its potential for subtle exploitation of our agreement to its purported "objectivity." Because a viewer might potentially be disarmed by its claim to be a natural representation of "fact" and "event," *See It Now* has the capacity to cloak that representation with a second-level message that seeks to prompt our judgment of what we see and hear.

In short, the tension that animates this moment of critical focus accommodates the potential strain between the conventions of reportage and the conventions of argument. Another way to fix this critical locus is to ask, if we posit a category of zero-degree reportage—one that seeks the transparent rendering of the facts of experience and is wholly objective—whether the overlay of other genres permits a second-order message to arise in the text. In these programs, a site for disclosing the implicit messages occurs at the point of tension between reportage and argument, between the documentary as a claim to transparent actuality and its methods of realization that borrow from the domain of argument and poetic.

To consider genre in this way is of course to draw attention to the essentially ideological status of genre. That is, the concept of genre as it relates to these texts brings into play, first, the system of production, second, a structural analysis of the text, and, finally, the reception process, with the audience conceived as an interpretive community. Rick Altman relates the concept of genre to that of the interpretive community. For him, genre serves to limit the free play of signification. The genre usurps the function of an interpretive community by providing a context for interpreting the documentary and by naming a specific set of intertexts according to which a new documentary form must be framed and read. The genre limits the field of play of the interpretive community. Altman sees this limiting function as an ideological project because it is an attempt to control the audience's reaction by providing an interpretive context.

Generic decisions prompted by discourses are not neutral ones, he argues, but rather ideological constructs that provide and enforce a prereading.[37]

In a similar way, Steve Neale sees genres as part of the dominant industry's "mental machinery," not just as properties possessed by texts. Neale defines genres as "systems of orientations, expectations, and conventions that circulate between industry, text and subject." The genre of television news documentary, then, is both a "coherent and systematic body of texts" and a coherent and systematic set of expectations grounded in dominant ideology.[38] The genre provides a "form" that the producers use to shape their own rhetorical choices of what to include, how to arrange it, what to leave out. In this way, genre is a potent critical tool. It coordinates the decisions of makers, the structuring of the text, and the interpretation of a viewer. As such it has a potential for subversion and for suasive engagement.

*Rhetorical Form as Ideology*

When we speak of significant form in critical analysis, we are usually referring to recurrent and abstractable patterns in texts. That is, of course, a necessary and indispensable sense. But one other locus of form merits our attention. It is more elusive and problematic than discursive form because it is not directly observable, but its exploration may well be the ultimate fulfillment of our critique of these *See It Now* texts. The form to which I refer is the form of consciousness affected by and manifested in the symbolic systems of discursive texts.

It is fairly commonplace to consider ideological meanings as they are found in the material of discourses—to illuminate the various beliefs, assumptions, and explanations that are implicit in them. But can the very type of form that a text uses itself be imbued with ideological implications? Is there an ideological significance to the patterning of documentary discourse? For instance, does the *See It Now* presentation of a reality "seen now" and "live" embody notions of a peculiar proclivity toward unmediated presentation and further toward a notion of debate and dispute as essentially desirable—as an unquestioned facet of a democratic system? Such questions must be asked if we are to explain the way that *See It Now* does its ideological work: how its significant form can be interpreted as bearing ideological meanings.

It seems commonplace that what binds social groups together is oftentimes less the beliefs they hold than the manner in which they

give their beliefs expression. Groups often share stylistic prefer-
ences and more or less regular patterns of argument. But it may also
be argued that such stylistic and formal proclivities are representative of cultural assumptions that lie beneath, and that if we understand the representational conventions of discourse, we might be
in a position to reveal something of the sociology of the culture
which produced it. The explication of documentary semiotics and
their associated culture is at the center of our examination of these
texts and I shall presume that representation itself is an active
articulation of ideology.

In sum, I have described a method of opening the *See It Now* texts
to rhetorical analysis. Based upon textual criticism, it offers to put
the critic in closer contact with the text, prompting a reenactment
of the text and a repositioning of critic with audience; in this way, it
offers the potential to understand the messages that move between
audience and text. It ensures that any interpretation of *See It Now*
will develop from the particularities of its rhetorical practice as it is
bound to this specific situation in the world. This practice, furthermore, attends to the interplay of the verbal and the visual levels of
the text and the layering of genre upon genre. In short, it holds in
suspension the concepts of source, of textuality, and of response and
recognizes that there is a complex web of influence among these
concepts. Finally, it recognizes always that the meaning of these
texts is a process of negotiation as the text unfolds and is read—the
meaning may not be "read off" by hunting down significant symbols
or motifs.

What is needed now is demonstration. Our sample in this instance is the opening title sequence for *See It Now* as it was broadcast in the 1953–1954 television season.

## Television as an Open Medium

Ronald Primeau suggests that television texts activate the viewer's sense of memory because they are formulaic. Such activation
functions to reduce the complexity of apprehension and to facilitate
drawing upon an already established ethos of program and performer. For Primeau, this regularity is part of the persuasiveness of
the program. If Primeau is correct, then the opening title and credits
sequence of *See It Now*, like nearly everything else in the programs,
attests to its makers' craft.[39] *See It Now* begins with a very quick
fade up; a volume meter fills the screen. Beside it is a small sign:
"CBS-TV CONTROL ROOM STUDIO 41." We hear the steady voice of an
off-camera announcer: "Stand-by now for *See It Now* with Edward
R. Murrow, which originates in Studio 41 in New York City." As he

speaks, the needle on the meter tracks his voice. We cut to a close shot of a television monitor; the picture on it says "STAND BY." The theme music swells on the sound track, and the picture on the monitor changes: "STAND BY DEXTER, MICHIGAN." The camera pans to the left, and we see another screen beside the first—we are looking at a panel of television monitors. The second screen says, "STAND BY DETROIT." As the camera pulls back to widen our view, we see, below the monitors, the back of a man's dark and carefully groomed head. Though he is not facing us, we can tell that he is scrutinizing the screens above and in front of him. Cigarette smoke curls up and wreaths his head as he watches.

Even these first moments reveal important elements. First, in *See It Now*, we are immediately dislocated from our usual perspective as viewers of television. That is, no longer are we on the outside, merely observing. Instead, in the *See It Now* opening sequence we find ourselves inside the television control room. Around us is the equipment and the electronic gear that we associate with the "world of television." As the announcer urges us to "Stand By," and as the control panel monitors repeat "STAND BY," our vantage point shifts radically: suddenly we are addressed as part of this "*See It Now* world."[40]

Such foregrounding of the television medium is significant, and two motifs are evident. First, we sense in this sequence the power of the institution of television that lies behind the program, apparent in the props and in the jargon of live television.[41] But we are also aware of the institution of the Columbia Broadcasting System itself. The *See It Now* text is linked with the institution via the CBS logo and studio. By virtue of its sponsorship by the Columbia Broadcasting System and by the Aluminum Company of America (ALCOA) the program's stature is enhanced.

Moreover, the potential of these conventions is of considerable interest. As *See It Now* becomes self-referential, and as we are moved from our usual perspective on the medium, so we are invited to consider the "*See It Now* world" differently from the one we know day to day. Relocated in the control room of a television studio before a panel of television monitors, we are invited to shift our perception of events to another key: to "see" things in other places "instantly," in other words, to see "the world" differently. Likewise, we are invited, quite unconsciously, to substitute a code of "television veracity" for our everyday standards of judgment. Part of that "veracity" is embodied in our expectations about "live" television.

*See It Now* evokes these expectations both in its lingering visualizations of the panel of monitors and in its introductory narration, which is a mantralike repetition of "see" and "now."[42] Even the title, *See It Now,* draws upon our expectations about "live" television and invites an attitude toward the medium.[43] The text draws upon the illusion that live television "reality" comes to us undistorted. We are asked to assent to the images we see as not only "real" in an ontological sense but also "unrehearsed," "live," and hence, free from prior interpretation.

Our first perspective in the program is looking at the monitors that sit just over Edward R. Murrow's shoulder. Like us, when we see him Murrow watches their screens; clearly, whatever we will learn of the world will come over the monitors that glow before him. Thus, we are invited to watch events with Murrow. As the world of *See It Now* appears on these monitors, television itself is nominated as a selective instrument of sight.

Yet this happens quickly; the picture dissolves to another view of the control room. We see a second man who sits before a flat panel studded with levers, dials, meters. Beyond him a studio television camera is framed in a circle of light, the CBS logo prominent upon its side. A cameraman focuses and refocuses the lens. We hear the theme music; the announcer continues: "ALCOA, Aluminum Company of America, in cooperation with CBS Television, presents the distinguished reporter and news analyst Edward R. Murrow, in *See It Now. See It Now* is produced by Mr. Murrow and Fred W. Friendly."

At the same time, words in large block capitals appear to zoom out from the scene of the television director and cameraman: SEE IT NOW. The director, hunched over his panel, pushes another switch before him. Murrow's name replaces SEE IT NOW on the screen. And at the appropriate moment, Murrow's name dissolves and is replaced by Friendly's. More voice-over narration: "A weekly presentation of the Aluminum Company of America, the nation's leading producer of aluminum. . . . Now, speaking to you from the control room of Studio 41, is the editor of *See It Now,* Edward R. Murrow."

Through the narration, Murrow's stature is confirmed, and his ethos is certified.[44] Rather than being introduced by the voice-over narrator as simply "Edward R. Murrow," Murrow is described as the "distinguished reporter and news analyst." Moreover, the introduction defines *See It Now* as a product of personal authorship: Murrow's name is spoken four times; it is superimposed an additional time. In a word, the text draws upon what we already know of Murrow, but this knowledge is referenced and directed by the narrator.[45]

Murrow's ethos is certified through the visualizations as well. As we see him sitting in front of the monitors, seemingly controlling the flow of images into the control room of Studio 41, we are invited to regard Murrow as having a special and privileged knowledge. Thus the text consistently suggests that Murrow will give us the "facts." Murrow is the gatekeeper and our access to the world outside the control room. And one of Murrow's privileged functions within *See It Now* is to contextualize what we see: introducing, describing, defining, linking—framing our perception and coaching our understanding.

In this regard, the opening sequence emphasizes *See It Now*'s origination from a specific location. The program is broadcast from Studio 41 in New York City. Such emphasis on verifying its connection to the "real world," such "grounding," reveals a theme that runs throughout the programs. Consistently, *See It Now* will use the words "this is" to introduce a camera sequence of places or people— a reminder, however subtle, that what we see is "what is there," without manipulation on the part of the makers, and that what we are offered in such a sequence is unmediated "reality."

And so, in this opening sequence, in three shots, without a word from Murrow, we find the title sequence of the *See It Now* program giving concise expression to some of the strategies of appeal that will appear in "The Case of Milo Radulovich," indeed in all of the *See It Now* broadcasts. The way the audience is asked to participate, the use of Murrow's ethos, the translation of events to fit the *See It Now* frame, the strategies the program uses to certify its connection to the world, and its emphasis upon the medium—all are already present.[46] The opening sequence is an economical rendering of motifs that prepare us for what comes after. Appealing in itself, it points our expectation toward the rest of the program.

## Conclusion

The perspective I have proposed is a distinctive one and capable of yielding a distinctive interpretation of these documentary texts. This method keeps equal attention focused upon production, textuality, and reception of the documentary text. But the method's value may be evaluated only to the extent that it explicates the *See It Now* telecasts and the ideology they represent. We must now turn to this explication.

In chapter 4, I will analyze "The Case of Milo Radulovich," the first of these *See It Now* programs to be telecast. Chapter 4 will concentrate upon the way the text transforms the story of a single individual into a representation that has the potential to stand for all victims of McCarthyism. This "magnification" of the single example is our critical focus, and the question will be how the visual text moves our sympathies from the specific example to its more universal implications.

Chapter 5 analyzes "An Argument in Indianapolis" and brings the issue of depiction directly to the surface. Our interest revolves around the manner in which depiction is used as argument. In addition, this chapter will introduce what will be the recurring problem of impartiality and bias. We will compare the traditional assessments of the fairness of "An Argument in Indianapolis" with our estimation arrived at via textual criticism.

In chapter 6, our attention is focused on the most famous of the *See It Now* broadcasts, "A Report on Senator McCarthy." There we will continue to consider the questions of objectivity and argument and will seek an accommodation between the generic expectations of the program and the text's increasing evidence that it strives not just to inform but also to solicit our judgment.

Chapter 7 is devoted to "Annie Lee Moss Before the McCarthy Committee," a program broadcast scarcely a week later. In style, "Annie Lee Moss" is quite different from the ones that preceded it, and it is often taken as the "fairest" of the four telecasts. I will investigate the grounds for that characterization and will propose that, as the documentary text invites our assent, it simultaneously seeks to close the distance between itself and other discursive genres. Here I will examine rather directly the intertextuality of the television news documentary.

# Part II

4

# A Little Picture of an Enormous Problem: "The Case of Milo Radulovich, A0589839"

At ten thirty on Tuesday evening, October 20, 1953, Edward R. Murrow turns in his chair and looks into the television camera before him. "Good evening," he says.[1]

A few weeks ago there occurred a few obscure notices in the newspaper about a lieutenant—a Milo Radulovich—a lieutenant in the Air Force Reserve, and also something about Air Force Regulation 35-62. That is a regulation which states that a man may be regarded as a security risk if he has close and continuing association with Communists or people believed to have Communist sympathies. Lieutenant Radulovich was asked to resign in August. He declined. A board was called and heard his case. At the end, it was recommended that he be severed from the Air Force, although it was also stated that there was no question whatever as to the lieutenant's loyalty. We propose to examine, insofar as we can, the case of Lieutenant Radulovich.

"The Case of Milo Radulovich," as the program came to be known, made clear that Edward R. Murrow and Fred W. Friendly were entering *See It Now* in the debate over national security, the rights of the individual, and the responsibilities of the state—the program's first direct and sustained examination of the issues that preoccupied the public mind and dominated public discourse in the decade after 1945.[2]

Moreover, in focusing upon the apparatus of national security and questions of individual loyalty, *See It Now* was clearly aiming directly at one of the central abuses of the era. As Friendly remembered it, the story of Lieutenant Radulovich was "television's first attempt to do something about the contagion of fear that had come to be known as McCarthyism."[3]

Media historians agree: they call the Radulovich program "a classic case," "a story that dramatized the problem of guilt by association," and a television broadcast that "symbolized the McCarthy Era." As one historian puts it, in sustaining an inquiry not only into a blanket regulation but also into the mentality embodied in its sweeping application, "The Case of Milo Radulovich" indicted the paranoia of an entire generation.[4]

## Particular Story or Universal Symbol?

A moment of considerable interest, then, is how this text sustains such ideological argument. But there is a gap in our understanding of "The Case of Milo Radulovich": while critics agree that the plight of the lieutenant "symbolized" an era, and "stood for" a class of victims, the precise development of this symbolic identity and its ideological implications have been taken for granted.[5]

The oversight is curious, especially since, on the surface, the strategy of the *See It Now* rhetors is conspicuous and self-conscious: in planning the program, they realized the necessity of finding "the right incident, the small story, which would provide [them] with the 'little picture'—shorthand for a real situation which would illustrate a national issue."[6] And in the telecast version of the program, this strategy, the use of the "little picture," the specific story of Milo Radulovich, is self-evident.

In short, this *See It Now* program raises crucial questions about the documentary form. Specifically, it draws our attention to the problem of focus and depiction in modern, mass-mediated visual forms. The problem may be briefly described in the following way. At the heart of the documentary enterprise is the technological capacity to record a visual/aural record of a particular piece of the world (a recording that comprises the evidentiary quality of the documentary account).[7] From this capacity, critical questions follow immediately—among them, what is the relationship between the record of a "specific reality" and more general propositions about what is going on; for example, how does the documentary record of one individual worker's situation connect with the general problem of "unemployment in the Midwest"? While this tension between particular and general animates most "realist" texts, it is exacerbated in visual forms because of the obvious recognition that what the camera records is radically "particular" and seems, initially, to foreclose more "general" implications.[8]

The bridging of the particular/general gap in the documentary form is especially crucial when we consider its role as a persuasive document. As Nichols points out, the problem in documentary conflates traditional notions of argument and evidence: "documentary has a tension arising from the attempt to make statements about life that are quite general while necessarily using sounds and images that bear the inescapable trace of their historical origins."[9] James A. Wood succinctly described this inherent tension and argued that while visual forms powerfully present the single example (we accept the film image as "tied" to reality), precisely because the film image is so specific, it may prevent generalization, stranding the viewer at the level of the single case.[10] For persuasion to succeed, Wood said, it is essential to invest the specific case with implications beyond the local and singular. In other words, an audience's willingness to acknowledge some one "particular" as "general," "typical," or "representative" gives persuasive potency to the documentary form.[11]

Does "The Case of Milo Radulovich" transcend the individual story of one man's plight? If it does, how then does Milo Radulovich come to stand for other victims of McCarthyism? The answers to these questions are interconnected; we shall see that they involve notions of representation and the "way we come to know" Milo Radulovich.

The present reading of "The Case of Milo Radulovich" may thus be regarded as addressing two interconnected issues. First, examining the text from the point of view of its symbolic movement, it identifies previously unacknowledged rhetorical action and shows how the program solicits our judgment of both the individual tragedy of Lt. Milo Radulovich and, more broadly, the social tragedy of McCarthyism. Second, the analysis permits us to probe the question of representation and depiction in documentary argument. I contend that for this documentary each issue is part and parcel of the other, that "The Case of Milo Radulovich" relies upon a simultaneous particularizing and universalizing symbolic movement to represent Radulovich and the ideology of McCarthyism.

Representation itself is a rhetorical action; it is a symbolic operation, and the representation of the individual in a form that both magnifies and narrows is the business of synecdoche, the trope of representation.[12] I argue here that it is profitable to characterize the movement of the program, which prompts our assent to the plight of a single individual while at the same time suggesting how that individual can stand for a larger complex of public issues, under the rubric of synecdoche. What we shall see is that such "representativeness" is a textual fabrication—a rhetorical strategy of this *See It Now* documentary.

To address these issues, then, I first set the program in context, then analyze the textual dynamics that characterize "The Case of Milo Radulovich." The program develops its central figure as representative by "fixing" him within the "common sense" of his neighbors in the small town. Moreover, this group of citizens is crucial to the action of the text, for, like the figure of Radulovich, they are constructed as "representative" and function to constitute the *See It Now* audience by articulating the political, social, and moral implications in the case of Milo Radulovich and by modeling the ideal response to his story. We shall see that through the two-way operation of representation, general to specific/specific to general, the text manifests its ideological claim.

## McCarthyism: Loyalty and Security

As we have seen, questions of loyalty and security, indeed the very issue of "guilt by association," preoccupied the public mind in the postwar decade. Perhaps at no time did it command more attention than in the late summer of 1953. Then the McCarthy subcommittee, minus its Democrats and fresh from its sensational and widely publicized inquiry into the Voice of America, conducted several simultaneous investigations. Sometimes operating as a one-man committee, McCarthy drew the constant attention of the press and became a regular on daytime television in Washington and wherever he traveled for his hearings.[13] In early fall, the senator announced an investigation of "communist infiltration into the Army" and began closed hearings at the Signal Corps Center, Fort Monmouth, New Jersey, during the first week of October. Within the week, bowing under pressure and publicity, the army released a number of employees identified by McCarthy as "security risks." The senator gloated as the number of dismissed employees continued to grow, and he assured reporters that his subcommittee had unearthed a trail of breaches in security and "extremely dangerous espionage" that could "envelop the whole Signal Corps."[14]

But despite headlines in the autumn of 1953, the issues of loyalty and security had a longer history, one revealing how deeply the roots of suspicion reached into the national psyche. In March 1947, President Harry Truman had reluctantly implemented what became a loyalty program for the executive branch of the federal government.[15] Executive Order 9835 directed that members of the executive branch would be subject to "checks" but must be retained in their positions if the check revealed a reasonable doubt as to their disloyalty. But four years later, under pressure from McCarthyites, Truman modified the directive so that employees could be dismissed from their positions if there was any reasonable doubt as to their *loyalty.* And a few years later, the still more stringent Public Law 733 demanded immediate dismissal in all doubtful cases.

Upon taking office and under the growing influence of those convinced of Communist infiltration, President Eisenhower extended Truman's tight security provisions to every government agency and to every type of job. In May 1953, Executive Order 10450 revoked the guarantee of an impartial dismissal hearing while subjecting all present and future employees of the executive branch to broad character scrutiny. But more ominously for civil libertarians, the order eliminated the distinction between a loyalty risk and a security risk, making "national security" the only yardstick for retaining a position in the government. The administration rejected arguments that some security risks might not be disloyal and instead emphasized that a person's character, habits, or associations made that person vulnerable to blackmail. The result was that people were subject to firing for personal traits, such as alcoholism, homosexuality, "infamous" conduct, or the rumor of such activities.[16]

Thus, by the fall of 1953, any employee alleged to be a security risk could be dismissed from government solely on the basis of habits of personal life or for associating with suspected "fellow travelers." Furthermore, the information gathered by the investigators remained closed to the defendant on the grounds of "security." In early October of 1953, Eisenhower's order was amended to make even the taking of the Fifth Amendment before a Congressional Committee sufficient grounds for automatic dismissal.[17]

## The "Little Picture"

In such a chilly social and political climate, Murrow and Friendly moved, quietly at first, to speak of the relations between the government and the individual. They had decided to produce a program dealing directly with the issues of McCarthyism's abuse of loyalty and security provisions. To make it most effective, they waited for the "little picture" that would dramatize the conflict.[18]

With the McCarthy investigations at Fort Monmouth dominating the national headlines, Murrow passed along to Friendly a clipping from the *Detroit News,* a local story: "Air Force Tries to Oust Vet;

Links Family to Reds." "Here, read this," he said, "it may be our case history. . . . Let's have someone check it out."[19]

Friendly immediately dispatched reporter Joe Wershba to Dexter, Michigan, for a preliminary investigation. Wershba found Radulovich to be "attractive and articulate" and more than willing to participate in the program. A cameraman was sent to join him, and soon film began to return to *See It Now*'s New York offices.

The first interviews with Radulovich and with his father had an immediate impact on Friendly, Murrow, and the entire staff. Murrow, impressed with the lieutenant's conviction and self-control, demanded and got more interviews and then pressed for more air time than the standard ten-minute segment; both Murrow and Friendly recognized that the entire half hour must be devoted to Radulovich alone.[20]

Seeking the Air Force's version of the case, Friendly solicited comments from a high-ranking Pentagon spokesman. "Does Murrow know about this?" the official asked. And, a few days later, two senior Air Force officers, a general and a lieutenant colonel, visited the producers at CBS to discourage production of the telecast. In *Due to Circumstances Beyond Our Control . . .* , Friendly describes the scene. Stressing "this problem of security during the Cold War," the general seemed unconvinced that the broadcast would ever be aired. Murrow insisted that *See It Now* desired to do a fair, balanced job of reporting but would be unable to do so if the Air Force refused to comment. Stalemated, the meeting concluded with the general's chilly reminder: "You have always gotten complete cooperation from us, and we know you won't do anything to alter that."[21] But Murrow and Friendly determined to go ahead with the Radulovich telecast even without the Air Force's statement.

Recognizing the importance of the program they were assembling, Friendly pondered the best way of publicizing it. He asked the CBS management for extra advertising funds and for approval of special advertisements. Both were denied. Then Friendly turned to *See It Now*'s sponsor, the Aluminum Company of America, and asked ALCOA to place an advertisement for the broadcast in the *New York Times*. After several days of delay, ALCOA refused to finance the ad but reluctantly agreed to drop the broadcast's scheduled middle commercial.

Convinced that the issues were great and the material compelling, Friendly and Murrow decided to use their own funds for an advertisement in the *Times*.[22] It consisted of a small photograph of Radulovich, the title of the program, the time, and the local station. The advertisement was signed not with the CBS corporate logo but by "Ed Murrow and Fred Friendly."[23]

Wershba and cameraman Charlie Mack shot nearly five hours of film. It was edited down to the necessary half-hour length in only three days—what Friendly described as a "pressure-cooker" atmosphere. Murrow asked that three or four minutes be left on the end for a "tailpiece." "Leave me enough time," he said, "because we are going to live or die by our ending. . . . we simply can't do an 'on the other hand' ending for this."[24]

The final cut of the Radulovich program was not finished until shortly before broadcast time, and the staff never did rehearse the entire program from start to finish.[25] The hectic production procedures of those days meant that there was always great tension in the studio when any program aired. With parts of the final mix coming from three studios and cutting rooms, some hand carried, some over telephone wire, it was never known whether all the individual elements would be ready in time for the telecast.[26]

But for "The Case of Milo Radulovich," the tension was even higher than usual. And as they awaited the "on air" signal, Murrow commented that, whatever happened, "things will never be the same around here after tonight." Despite any tension Murrow may have been feeling, he seemed calm as he sat in the control room of Studio 41 in New York and watched the program credits begin to roll on the monitor in front of him.

## Textual Analysis

"The Case of Milo Radulovich" divides naturally into three distinct segments. The first concentrates upon the person of Radulovich himself, selecting details to fashion a portrait of the lieutenant and his character. The second section has two subparts: the first introduces a "chorus" of citizens who discuss the case and its implications; the second subpart takes us to a meeting with Radulovich's family. The third and final section, Murrow's conclusion, builds upon the first two. Since each section develops one part of the symbolic movement, functions to shift attention from individual to symbol, and is part of a developing action upon the audience, I will consider them in original sequence.

As the announcer finishes and introduces Murrow, the camera pans left to reveal the newsman. Seated before the control panel where we first saw him, Murrow has turned and now directly faces us, the control board with its monitors and meters on his left, an enormous microphone in front of him. Seen in close shot, Murrow holds his familiar cigarette. He begins with a nod and his customary "good evening."

I have already noted Murrow's opening remarks about a "few obscure" notices that recently appeared in the newspapers. But such references are only the first that will firmly anchor the "story" of Milo Radulovich within the world of verifiable experience—within the world of "news."[27] In other words, *See It Now* reminds that its "world" is the world of public experience. As news documentary, then, *See It Now* solicits a heightened awareness of its purpose and our special attention toward its subject: its concern is the public realm.

If we look more closely, in style and tenor, Murrow's introduction is curious: the "obscure" notices in the papers concern "a lieutenant, a Milo Radulovich." They concern "a lieutenant in the Reserve." The notices are "something about" an Air Force regulation. Overall, there is a striking lack of specificity in Murrow's description,. and so the Radulovich case is cast in the tone of a peculiar generality.

Furthermore, Radulovich "was asked" to resign; a board "was called"; and after the hearing, it "was recommended" that the lieutenant "be severed" from the military, though no doubt of his loyalty "was stated." The actions of the Air Force are described in the passive voice, a tactic that not only completes the tone of generality but also detaches the actions from their human agents. Throughout, the agents arrayed against Radulovich will remain impersonal, mysterious, like the evidence against him, forever closed to the accused officer.

Although the lieutenant's accusers are depersonalized and made more general in the language of the opening, we are prompted to think of Radulovich as "active." The lieutenant has "declined" to resign, and this act of self-assertion sets him in contrast to the impersonal and impassive board that sits in judgment.

Thus the text discloses an early perspective on its subject as revealed in the style and the voice of Murrow's introduction. Overall, it reveals a lack of specificity in Murrow's casting of the story, a tone of generality that hints at larger issues beyond the particular story of Milo Radulovich. The strategies that *See It Now* will use to develop this perspective are to become clear in the subsequent segments.

To signal the end of the prologue, Murrow turns to his left and looks up at the panel of monitors. "We propose to examine," he says, "insofar as we can, the case of Lieutenant Radulovich." We dissolve to a shot similar to the one that opened the telecast: Murrow's back is to us, he is looking up at monitor 2, which says "Dexter, Michigan." The camera begins a slow pan to the left and tilts up. As we watch, the graphic dissolves to a close shot of a statue. Murrow completes the introduction: "Our reporter, Joe Wershba. Cameraman, Charlie Mack."

This device—Murrow's turn and look, the camera move toward the monitor, the dissolve from "stand by" to image, the subsequent "take" on the film itself—is the standard *See It Now* transition. It parallels the opening title sequence in its evocation of the gatekeeping role of Murrow and its mythologizing of the medium: we are instantly "transported" from Studio 41 to Dexter, Michigan.[28] Furthermore, it also heightens the illusion of a "live" transmission from the field location that *See It Now* seeks to sustain.

*Everyman and Hero*

Reaching the end of his introduction, Murrow turns to the panel of TV monitors behind him and announces: "This is the town of Dexter, Michigan, population 1,500." The scene dissolves to the picture of a War Memorial statue. Again, Murrow: "This statue is at the head of Ann Arbor Street." A cut to the inscription on the statue, which Murrow reads: "Erected by the citizens of Dexter to heroes who fought and the martyrs who died that the Republic might live."

The scene changes; our view pans left, showing modest white frame houses across from the park. They sit far back from a street along which traffic cruises sedately. The homes are widely spaced, their front porches nearly obscured by leafy elms. Here in Dexter, Michigan, nothing seems amiss; nothing is unique or unusual. The town is quiet, familiar—a typical Midwestern hamlet.

As the camera sweeps across the houses and streets, it reaches a small business district. The buildings are narrow and one story—the central square in a small town. We see the street disappear on the other side of the square; the sun is low, reflecting off the cars as they converge, then cross.

Then Murrow again, ironically echoing the words inscribed on the monument, "This is the story of Milo Radulovich—no special hero, no martyr. He came to Dexter one year ago, after ten years in the Air Force. . . . Won a general commendation for working on a secret weather station in Greenland. Now he is a senior at the University of Michigan eight miles away. His wife works nights at the telephone company. They live at 7867 Ann Arbor Street." Ordinary, prosaic, yet carefully chosen, these details begin to sketch a portrait of Milo Radulovich. The résumé we receive is commonplace and from the everyday world.

The accompanying visualizations carry the same theme: the text cuts from a wide shot of the town square to a close-up of a street sign, framed by a leafy oak tree; it reads "Ann Arbor St." Quickly, another cut, and as Murrow gives the address, we see a wide shot of a large frame house. Laundry hangs on the line in the yard. Again a quick cut: we see an extreme close-up of the numbers "7867" fastened to the wall just beside the front door on the wide and whitewashed porch. Murrow's dramatic words follow: "This," he says, "is Milo Radulovich," and suddenly we are inside the Radulovich home.

The sequence reveals in miniature the strategy of "The Case of Milo Radulovich." The movement across the town of Dexter, from the statue of the Hero and Martyr that stands in the city park, to street to house to front door, ever closer to Milo Radulovich, a most typical man, is a paradigm of the dynamics of the whole. Within the text, we will be invited to move symbolically between Hero and Everyman, and *See It Now* will seek to transfer the symbolic heroism of those "who died that the Republic might live" from the memorial in a village square to "an" ordinary man, to "a" Lieutenant Milo Radulovich, who will be transformed into—while "no *special* hero"—a hero nonetheless.

In juxtaposing everyday details about its central figure over scenes of a quiet village, *See It Now* has signaled a salient theme and has presaged its tactics: the text will present Milo Radulovich subtly interwoven with the town and townspeople of Dexter. He will exist as a figure on the ground of the social world of the small town. That is, this text will solicit response by offering viewers the chance to come to "know" Milo Radulovich through the comments of his neighbors and fellows. For its promised transformation to be effective, however, the text must first encourage its auditors to see the central figure as a concrete, specific, and altogether typical tragic case.

We first see Milo Radulovich in head-and-shoulder close-up shot. He is modestly handsome, dark sweater and open collar. Framed by a table lamp behind him, he speaks to an interviewer slightly off camera. "The Air Force does not question my loyalty in the least," Radulovich says. The "allegations" are that he "maintained a close and continuing relationship" with his father and sister. "My sister and dad have read what are now called subversive newspapers, and my sister and father's activities are questionable. That's the specific allegation against them."

As our view changes to an even closer shot, Radulovich characterizes "blacklisting" in tragic, human terms. "Well, I think I am being a realist about it. Anybody that is labeled a security risk these days . . . simply won't be able to find employment. . . . In other words, I believe that if I am labeled a security risk—if the Air Force won't have me, I ask the question: who else will?"[29] As he describes it, Radulovich's predicament contrasts sharply with the normalcy that has dominated the text so far in its depiction of the town and of the young man.

But with Milo's question left hanging, unanswered, *See It Now* cuts abruptly to a large signboard: SELFRIDGE FIELD. Murrow tells us, "This is headquarters of the Tenth Air Force, where the Radulovich hearing took place." We see a wide shot of an impersonal building.

What is most striking in this segment is how the images carry the force of argument. As the sequence progresses, we see no Air Force officials, only the signs outside the administration building listing the commands headquartered within. This absence of human beings emphasizes the increasing depersonalization of the Air Force within "The Case of Milo Radulovich."

The image of a distant bureaucracy is rendered unmistakable: we cut to a tall chain-link fence. It is topped with barbed wire. "No reporters were permitted at the hearing," Murrow says, "and the Air Force refused to provide us with a transcript." The camera begins a slow pan to the left across the fence. We are reminded in movement and in pacing of the slow pan that opened the program, the sweeping from Dexter's bronze hero to the town beyond. In the distance, through the gate, we see a bit of the air base. And as the camera swings left, it finally comes to rest on an uncomfortable Air Force police guard. He motions the camera away, blocking our view.

Though this camera move is a mirror of the earlier one, we see an ironic reversal. Earlier we moved from the image of the hero to the town beyond, a town that had been preserved by the actions of the hero. But now the sequence asks us to see the military as a perversion of that vision. In place of the Hero is an embarrassed young guard who seeks to keep us away. In contrast to the open and placid society of the town, we confront a depersonalized and faceless bureaucracy that bars our access.

Murrow quickly introduces Radulovich's attorney for "his report" on the hearing. We cut to a medium shot of attorney Charles Lockwood. The lawyer is indignant; his rimless spectacles emphasize the narrowness of his face as he rapidly speaks into the camera.

"The president of the Hearing Board placing a sealed envelope in front of him [Radulovich]. . . . 'These are the allegations. Now proceed to exonerate yourself.'" Attorney Lockwood shakes his head: "We put in several disinterested witnesses, who . . . gave unchallenged testimony. . . . The Air Force did not produce a single witness. We were not told who the accusers were. We have no right to confront them or cross-examine them. But at the conclusion of the trial, although we had met the allegations, the Air Force made findings . . . that every single allegation was true."

From the attorney's perspective, after thirty years of law practice, the case is a perversion of justice: "As a matter of fact, we have had no hearing at all. We have had no day in court." Radulovich is charged with nothing less than "guilt by relationship," he says, "a cruel and inhuman practice" usually rejected by civilized nations.

As we watch, this "report" by Radulovich's lawyer is given a special status in the text through its manner of presentation. While all other "witnesses" speak to us through an off-camera intermediary (like Radulovich, who seems to speak to someone sitting just off camera to the left), the lawyer speaks directly to us. In "The Case of Milo Radulovich," only Murrow and the lawyer are allowed to address us directly. Thus, Lockwood's eyewitness account that the hearing was a "perversion of justice" is invested with special importance by way of its stylistics of presentation.

So far, then, through detail about Radulovich and about the accusations against him, *See It Now* constructs Radulovich as both a typical man and a specific victim of McCarthyism's "guilt by association." But in addition to constituting Radulovich's individual story, these details encourage a natural pathos for him.

It seems reasonable that auditors might find their emotional reaction intensified as they are invited to perceive Radulovich caught up in a bizarre and nightmarish scenario. Such tactics, of course, are neither surprising nor novel; even Aristotle's *Poetics* advises that the tragic hero should be someone "average."[30] Moreover, such tragedy acquires the potential for pathos, Aristotle continues, for "what we fear for ourselves excites our pity when it happens to others."[31]

But the lieutenant must also simultaneously assume more representative stature, and *See It Now* must build upon the specifics of the lieutenant's individual case. This move, from particular to universal, is accomplished in the crucial second section of "The Case of Milo Radulovich," which follows. This section features a series of comments by the lieutenant's neighbors. More important, however, it functions by way of a remarkable system of visual stylistics.

*The Chorus of Citizen-Witnesses*

The segment begins with a close shot of a road sign announcing the city limits of Dexter, Michigan. Traffic passes; an auto horn sounds. For over a hundred years, the town "has had no spectacular news stories," Murrow says, "but they are willing to discuss the case of Milo Radulovich."

Murrow introduces the first "witness." John Palmer is chief marshal of Dexter and has "known Radulovich a year." The marshal says he is confused as to how "they" could indict Milo because his father "read a paper that he wasn't supposed to read." Radulovich "can't condemn his father and cast him aside," Palmer says. "I couldn't do that. Neither could any other boy who had a father."

When asked about the rumors of the Raduloviches leaving Dexter, Palmer says: "I wouldn't do it. I'd stick right around and see it through. You never want to run from anything—that's the way I look at it. . . . still be a good neighbor to us like he has in the past. We'd like to have him here, if he'd stay." Thus, the theme of community and social life moves to center stage; Milo is a "good neighbor" and so stands solidly within the social world of Dexter. As those who know him tell about him, the audience too may come to "know" Milo Radulovich.

Of special interest, however, is the way in which this segment develops visually: after Palmer, again, there is an abrupt cut, followed by a wide shot of the village business district. But this time, strikingly, the shot offers a quite different perspective: our vantage point is that of a passenger in an automobile. The shops move by as we turn; we hear the sound of the auto accelerating. Murrow speaks over: "Next we go down Ann Arbor Street, to the dry-cleaning store managed by Mrs. Madeleine Lewis." Mrs. Lewis tells of organizing a petition drive in support of Milo Radulovich.

The journey continues. Once more the perspective is within the auto: we seem to be "driving" through Dexter. Murrow narrates as we pass stately houses, lawns framed with tall trees. "After Mrs. Lewis, we go to see A. G. Wall, the town dentist. For twenty-nine years he was Dexter's mayor." Wall, a relaxed, older gentleman, echoes the others. The only thing that seems certain, Wall says, is that the "boy's" relatives are "Communist-inclined." But "I can't see how they can hold a man responsible for the views and actions of his relatives," he concludes, "because of the fact that you can't control them."

Without introduction, the camera cuts quickly to another man seen in head-and-shoulders framing. He squints in the sunlight. "I don't see why he should be held responsible for what his father and sister do," says the man. "I know I wouldn't want to be held responsible for what my father did."

"That was Ernst Alsasser," Murrow says. "He runs a gas station." The scene shifts, Alsasser looks down, and in the wide shot that follows we see him, sleeves rolled, pumping gas. A quick cut and we, again, look out the front window of a moving car. Traffic, a horn—and the camera eases to a stop at a signal.

The motif of traveling, the repetition of the unusual camera shot from within the automobile, and the chorus of citizen-witnesses are stylistic features that work in concert to initiate the shift in perspective that "The Case of Milo Radulovich" demands. At this point, the audience is invited to listen to common people speak, to share the perspective of his "neighbors" on Milo's predicament. That perspective is uniform and predictable: "relatives are unreliable"; "you can't choose them"; "an innocent man stands and fights"; "be a good neighbor." As they address us, Radulovich's neighbors attest to his innocence, and the uniformity of their comments certify that Milo is "one of them."

But while the motif of driving and the camera shots are striking and appealing devices in themselves, they also serve to direct attention to these speakers visually. In this segment our usual vantage as viewers is altered dramatically, and the text repositions us in relation to what we see. We drop the expected objective subject position outside the "action" of the text and instead are positioned within the text, moving through the community, stopping to hear comment. As *See It Now* realigns and repositions its auditors "into" the text, it suggests the audience's community with the chorus of Dexter citizens. Reacting to the case of Milo Radulovich, the chorus models the reaction that the program demands of its actual audience—the attitudes, knowledge, and predispositions we are to manifest.

The final interview in the segment is illustrative: the subjective, moving camera stops before a neatly kept home; a young man with a crew cut, a neighbor of Milo Radulovich, stands in close-up, his tee shirt revealing brawny shoulders. "This is Steve Shorter," Murrow says in introduction, "he drives a truck." If the military, "or who they are that are purging this man . . . , gets away" with it, Shorter says, then "they are entitled to do it to anybody. You, or me, or anybody else. If it comes to the point where you and I are held responsible for the activities of any member of our family, then we all better head for cover."

Shorter's statement, like those of the others in the "chorus" of Dexter citizens, resonates on several levels at once. First, in rather straightforwardly raising questions of morality and public policy, the chorus's comments cast the story of Milo Radulovich in a different light, both highlighting certain evocative aspects of his predicament and bringing out its moral and more universal significance.

But, as we have also seen, the chorus of townspeople also increases the dramatic momentum of "The Case of Milo Radulovich," providing a way for the audience to experience the situation of the central figure. How this effect is finally achieved might be explained in terms of its direct analogue—the chorus of the classical Greek drama.

The chorus was an identifying feature of Greek drama, appearing in several distinct forms as the genre developed from early to later periods.[32] Nevertheless, certain functions remained more or less consistent. The Greek chorus furthered dramatic action by serving as "ideal spectators," and in reacting to episodes, the chorus responded to the issues raised and provided a pattern for audience response, showing an audience how and where catharsis was appropriate.[33] An actual audience could measure its response to that of the chorus, whose members represented "common humanity" much like themselves.[34]

A second function of the tragic chorus is also significant for our understanding in this case. The chorus worked to clarify meaning or the significance of action.[35] In its guise as "humanity" or the "people of the city," the tragic chorus elevated commonplace details into universal verities furnishing a background of moral and commonplace sentiment with the potential to bring the passion of the central figure into sharp focus.[36] In other words, in "saying" what moral or political implications the development of the action suggests, the chorus underscores the moral and provides a way for the audience to acknowledge the universal within the particular story.

Thus, in this *See It Now* text, while the chorus of citizen-witnesses is quite literally Radulovich's neighbors who comment upon his story, as the "voice of the people"—representatives of "humanity"—they function to shape the meaning of the story and to suggest its moral and political aspects. And in their simultaneous guise as representatives of the intended audience, the chorus guides and instructs us in our response. As in classic Greek drama, the townspeople of Dexter take on the role of more universal personae—developing a moral interpretation and modeling the reactions demanded of the actual audience.

In this text, through the coaxing of the subjective camera and the "traveling frame," through the evocation of conventional wisdom, the *See It Now* rhetors invite us to find ourselves in the representation offered by this group of townspeople. Thus, not only is Milo Radulovich "one of them," but through the visualizations in the text that pull toward the chorus, through the sentiment displayed, the audience is invited to realize Milo is also "one of us." In doing so, the *See It Now* text simultaneously constructs its audience and demonstrates the desired reaction to Radulovich's story. As we shall see, this has significant implications.

## Disarming the Allegations

With its depiction of "Milo Radulovich-Everyman" in place, its modeling of its audience accomplished, *See It Now* turns to undermining the actual allegations against the lieutenant. The change in tactics is signaled by an audio cue: a loud, prolonged ship's horn. We cut to a wide panorama of city wharfs and freight yards with a city skyline in the distance. Our vantage is elevated, and we look down upon the waterfront. Murrow's narration locates us: "Detroit is fifty-three miles from Dexter. Milo and Nancy Radulovich go there every six weeks, according to the testimony, to visit his father, John Radulovich."

But though the tactics have shifted, the text's strategies have not: our introduction to John Radulovich mirrors our introduction to Milo himself—we come to John Radulovich through the accumulation of everyday details and through the reactions of others. To begin, Murrow renders the elder Radulovich with an economy of detail: he has worked in the "Hudson automobile plant" for twenty-six years and before that as a miner.

We go "to see Claude Bland, an officer of Radulovich's Local UAW." There is a cut to a portly man standing before a union meeting hall. Bland firmly states that the union "doesn't want any part" of Communists and would remove any from its rosters. Furthermore, the charges against the elder Radulovich are "preposterous," Bland says. "I've heard reports that he read papers, which, to me, doesn't mean a thing, because naturally people of foreign extraction will naturally read papers printed in the language with which they were more familiar. That's—They said he read Serbian papers." Asked by reporter Wershba if the elder Radulovich could be considered a "subversive," Bland answers, "Not in any way, shape, or form. I have known him since 1937. I worked with the man in the department, ate lunch with him on many occasions. I never heard the man say one word regarding the Commonist [sic] philosophy."

But Bland's interview hardly prepares us for one of the most moving segments of the program—our direct encounter with Milo's father. Again, it commences with a mirror of the scenes of introduction to Milo: we cut to a modest brick house framed by trees, then to a closer shot of the front of the house. Once more, Murrow supplies carefully chosen detail: "Milo Radulovich's father lives at 3953 Nottingham Street. He owns his own house." Murrow says ironically, John Radulovich "denied subscribing to the *Daily Worker* and said he subscribed to the Serbian language newspaper . . . because he liked their Christmas calendars." Again, as in Dexter with Milo, the ordinary and the normal are contrasted with the extraordinary and the bizarre.

We see John Radulovich and his wife in their living room: he is bald and wrinkled; his wife bespectacled, gray. Obviously uneasy, John Radulovich squints at the camera, shifts his weight, looks down, and begins: "Here's a letter I write to president. I want to read to you [*sic*]." Suddenly, it is clear that the elder Radulovich speaks English with great difficulty and can hardly even read the letter he has written. He stops and in a thick accent begins again. His wife helps him; the letter is made more touching by the old man's struggle to read it.

I am American citizen who come here thirty-nine years ago from Serbia. I serve America in the Army in the first world war. . . . My whole life, my whole family, is American. Mr. President, I writing to you because they are doing a bad thing to Milo. They are wrong. The things they say about him are wrong. He has given all his growing years to his country. He is good for this country. Mr. President, I am an old man. I have spend my life in this coal mine and auto furnaces. I ask nothing for myself. All I ask is justice for my boy. Mr. President, I ask your help.

When he finishes, John Radulovich looks up at the camera, squinting in the lights.

Next, *See It Now* introduces Milo's sister. She "neither defends nor explains her political activities," Murrow says. And Margaret Radulovich Fishman is deliberate: "I feel that my activities, be what they may—my political beliefs are my own private affair." This very brief interview with the sister has less impact: she is not introduced in the same way as the other central figures. Murrow supplies no details about her, and the visualizations offer no sequence establishing spatial location or setting. Instead, the remarks of the sister are quickly passed over. Her statements, coming after the pathos of the "old John section" and not grounded by the personalization of her character, have little effect. What might be damaging to our developing portrait of Milo Radulovich is mitigated by its placement and by its style of presentation in the text.[37]

There is only one more witness to hear. We cut to the extreme close-up of the house number nailed to the outside of the Radulovich home: "7867." Murrow announces our change of location through the same spatial motif that has, so far, patterned the text:

"Back in Dexter, we returned to the wooden frame house on Ann Arbor Street and talked to Milo's wife." Spatially we have returned to where we began.[38]

The scene inside the Radulovich home is set via a wide establishing shot. On our left is Milo; beside him on the couch, his wife Nancy. The furnishings behind the couple are modest: a lamp, curtains, some curios on the end table. Facing them in a chair is the reporter on the extreme right of the screen. "Nancy," he asks, "considering you are a mother with two kids—deep down, wouldn't you have preferred that Milo would have kept sort of quiet about this and maybe it would have passed over? And nobody would have known about it?"

Nancy Radulovich's manner is sincere. Her words, obviously heartfelt, echo those of the chorus of citizen-witnesses: as they had suggested Milo not run from trouble, Nancy, too, characterizes him as a "fighter." Moreover, she will stand beside her husband. "I wouldn't want him to take it lying down," she says. "If he did, he would be admitting to something that we aren't guilty of. . . . I don't regret anything—him coming forward and fighting it."[39]

What remains is for the text to reintroduce its hero, Milo Radulovich, but now we have been prepared to see Milo in a quite different light. Now, seen through the comments of his neighbors, through the empathy of his father and the faithfulness of his wife—through, in other words, the universal form, we are invited to attend to him in a different fashion. His importance is magnified, and his comments about family underscore a central motif.

First, Milo defends himself: "what my sister does, what political opinions or activities she engages in, are her own affair. Because they certainly do not influence me." Radulovich is animated, his face expressive, his fingers punctuating sentences in the air. Indeed, his anger is clearly evident and at times rises to the surface. When reporter Wershba asks the lieutenant why he spoke out, Radulovich says, "I certainly didn't believe in my own heart that I was a security risk. I didn't believe . . . that I should take this lying down."

But Wershba's last questions turn to the context of the situation in 1953. Quietly, the reporter asks about Radulovich's young children. There is a pause; Milo looks around at his wife, at the middle-class parlor. His answer brings together the separate motifs of private and public worlds. "If I am being judged on my relatives, are my children going to be asked to denounce me? Are they going to be judged on what their father was labeled? Are they going to have to explain to their friends, et cetera, why their father's a security risk?"

Now the contrast between the world of neighbor, family, and community and the public world of security checks, loyalty oaths, and McCarthyism is established. Here the text links home and society, family and politics. "I see a chain reaction," Radulovich warns, using an eloquent yet disturbing image, "that has no end . . . for anybody."

## The Social World

It is no coincidence that nearly all of the "The Case of Milo Radulovich" takes place in or before homes or community social centers. Earlier I mentioned how the ethos of the heroic central figure seemed to be part and parcel of his place in the social world around him. Over and over, citizens of the town tell us about the Radulovich "case" as they sit in their parlors or stand on their front porches. The Raduloviches talk about their children. Old John and his wife sit in their living room. Such continual reference to the domestic is striking; the program centers itself in the world of small-town America, of neighbors, and shady main streets.

But what we hear them say simply does not fit. The perverse contrasts with the normalcy that figures in the depiction of the town and the lieutenant. "These days," Milo says, "anybody labeled a security risk," will not be able "to find employment." These days, that is, beneath the placid surface of the small midwestern town, in the corners of this middle-class parlor, there is the unexpected—the subversive and the hidden intimidations of McCarthyism.

But an antidote is suggested by the *See It Now* rhetors. In its celebration of the ordinary, the mundane, the everyday, in its depiction of the town, of its citizens, of Milo Radulovich as typical and unremarkable, even in the remarks of Old Radulovich's fellow worker, the text juxtaposes the social world and one's private knowledge of a neighbor with the political world and public allegations of subversion. In the world of the *See It Now* text precisely this familiarity sustains trust.

Thus, in the end, Milo Radulovich is portrayed as innocent because he is like us; he is "one of us," nothing special. We find that *See It Now*'s "Case of Milo Radulovich" represents the familiar social world, invites us to join that world, and solicits our judgment from within it—a judgment made more poignant with its overtones of the universal.

## Murrow's Conclusion

Having now established the dimensions of its central figure and suggested how we are to react to his plight, *See It Now* moves quickly to its conclusion. The final section of "The Case of Milo Radulovich" is Murrow's "endpiece," a feature of nearly all *See It Now* programs and the only part of the "Radulovich" text that is clearly "marked" as argument.

As in the opening, the final sequence begins with the medium shot of Murrow and the control panel behind him. Murrow looks up and addresses the audience. "This is the transcript of the Radulovich hearing," he says, nodding at the papers before him. "I would like to read you just a bit of it."

Yet the reading itself is curious. Murrow's style is staccato: the sentences short, clipped. But it also underlines the universal in the "small story" of Milo Radulovich. In Murrow's version, the participants lose their specificity and are identified only generically, as types, as "the chairman of the board," "the lawyer," "the witness," and "the defendant." The Recorder: "I would like to introduce into evidence, as Exhibit F, the classified investigative file." The President of the Board: "It will be received and will be considered by the Board." The Lawyer: "Is it being received as a closed envelope?" The President: "It is a confidential investigative file." The Lawyer: "It is a report to the Air Force by someone, or some agency. Is that right?" Paralleling the tone of the introduction, he portrays the participants less as specific people than as characters or personae in a bizarre morality play. In Murrow's reading, the entire "case" is transformed into parable.[40]

With a final look of distaste, Murrow sets the transcript aside. The camera begins a slow zoom into an extreme close-up of Murrow, who swivels in his chair, takes a paper from the desk, then turns again into the camera. Once more, Murrow directly addresses us; again, the tone is formal, the voice calm and deliberate—the sense, one of gravity. "Perhaps you will permit me to read a few sentences just at the end, because I should like to say rather precisely what I mean."

Murrow offers the Air Force "facilities for any comments, criticism, or corrections it may wish to make in regard to the case of Milo Radulovich."[41] He summarizes the current status of the case and says that the final decision will be that of Air Force secretary Harold Talbott. But Murrow wonders how any decision can be made: "We are unable to judge the charges against the lieutenant's father or sister, because neither we, nor you, nor they, nor the lieutenant, nor the lawyers know precisely what was contained in that manila envelope. Was it hearsay, rumor, gossip, slander, or was it hard, ascertainable fact that could be backed by creditable witnesses? We do not know."

Still reading, Murrow explains one of the crucial distinctions of the era of McCarthyism—that between the loyalty risk and the security risk. "There is a distinct difference between a loyalty and a security risk. A man may be entirely loyal, but at the same time be subjected to coercion, influence, or pressure, which may cause him to act contrary to the best interests of national security." Yet, Murrow emphasizes, the board in the Radulovich case found "no question of his loyalty." Moreover, "no evidence was adduced to prove that Radulovich's sister is a member of the Party, and the case against the father was certainly not made."

Now the camera moves in for an even closer view of Murrow. "We believe," he says, "that 'the son shall not bear the iniquity of the father,' even though that iniquity be proved; and in this case, it was not."[42] Finally, Murrow lowers his tone. "Whatever happens in this whole area of the relationship between the individual and the state, we will do it to ourselves—it cannot be blamed upon Malenkov, or Mao Tse-Tung, or even our allies. And it seems to us—that is, to Fred Friendly and myself—that that is a subject that should be argued about endlessly."

This tactic reproduces the pattern founded from the first of the program; in the tone of generality in Murrow's opening, the commonplaces voiced by the chorus of citizen-witnesses and their reactions to Milo's story, in the warnings of a dangerous "chain reaction" for "everybody," *See It Now* has consistently teased out themes of larger issues in terms of the "small picture." Such a strategy certainly makes the issues relevant for the audience. But in addition, Murrow's reading of the transcript, like his introductory comments, serves to frame the story.

Murrow's conclusion recontextualizes the case within its local and immediate political situation and emphasizes the larger set of ideological issues. In this way, Murrow's conclusion, taking us from general to specific, completes the symbolic movement within the text. It accepts the lieutenant's case as universal, relieves stress upon the "immediate effects" of McCarthyism and articulates the moral, political, and ideological issues embodied in the plight of one typical man.

## Response to the Telecast

By the time it ended, there seemed little question that "The Case of Milo Radulovich" was intended to be provocative, and the immediate reaction was swift and unambiguous.[43] Friendly describes how the telephone lines "lit up" immediately after the broadcast,[44] and in the weeks that followed, of the nearly 8,000 letters and telegrams sent to CBS and to ALCOA, opinion ran "100 to 1" in Radulovich's favor.[45] The program had a 54.4 percent coverage and approximately 2,229,000 homes listening—about 10.9 percent of American homes equipped with television receivers.[46]

Television reviewers, too, were ecstatic about the program. Jack Gould called it a "superb and fighting documentary."[47] Robert Kass agreed, saying the program was a "splendid show . . . , vivid, vital journalism, TV style."[48] While another review responded to the program's emotional treatment of the distress of Lieutenant Radulovich: "Murrow told the lieutenant's story in a quiet, angry way that was most moving."[49]

Yet there was, amid enthusiastic response, the sobering realization that a threshold had been crossed. The Radulovich broadcast represented a decisive step forward, taken by television as a medium, to address issues sparking national controversy and to participate in an ongoing public debate. One historian called it a half hour of "undiluted controversy."[50] And television critic Gould observed that "the program marked the first time that a major network, the Columbia Broadcasting System, and one of the country's most important industrial sponsors, the Aluminum Company of America, consented to a program taking a vigorous editorial stand in a matter of national importance and controversy." *See It Now*'s position, Gould said, was clearly opposed to the "curtain of silence which so often descends on difficult security questions."[51]

But their willingness to engage in controversy left the *See It Now* rhetors vulnerable, for in the social and political climate of the times, controversy was often suspect. Despite the commendations of the establishment and the more liberal press, hostile columns began appearing amid the choruses of praise. The *New York Herald* would refer often in the coming months to "Egghead R. Murrow and his partner in port-side reporting."[52]

Still, quite apart from its subject matter, "The Case of Milo Radulovich" represented a turning point in TV documentary.[53] To many, the telecast was most important as the first step that the infant medium of television had taken toward respectability. As Jack Gould pointed out, the measure of the achievement of the Radulovich broadcast could only be judged against the backdrop of the usual television approach to "public affairs." Until "Radulovich," "broadcasting all too often has been found timid and wanting." Robert Kass agreed that the program "points out how little originality and fearlessness we have seen in six years of large scale television."[54] And in its 1953 annual review, *Variety* called "The Case of Milo Radulovich" "easily the most important single contribution made to television in the year,"[55] while another industry journal described the program as "a milestone in the realm of pictorial editorialization which brought to the TV medium a new found respect."[56]

Friendly saw in such reactions a recognition of the potential influence of television. He claimed that the approving critical response for "The Case of Milo Radulovich" was "the realization that television could be more than another arm of show business."[57] Moreover, Friendly regarded "Radulovich" as a watershed program: until then, *See It Now* had been rather ordinary television, he argues, but in the Radulovich production was discovered the "missing ingredients" of "conviction, controversy, and a point of view."[58]

The program is significant in another way as well. For some analysts, the Radulovich telecast was the opening of a "campaign" against McCarthyism, and they saw it as furnishing background for the later programs in the series.[59] Friendly later admitted that the positive reaction to the Radulovich program persuaded the producers to proceed with the program that was to become the most famous of the *See It Now* broadcasts, the "Report on Senator McCarthy."[60]

## Representation and Synecdoche

In seeking to understand "Radulovich," however, I suggest that making the question of the representativeness of the story the focus for analysis has allowed us to see several salient features. First of all, in "The Case of Milo Radulovich" the visual format is vital. Within the text, the presentation of Milo, the chorus of his neighbors, and his father or sister shows how the text proposes that we regard them. In addition, however, as I noted with respect to the pivotal segment of the text, the subjective camera and moving frame build a way to invite us "into" the text and so connect the chorus of townspeople with our own reaction, both modeling the reaction sought by the text and indicating the universal quality of Milo's story through the realization that he is "one of us." In "The Case of Milo Radulovich," clearly, *how* something is represented cannot be separated from *what* is represented.

Also, throughout the analysis, I indicated some ways that Milo Radulovich comes to embody both a particular and a thoroughly unremarkable young man caught in a private plight and at the same time a symbol of a public problem. I have said several times that the program has a specific symbolic movement, one that I argue moves from specific to general and back again. By moving to another level of critique, I can describe this effect more clearly.

Aside from this particular yet evocative story of a particular Air Force lieutenant, I argued that the text invites us to see, beyond the private and individual tragedy of Milo Radulovich, the realm of the universal and to give a grander ideological significance to his story. Radulovich's private tragedy becomes representative of our public failing, and this universality makes his plight that much more evocative. It is interesting that we find this same notion of representation defined in the rhetorical figure of synecdoche.

In "Four Master Tropes," Kenneth Burke describes what he calls an "evanescent moment." Addressing the classical tropes of metaphor, metonymy, synecdoche, and irony, Burke considers them not in their figurative use but for "their role in the discovery and description of the truth."[61] As for synecdoche, while the tradition defines it as one of the figures of substitution—"genus for species or species for genus for the sake of vividness of effect,"[62] or later as "given persons or people, given places or times, [standing as] tabernacles for greater wholes"[63]—Burke is far more expansive. For him, synecdoche is "representation," the representing of "part for the whole, the whole for the part . . . cause for effect, effect for cause, etc." Every synecdoche, Burke concludes, implies a "convertibility between the two terms . . . an individual is treated as a replica of the universal, and *vice versa.*"[64]

## Rhetorical Functions of Synecdoche

How does "The Case of Milo Radulovich" invite us to see, and to see beyond, the individual case of Milo Radulovich? In this "small story," the case of one particular man is given larger ideological meanings, while at the same time the ideological is enacted in the particular—given names, places, action, attributes—and is naturalized within commonsense wisdom. We may usefully and accurately describe these operations as synecdoche in the following ways.

First, the appeal of the program rests upon the synecdochic amplification from particular to general. For the *See It Now* rhetors, the "representative-ness" of the "case" of Milo Radulovich is plainly a careful and necessary fabrication. As we have seen, the program seeks to fix the Radulovich story by attending to details and to specifics of the case. This everyday "hero" is framed within the commonsense wisdom of his fellow citizens in the small town. But it is most important to recognize that the basis for the appeal is "what everyone thinks about the world." Specifically, the situation that is presented roots itself in the commonplace—the world of small-town America, of neighbors, and shady main streets. Certainly, the appeal of such images runs strong and deep in the American cultural consciousness. They have been vivified in the myths of small-town sociability and the virtue of the common man. From this perspective, Milo Radulovich takes on added significance as a commonplace "stock figure" similar to the "bashful heroes" familiar in American motion pictures.[65] Through *See It Now*'s presentation, Radulovich represents the heroic everyman caught in the political crossfire of McCarthyism.

Second, the program reverses this effect and draws upon the synecdochic reduction from general to particular. Using the story of the lieutenant as the index of a complex ideology, "The Case of Milo Radulovich" articulates more universal ideological themes in terms of a specific and intelligible representation.[66] Moreover, I suggest, via this less acknowledged synecdochic movement *See It Now* accomplishes its ideological work.

Its explicit strategy, of course, is to show the effects of McCarthyism on the common man, and in *See It Now*'s treatment of Radulovich's specific problems, we see "what it means in human terms." In addition, however, the program "uses" the figure of Radulovich and the chorus of neighbors as markers for a counterargument to the ideology of McCarthyism. *See It Now*'s "commonsense" perspective on Radulovich's story implies, as I have noted, a populist ideology that bases its position on a set of assumptions about "what everybody thinks." As a result, the argument of *See It Now*, grounded in this populist "everyday" perspective on events, efficiently undercuts partisan politics. As a replacement for this partisanship, *See It Now*'s perspective on McCarthyism, posing "ordinary people" as its source, presents necessarily ideological positions simply as a set of natural, taken-for-granted "truths." In this way, *See It Now* is able to present its own perspective on McCarthyism both as apolitical and as part of a "commonsense" consensus. *See It Now* is able to articulate covertly a political response to McCarthyism that counters McCarthyism's cloak of suspicion with the myth of "Main Street," and in it the discourse of populist morality suppresses the discourse of politics.[67]

If we reestablish connections with the context of the program's era, this strategy seems an efficacious one for the *See It Now* rhetors for several reasons. Framed within the public argument of its time, the movement from specific to universal and back again takes on ideological implications. First, while McCarthyism flourished, to openly oppose the movement was to open oneself to charges of being a "fellow traveler" or "sympathizer," and the tactics of the McCarthyites were uniformly to discredit the ethos of opponents by rendering them suspect. But the *See It Now* rhetors seem to have located an antidote. In using a specific representation that embodies the "problems" of security, loyalty, and the blacklist, the program makes clear the effects of McCarthyism on the individual. In appealing to the commonsense wisdom articulated by the young lieutenant and the chorus, the program develops an ideological argument and embodies it in terms of one specific situation.

Second, but more consequential, it seems that the *See It Now* rhetors found a way to speak out against McCarthyism by a kind of "populist ventriloquism":[68] that is, by constituting and then speaking for an audience. For the actual audience of "The Case of Milo Radulovich" we can imagine that its synecdochic action might have considerable potential appeal. It is abetted not only through identification with the content of commonsense wisdom but also through the forms within which that perspective is constructed. For instance, Murrow's voice-over and narration rely exclusively upon the first-person plural "we." Though perhaps a manifestation of Murrow's individual style,[69] in this text, the reference shifts from the "we" of the program rhetors to the collective "we" of the intended audience. I suggest that this shift is a crucial part of the way the program attempts to forge its ideal audience. *See It Now* speaks "for" its auditors through the mobilization and visual presentation of the chorus, and this visual/aural collective "we" positions the auditor as witness, participant, and supporter of the case of Milo Radulovich. If successful, *See It Now* will be accepted by its audience as their representative, speaking for them and speaking to them from a perspective (common sense) and with a language they all share.[70] Thus, the program constructs a model of its ideal auditor through its visualization of the chorus of townspeople and positions its audience as members of a group—the people—a populist identity, moreover, that is constituted by the text itself.

In sum, this *See It Now* text contrasts the American small-town social world and one's private knowledge of a neighbor with McCarthyism's public allegations of subversion and guilt by association. The text invites us to see ourselves in the "small stories" of Radulovich and his neighbors. Presenting them as unproblematic reflections of "us" and "our world," *See It Now* hides its constructedness while at the same time constituting its audience after the model of the specific Dexter townspeople. The work of this *See It Now* text thus depends upon its ability constantly to prompt its audience to reconstruct this synecdochic equivalence, this perfect symmetry between the individual person and the wider problem of McCarthyism, between the individual members of the chorus who are seen and speak and the universalized "we" in the audience who see and are invited to "speak" against McCarthyism.[71] Thus, within this *See It Now* documentary, the rhetorical figure of synecdoche ties together the three sections of the text. But in addition, synecdoche unites historical person and heroic persona, textual chorus and actual audience, in an intricate and parallel dance.

It is perhaps now clear how synecdoche suggests one way to understand how the *See It Now* rhetors prompt our assent to the plight of an individual while at the same time suggesting how that individual can stand as a "small picture" of a larger complex of historical and situational problems. Milo Radulovich as individual stands for the universal; and as representative of the universal, his individual plight attains a special pathos.

In focusing upon the role of the interesting segment that featured the chorus of Dexter townspeople, I suggested that there the text disclosed how it sought to bridge to its audience through the reactions of a group of typical citizens. Consequently the chorus of citizen-witnesses both comments upon the story of Milo Radulovich and represents an intended audience, which informs our response. The chorus does not merely voice support or elicit our "pity" for Milo Radulovich, for once we find ourselves aligned with it, the citizen-witnesses clearly model the sensibilities that we should manifest and the proper way of judging the lieutenant's situation.

## Depiction and Representation

As "The Case of Milo Radulovich" demonstrates, Burke's conception of synecdoche can enrich our understanding of documentaries. It also suggests implications for the more general problem of representation and depiction in documentary argument.

The news documentary falls between the blunt "evidentiary" reality of the newsreel and the imaginative constructions of rhetorical invention, and its potential for public argument seems dependent upon this position. On the one hand, such documentary argument is based upon the ontology of the photograph itself—"the indexical relationship with the pro-filmic event."[72] But to engage the public mind, documentary must enrich and magnify this specific historical moment. As Bill Nichols has remarked, "The subject of the documentary must be presented as an agent or event in history by way of a filmic representation that introduces ideology and myth without overturning indexical reference."[73] As "The Case of Milo Radulovich" makes clear, this transubstantiation into the imagery of the ideological or mythic requires our assent to the "reality" of the historical.

The shuttling back and forth between the indexical or historical and the symbolic, ideological, or mythic that defines such documentary rhetoric seems to have its equivalent in the two-way movement between specific and universal. Of course, here once more we come under the influence of the cognitive operations described by the trope of synecdoche, but we do so in a way quite different from the traditional. This approach enables us to transcend the traditional question of how documentary argument escapes "the tyranny of the specific case."

Documentary argument layers a second-order signification over the indexical photograph. This wash of the symbolic or mythic has the potential to highlight the more general moral and ideological implications within the specific.[74] At the same time, the ideological is enacted in the historical event. In short, the rhetorical documentary does not "escape"; instead, the form operates "bimodally"—historical and symbolic are mutually dependent. Thus, side by side and mutually dependent within documentary argument are the specific, the historical and the universalized, the exemplary, and the symbolic.

When seen in this way, the trope of synecdoche is perfectly suited to describe the persuasive dimensions and rhetorical action of many television news documentaries. Via the cognitive operations described by synecdoche, it appears, the news documentary magnifies the specific case while enacting the universal within the concrete. In this regard, Michael Osborn has said, "as knowledge becomes more complicated and remote, and as more people become responsible for informed judgments and decisions, synecdoche, which makes the world accessible through concrete representation, seems likely to become increasingly vital."[75]

Moreover, in answer to the question posed in the opening of this chapter, it is now clear that the documentary discourse escapes the tyranny of the specific case through synecdoche. It may well be that we interpret *See It Now*'s perspective on issues in the public realm through the figure of synecdoche acting upon—working with and on—representations like those of Radulovich and the townspeople of Dexter.

# 5

---

# Depiction and the Defense of Plurality: "An Argument in Indianapolis"

For November 24, 1953, television listings announced the evening's *See It Now* telecast as "The Indianapolis Controversy over Formation of a Unit of the American Civil Liberties Union."[1] But those who tuned in saw an unexpected opening segment.

After the standard title and credits, Murrow is framed in a close shot: "Good evening." In his hand is the characteristically uplifted cigarette. "Five weeks ago tonight," he says, "we reported at some length on the case of Lieutenant Milo Radulovich."[2] "The case has been under consideration of the Air Force ever since. At the conclusion of our report five weeks ago, we offered the Air Force the opportunity to offer criticism, comment, or correction. Today the decision was reached on Lieutenant Milo Radulovich." We cut to a position over Murrow's shoulder. He turns and looks up at the monitor before him on the control panel. "And here," he says, with a dramatic flourish, "is the Secretary of the Air Force, Harold E. Talbott."

The camera tightens ever so slightly upon the monitor above Murrow. It reads: STAND BY WASHINGTON. And then we see the secretary—he is sitting stiffly behind a desk, and his words are addressed to the commentator. "Mr. Murrow," he begins:

It is my sworn duty to uphold and protect the security of the United States. I am also keenly aware of my responsibility to protect the individual rights and privileges of each man and woman in the United States Air Force. The preservation of our American way of life requires that we must be alert to safeguard our individual liberties. I have given the case of First Lieutenant Milo J. Radulovich the most serious consideration. I have decided that it is consistent with the interests of the national security to retain Lieutenant Radulovich in the United States Air Force Reserve. He is not, in my opinion, a security risk.

Unexpected as it is, the announcement is stunning—the Air Force publicly reversing its decision to remove Radulovich from the service. Those involved were ecstatic: earlier in the day, when it first became known, there had been an impromptu celebration in the *See It Now* offices. For Radulovich's sake, the staff was "more pleased about this than anything else," said Joe Wershba, thinking back on that day. "It was clean. No rough edges. It was a victory."[3]

Indeed, it was a victory. And this outcome of the Radulovich case may have prompted Murrow and Fred Friendly to become more deeply involved in the great argument of the day over McCarthyism. For the *See It Now* rhetors, "victory" in the Radulovich case was an encouragement, and for some others—some of those on the outside of the program—it was a sign that *See It Now* could be counted on to speak out against the stifling of controversy and the urge for conformity that characterized the era.[4] But whatever messages the "victory" might have sent severally, for the audience watching on November 24, the opening could only have reinforced the credibility and ethos of Murrow and the program itself. For this audience, the Air Force's reversing of its decision in the case of Lieutenant Radulovich may well have had the more local effect of paving the way for the Indianapolis story that followed.

## The Question of Bias

After a short commercial break, *See It Now* returns. Murrow looks up to the camera, the control panel to his left.

This next report we call "the argument in Indianapolis." There was considerable argument there last week between the American Legion and a group of people who wanted to start a local chapter of the American Civil Liberties Union. This report was all filmed in a period of five days, and all the arguments will be presented by the people who actually participated.

From the very first words of the program, which came to be known as "An Argument in Indianapolis," *See It Now* announces its intention to "present the arguments" of those involved in the Indiana dispute. This is an interesting assertion, for it announces the program's pretense to neutrality. In other words, *See It Now* purports to be merely the medium for the more or less objective presentation of positions of those involved in the "argument." The textual claim is that the program has effaced itself from the "argument," and so this apparently innocent statement works to dissipate or nullify potential charges of bias or partiality on the part of *See It Now*.

Still, the claim of impartiality has prompted considerable disagreement. For most media scholars, the conclusion has generally been that "An Argument in Indianapolis" is unbiased and impartial. Analyses of the program have, for the most part, lauded it as an example of how a news documentary might present a "fair" report on an event. Murray Yaeger's early appraisal is a typical evaluation. Yaeger classified "An Argument in Indianapolis" as an "unbiased controversial" program because it presented "both sides of the story."[5] He found the program more "report" than "editorial," chiefly, Yaeger says, because it used only "minimal comment" by Murrow and concentrated instead upon the actual people and their situation as told in their own words.[6]

In subsequent analyses, most attention has focused upon the novel segment presenting the parallel meetings of the Legion and the ACLU—a section that occupies the center of the program and is its longest single segment.[7] For instance, critic Gilbert Seldes cited the cross-cutting of "An Argument in Indianapolis" as a prototype and as one of *See It Now*'s technical contributions to the documentary genre. The editing results, he says, in an effect of "angry debate" between the two sides and showed that the issues involved were not trivial but intense. Furthermore, argues Seldes, the intercutting "had the effect of almost mathematical impartiality" and revealed the way that news documentary could "handle" controversy without itself becoming embroiled in the actual dispute.[8]

But not everyone who has seen "Argument in Indianapolis" shares this sanguine perspective. In his book, *The Left-Leaning Antenna: Political Bias in Television,* an exposé of liberal sensibilities in the media, Joseph Keeley takes another tack. Keeley suggests that editorial opinion can be found in many other ways than just by what is said: "Doubt can be raised in many minds by something that does not even show in a newscaster's script."[9] To illustrate, Keeley describes the "debate" sequence from "An Argument in Indianapolis":

Harsh lighting made the Legionnaires look ghastly, and their voices came through sounding harsh and unpleasant. . . . When the cameras switched to the ACLU people in another part of the city, there was a tremendous difference. All these people looked like solid citizens, thoughtful and concerned about The Important Things [*sic*]. . . . However, what both groups said did not matter greatly. One could make up one's mind by the way they looked. [36]

Keeley's critique intrigues. And it clearly calls into question the claimed "neutrality" of "An Argument in Indianapolis." Is the claim to impartiality of this *See It Now* text justified? Answering this important question will frame this chapter.

But in responding to this issue, we will also implicitly be answering another, equally salient question: upon what grounds do we judge the question of impartiality? To say, as Keeley does, that we can make up our minds about the two opposing groups according to "how they looked" is to posit to the visual image and to the process of depiction a persuasive potency that demands explanation. In what way, then, does the depicted image invite an audience to shift its sensibilities to the event or person visualized? And how might what Michael Osborn calls "strategic pictures" function to establish premises of ideological argument?[10] Such considerations will, of course, take us to the threshold of another issue: the relationship of argument to the conventions of reportage, a relationship, moreover, that is crucial to the strategies of documentary.

## A Controversy in Indiana

The controversy in Indianapolis was originally a local issue, overlooked by the national press. It was, however, by any standard a bizarre story. A group of seventy Indiana citizens attempted to hire a hall for a start-up meeting of an Indiana chapter of the American Civil Liberties Union. On November 16, four days prior to the scheduled meeting, the use of the reserved auditorium at the Indiana War Memorial was canceled on grounds that the meeting was of a "controversial" nature. Suddenly every suitable meeting place in the area seemed booked, until a young Roman Catholic priest offered his parish hall for the meeting.

Murrow and Friendly became aware of the story through the Indianapolis newspapers and, prompted by an editorial in the *Indianapolis Times*, decided to investigate the dispute as a potential *See It Now* segment.[11] But their final decision to cover it was encouraged by two coincidental occurrences—both proceding directly from their defense of individual rights in "The Case of Milo Radulovich."

The first coincidence came without warning. Friendly received a call from the public relations director of the national Civil Liberties office about the affair in Indianapolis. The ACLU official admitted to Friendly that while the canceled meeting was not the sort of story that *See It Now* usually covered, the Radulovich program had set a precedent, and the ACLU realized that Murrow and Friendly were generally sympathetic. Furthermore, "Murrow was one of those people who understood what civil liberties really were."[12] Friendly responded that they were looking into the story and that he would keep the ACLU's request in mind.

But a second occurrence of the week lent a more personal and more ominous motivation to Murrow's and Friendly's decision to cover the controversy in Indiana. On November 17, Joe Wershba, the reporter on the Radulovich story, had been approached by Don Surine, a McCarthy investigator.[13] Surine promised to provide Wershba with documentary evidence that "Murrow was on the Soviet payroll in 1934."

The "evidence" was a copy of the front page of the *Pittsburgh Sun-Telegraph*, February 18, 1935. The headline proclaimed: "American Professors Trained by Soviets Teach in U.S. Schools." The article outlined a summer seminar at Moscow University that the Institute of International Education (IIE), as the primary American organization devoted to student exchange, had sponsored in 1934 and 1935. Surine told Wershba that the Moscow seminar was arranged through VOKS, the Soviet agency for cultural relations with foreign countries, and because Murrow had been the assistant director of the IEE for three years before joining CBS in 1935, he deduced that this made Murrow part of the "Moscow conspiracy." The threat to Murrow seemed plain. Clearly Surine meant that if Murrow remained quiet on matters such as those raised in the Radulovich program, nothing would be said about his past "Communistic affiliations."[14] When Wershba told him, Murrow brushed off the danger, saying nonchalantly, "so that's what they've got." But he could not ignore the revelation that McCarthyites were compiling data for a possible exposé.[15]

In this context Murrow and Friendly made the decision to proceed with "An Argument in Indianapolis." Only now, with a heightened sense of special urgency—two days after Surine's warning and a short twenty-four hours after Wershba saw the photostats—Murrow and Friendly sent reporters to cover the Indianapolis ACLU meeting scheduled for the next day. But what was originally expected to be a rather simple production was soon to become more and more complex.

As tensions mounted in Indianapolis and as the ACLU made ready for its first meeting, the American Legion planned a meeting of its own. State officers of the Legion, including members of its executive committee, were invited to Legion headquarters in Indianapolis to debate the merits of the ACLU. When the state commander of the Legion, Roy M. Amos, was approached for a statement on the morning of the scheduled meetings, and when Wershba revealed his intention to film the ACLU gathering, Amos insisted that the hastily called Legion meeting was equally significant and requested similar coverage. Wershba telephoned Murrow and asked for another camera crew. *See It Now* producer Ed Scott and cameraman Marty Barnett arrived in Indianapolis later that same day.[16] They rushed to Legion headquarters and quickly set up lights, microphones, and camera positions to record the Legion executive council.

The following morning the two producers arrived back in New York City carrying the exposed footage of the twin meetings while Barnett remained in Indianapolis for "cover" shots. With the broadcast scheduled less than four days after the meetings, the editing session was more than usually hectic for the staff.

Then, early the next week, with the program nearly completed, there was to be the sudden and dramatic last-minute inclusion of something more. It was not until 8:00 A.M. on the morning of the scheduled telecast of "An Argument in Indianapolis" that the *See It Now* producers knew of the change. Arriving home from the all-night editing session, Friendly received an urgent phone call from Murrow. Apologizing, Murrow said he had received an emergency message from the secretary of the Air Force, who wanted "Charlie Mack and his camera crew over at the Pentagon by nine o'clock" to film a statement.[17] But only when Mack phoned, hours later, did they realize that the Air Force would reverse itself on the air.[18] More footage was trimmed from the program to fit Talbott's statement into the allotted twenty-six minutes.

As a result, that evening, in *See It Now*'s second telecast on McCarthyism in a single month, Murrow faced the camera in Studio 41 to introduce "An Argument in Indianapolis." The story was preceded by a "short"—both shocking and gratifying—three minutes and ten seconds of Secretary Talbott reinstating Lieutenant Milo Radulovich.

## Textual Analysis

The opening statement by Secretary Talbott resonates on several levels: it "closes" the Radulovich story, and yet it "opens," and so interacts with, this broadcast about a controversy in Indiana. It justifies *See It Now*'s original perspective on the Radulovich case while it confirms the impact of the *See It Now* series. A closer examination of this brief segment and its lead-in discloses motifs central to the *See It Now* programs—motifs that might color an auditor's perception of "An Argument in Indianapolis."[19]

## The Reflexive Text

First, Murrow introduces the segment, not with a narrative about Milo Radulovich, or with the story of his appeal to an Air Force board of review, but with the narration of *See It Now*'s part in the Radulovich story: "Five weeks ago tonight, we reported [this story] at some length . . . ," he says. *See It Now* becomes, in this opening, self-referential—Murrow pulls the story of Milo Radulovich and his conflict with the Air Force back within the "world" of *See It Now* and focuses upon the role of the program in that story. That is, as Murrow frames it, the appearance by Talbott and his reversal is a response to *See It Now*'s "offer" of a chance for "criticism, comment, or correction" and seems, then, to have little to do with standard procedures or military policies of review in "loyalty cases."[20] Also, it reaffirms *See It Now*'s claim to "fairness" in reminding us that the Air Force appears at the invitation of the producers. In casting the story this way, *See It Now* is rendered a participant in the dispute, and so the program promotes the television medium itself as the "cause" of events. This way, *See It Now* is not the mere medium of "news"; it is a maker of news, itself a part of the story, an element in the resolution of a conflict in the public arena.

Furthermore, Talbott opens his statement directing his comments, remarkably, not to the audience, but to Murrow. On the one hand, this curious mode of address certifies the ethos of Edward R. Murrow. It reaffirms Murrow's status as one with access to those within the institutions of government and power. At the same time, such address enhances Murrow's status within the text: only through Murrow are we allowed access to those same institutions, and Murrow serves as the gatekeeper to the world "outside." Finally, Talbott's direct address to Murrow highlights the audience's position as spectator in the text. Murrow brings the world to us—his personal power and influence permit us to join in "seeing" the world "now."[21]

But the Talbott segment has additional themes. For instance, the secretary discusses the Radulovich case in the same terms that *See It Now* had used in the earlier broadcast. We must "be alert to safeguard our individual liberties," Talbott says; "the preservation of our American way of life requires that." Such a choice of similar descriptive motifs invites an appreciation of the influence of the program in setting the terms for discussion of the case. In a way, then, the audience is invited to read the Air Force's reversal as affirming the justness of the earlier program. And such a reading cannot help but influence judgment regarding subsequent *See It Now* episodes. That is, since *See It Now* seems now justified in defense of Milo Radulovich, then *See It Now* might well be justified in its other stands, and once a viewer has certification of its essential "correctness" in the Radulovich matter, then the viewer has a powerful reason to join *See It Now* on other issues. So the Radulovich decision has a kind of rebound or mirror effect: the Air Force's actions certifying the ethos and integrity of the *See It Now* program while at the same time thus inviting us to join the "correct" *See It Now* rhetors as they address the controversy in Indianapolis. Thus, *See It Now* presents its opening segment in such a way as to make it unmistakably clear that this is no mere "entertainment." The reflexive text promotes itself as influential enough to alter events in the world outside the television discourse. The Talbott statement constitutes a powerful message that redoubles attention to this telecast and invites increasingly deferential attention to "An Argument in Indianapolis."

For purposes of analysis, we may divide "An Argument in Indianapolis" easily into five natural segments. The first two are Talbott's statement and Murrow's introduction. In Murrow's introduction, as previously noted, the text reaffirms *See It Now*'s impartiality and objectivity and so claims neutrality in its presentation of the Indianapolis controversy. The third segment is the setting of the background of the story largely through the statements of "neutral" citizens, of representatives of the Civil Liberties Union and the Legion. The fourth and longest segment is the core of the text: the presentation of the "argument" between the groups in the form of what Murrow calls a "debate." The concluding segment is a peroration delivered by a local Catholic priest. Throughout, my analysis will focus on the way in which these segments work with one another and how the text buttresses its claim to impartiality.

### Controversy and Conformity

Deploying its standard visual conventions, *See It Now* begins the story. Murrow turns slightly and looks up at the monitors before him. We cut to the cover shot over Murrow's shoulder, and see STAND BY INDIANAPOLIS on the right monitor. The camera begins a slow move toward it—then a quick edit. We are looking down a broad avenue that is dominated, at its terminus, by a huge monument. We hear the sounds of traffic in the busy central city. Murrow speaks over: "That shaft is an Indiana landmark," he says. "A memorial to those who died in the War Between the States." "Three blocks north of here, is a memorial to the dead of World War I."

Our view changes. We see broad steps, and in an extreme wide shot, a trio of people climb them. "This is the Indiana World War Memorial," Murrow says. "It has an auditorium that seats 540." Quickly, he fills in background, telling us of the reserving of the auditorium, then the canceling of the reservation by the management shortly before the meeting. Murrow introduces the first of the "participants." He is "Roland Allen, a department-store executive," and he will, Murrow tells us, "begin the story."

Allen, bespectacled and slow of speech, stands before a gray curtain; he is portrayed as amiable and low-key. His statement is filled with colloquialisms, and he speaks directly to the camera, uninterrupted by editing or questions. "On the sixteenth of October, a group of sixty or seventy fine men and women—professors from Indiana University and Purdue University, physicians, lawyers, housewives, and other good folk—got together in a local hotel here to decide whether or not it would be wise to form an American Civil Liberties unit here in Indiana." But as a result of "a protest from the American Legion and the Minute Women" the use of the hall was disallowed. "And so," Allen says, "the old American problem of controversy came up; and many people mistook controversy for conspiracy."

Murrow quickly switches us to another interview: "Next, Wershba went to . . . [the] manager of the War Memorial, and asked why permission to use the auditorium had been withdrawn." We cut to a wide shot of the reporter with a microphone. He stands with another man inside the Memorial building. Then a closer shot: the manager admits that he originally considered the "local representatives" of the American Civil Liberties Union to be "very reputable people representing business and learning." But soon he began to get complaints from the American Legion and the Minute Women of Indiana. So, he says, "Realizing that this meeting must be of a controversial nature, which is not agreeable to the rules and regulations that govern the use of this Indiana World War Memorial, I thereupon canceled the meeting."

It should be noted at this early point in the development of the text how the theme of "controversy" has moved quickly to the center. The tension announced in these two interviews, the tension, that is, between controversy and conformity, animates "An Argument in Indianapolis." In fact, one of the objectives of this *See It Now* text will be to redefine controversy and conflict. But before we are ready for the new definition, the text must describe more of the situation in Indianapolis.

*Depiction of the Groups*

In keeping with its claim to impartiality, *See It Now* introduces us to the "other side," to those who want to stop the Civil Liberties meeting. We cut to a rather large Tudor-style home, then to the house numbers on the brick front. "This is 3650 Washington Boulevard, the home of one of Indianapolis's Minute Women," Murrow says. The door of the home opens, and the camera pans slightly left: a middle-aged matron wearing neat wire-frame glasses and a pillbox hat emerges. "This is Miss Marguerite Dice, a past officer of the organization," Murrow announces. The woman smiles uneasily at the camera, holds up a note card and begins to read her statement.

The War Memorial Building, Miss Dice reads, was erected "in memory of those men who gave their lives for the protection and preservation of the principles on which this country was founded." "What a travesty it would be to open its doors for a meeting to which Communists are welcome, when we know the open and avowed purpose of such is to overthrow our government by force and violence, as well as by infiltration."

We cut quickly to the state commander of the American Legion, Roy M. Amos. Murrow introduces him with the comment that the Legion was the source of the "heaviest objections." Amos looks down and forcefully reads the Legion position:

[We] can never agree that the Indiana War Memorial is a fitting place for a meeting of the American Civil Liberties Union. The Memorial is hallowed ground. It is a shrine sacred to the memory of thousands of gallant Hoosier patriots, many of whom died in Korea fighting Communism. As such, it must never be used as a sounding board for the advocacy of any policy of pampering Communists to the virtual exclusion of all others.

What is most remarkable about both of these interviews is their manner of presentation, and they naturally contrast with the earlier one with Roland Allen, the representative of the ACLU. To begin with, both Dice and Amos read their statements to us; they do not speak directly to us as Allen does. Also, they do not appear as relaxed or as comfortable on camera as the Civil Liberties man. Furthermore, Legion Commander Amos, sporting his Legion overseas cap, is presented in a shocking and abrupt close-up. Beetle-browed, Amos looks up nervously over the top of his spectacles and, after looking down to read, does not glance up again. The effect is heightened by lighting that is harsh and high contrast, leaving Amos a blazing white two-dimensional figure on an almost completely dark flat background. But Allen's statement earlier in the text is quite different and serves as a marker of the contrast to be developed in the unfolding of the program. Allen stands easily before an off-gray curtain. The lighting on his face, seen in medium shot, is soft and even, lending to his features a rounded appearance. Moreover, Allen is more animated: he gestures to emphasize a point, his face reveals his emotions as he speaks.

As will become clear, this contrast in style of presentation becomes a pattern. Over and over, those on the side of the ACLU speak extemporaneously, looking directly at the camera, their remarks low-key, their voices modulated and relaxed. The lighting and setting are more flattering and rounded. Those opposed to the meeting, in contrast, read their statements, avoid our direct gaze, and are uneasy and cautious, their voices emphatic and often shrill. Those people in the middle, those "neutral" (the manager of the Memorial, for example) always speak to a *See It Now* reporter, and the reporter seemingly stands as intermediary between them and the *See It Now* audience.

After Amos's statement, Murrow returns to the narrative of the ACLU's attempt to find a hall in which to meet. After the meeting was canceled, he tells us, the "good folks" had to find a meeting place. The visualizations carry us out onto the streets of Indianapolis, and we are invited by the text to reenact the search for a hall. Murrow's narration guides us, and the sequence is a striking use of the camera for emotional association. "On Tuesday, the Civil Liberties people called the Claypool Hotel," Murrow says. "A clerk told them the Chateau Room was available. Shortly after that, it was discovered that it had been previously booked." As he speaks, we see the facade of the Claypool Hotel, then its great sign on the side, and finally in a closer shot the hotel name on its awning over the sidewalk. The bizarre odyssey continues, the pacing of the text more rapid:

Then, the American Civil Liberties Union called the Continental Hotel on North Meridian Street—after that, the Riddick Piano Company, which has a large studio that is generally for rent. Next the Civil Liberties Union went to the Public Library and asked for their auditorium. After that, the Indianapolis YMCA. All of these places reported that they were either previously booked or for other various reasons unavailable for the Friday-night meeting.

With each place name, we see the outside of each building, its front door, and its outdoor sign—in every case, the interior is kept from our view just as its use is denied to the ACLU. The repetition of this section of the text parallels the frustrating experience of the Civil Liberties "folks" in finding a hall. And as we watch, we are prompted to share the frustrations of those citizens.

This sequence makes clear the text's invitation to align its audience's sympathies with those of the "good folk" of Indiana. Through the text's recreation of their experience in visual terms, *See It Now* invites the viewer to draw closer, to find a common ground for identification with those in the ACLU. Telling the story from their point of view subtly aligns the audience with the Civil Liberties group.

Then, ironically, Murrow tells us that the Knights of Columbus offered their hall, and a price of "fifty dollars was agreed upon." Again, a facade—this time of the Gothic K of C building. But again disappointment follows: the same evening, the Knights of Columbus auditorium was withdrawn. We cut to a shot of two men at a small table: one is the *See It Now* reporter. Murrow says, "We asked . . . why." The Knights' spokesman voices sentiments nearly identical to those expressed by the manager of the War Memorial Hall earlier: the fear of becoming "involved in the midst of a situation we had no desire to become involved in." Speaking to Wershba, he admits that "at first [we] could see no reason why it wouldn't be all right." But then, "we find that it was a controversial issue." Shaking his head in obvious concern, the Knight concludes that it is nearly impossible to "stay in the middle" these days.

Again, *See It Now* takes us back out to the streets; again, frustrated, we see cars moving down broad avenues. Murrow quotes from favorable editorials in each of the Indianapolis newspapers. We see other buildings. Then, a slow pan to the right and unexpectedly, there the tall spires of a cathedral. Murrow speaks over: "Then, less than two days before the meeting, an auditorium was finally offered. This is the corner of Vermont and New Jersey streets, just a few blocks east of the War Memorial Building. Victor L. Goosens, pastor of St. Mary's Roman Catholic Church, offered them his church's social center. It was accepted."

The program cuts to a shot of Father Goosens in his clerical collar. Seen in tight close-up (it is difficult to determine where the interview is taking place), Goosens offers a long and uninterrupted statement. He speaks directly to the camera, and his words are thoughtful. He explains that he was not afraid of involvement in the controversy, and instead, unlike others in the program, he consciously avoided the "middle."

It seems to me that there is something much more basic involved here than merely the idea of a meeting place. We have to be very careful . . . to recognize the rights of minorities. You know, all of us at some time or other are going to find ourselves in a minority group . . . and [if] it is possible for any group . . . to restrain another from peaceful assembly and from the right to express themselves freely, then, all our liberties are in danger. . . . What guarantee would there be that, later on, another group might not decide that when I or my people gather together for purposes of worship or the exercise of freedom of religion, that we should be stopped?

In speaking directly to us, by means of the style of interview we have been conditioned to associate with the Civil Liberties representatives, Goosens is thus aligned with that group. This conclusion is confirmed by the tenor of his remarks, and as a result, the words of the priest lend the "good folks" an additional ethical significance. Furthermore, in content Goosens's words echo sentiments that resonate in a common heritage, and Goosens sets the conflict between controversy and conformity within the American tradition. This contextualization of the conflict will have considerable ideological implications.

### The "Debate"

An audio cue signals the beginning of the "debate" segment, the fourth and longest section of "An Argument in Indianapolis." We see an extreme close-up shot of a small hammer striking a bell. In the pause, Murrow tells us that, a short distance from the Civil Liberties group's meeting in St. Mary's Parish Hall, the American Legion was holding, in protest, its own meeting.

The camera pulls back, and we see four Legionnaires standing at attention behind a dais. The room is dark, and the men stand out in stark contrast from the wall behind them. Two flags, country and Legion, enter and cross in front of the saluting officers. They are followed with strict precision by other members bearing shoulder arms. The group executes a sharp right-face and snaps to attention in front of the commander.

Quickly we cut to the Civil Liberties meeting. A man leads the pledge of allegiance to the American flag, which stands before him at the front of the hall. The room is bright, the meeting informal. *See It Now* shows us a wide shot of others in the crowded hall: they are young, old, men, and women—a diverse group. Murrow describes what we are about to see: "Because these two meetings, running simultaneously, so paralleled each other in subject and debate, we have chosen to present them as we have in political debates, with each side answering the other."

First the Legion. Commander Amos solemnly begins by welcoming the assembled Legionnaires: "You are assembled here tonight to receive information on a new development on the 'red firing line' in Indiana." To the Civil Liberties meeting: A neatly dressed young man confesses to the crowd that "I don't like to be told that anybody can't have a meeting. It gets my Irish up." He smiles. A quick cut back to the Legion meeting: a member stands, executes a sharp salute, and then marches to the lectern. The only reason the American Civil Liberties Union was granted use of the Catholic Parish Hall, he says, is because "the organization had not yet been declared subversive by the Attorney General." Another quick cut, again back to the Civil Liberties Union. We see Roland Allen standing framed between two American flags. He is relaxed; he smiles ruefully. "This week's adventures in our community remind me of the old American habit of answering a man who says he wants to talk. We say, 'Well, why don't you go hire a hall?'" He shakes his head. "This week we found ourselves having great difficulty in carrying out that old American habit."

But a remarkable shot follows: as if in response to Allen's light-hearted irony, *See It Now* cuts away to show the response of the audience. They laugh, nod. Another cut and we come to focus on one attractive young woman. The camera isolates her in close-up; she smiles pleasantly in agreement.

Suddenly the text cuts to the Legion meeting: Amos is reading a formal statement in his same ominous and weary tones. "The issue," he reads, "is the alerting of the people of Indiana to the fact that there is being established in Indiana a chapter of the American Civil Liberties Union." Amos never looks up from his statement. "This is an organization that is parading its avowed purposes of protecting the civil rights of individuals." He is a silhouette against a black background; his Legion campaign hat, his dark thick brows, his somber demeanor render him a menacing figure. Again, back to the parish hall. Framed before the American flags, a man talks gently to the group.

I have come to realize that a true conservative and a true liberal will find themselves side by side protecting the civil rights of their fellow men. For the true meaning of the word "conservative" means that you wish to conserve the best of the past, and pass it on the way you got it. A true liberal means a tolerance for the convictions of others and a willingness to hear them out.

And once again we see members of the audience at the Civil Liberties meeting. In the center of the frame, *See It Now* trains our gaze on a middle-aged woman who listens intently, nodding. Behind her a young couple watches the speaker.

The Legion meeting is in vivid contrast. Against the black wall, a Legionnaire in uniform reads a thundering denunciation of the Civil Liberties Union. The cadence of his accusation is ponderous—it sounds threatening, dangerous. I have, he reads, "documentary evidence at hand" that Civil Liberties speakers have "subscribed to, and been members of, organizations listed as subversive." We should, he vows, always refuse to allow the War Memorial, "dedicated to the memory of our war dead," to be used as a "sounding board for this philosophy or policy."

The cross-cutting between the two meetings continues. But by now, a clear pattern has been established. Certainly, what *See It Now* presents is hardly the "debate" Murrow promised. The speakers talk past one another, not joining issues, sharing little common ground. But certain important features are apparent. To begin with, here the viewer stands in a different relation to the *See It Now* text. It has already been noted earlier how "An Argument in Indianapolis" positioned its viewer as "seeing" through Murrow: Talbott's statement is directed to him; we watch and listen as Murrow summons witnesses and guides our responses. That is to say, for the most part, *See It Now* is a text essentially "closed" to the viewer as subject; the subject is usually positioned somewhere outside it.[22] But here, the text ruptures and opens to the audience, which finds itself "at" the meetings; the speakers speak to the viewer and they share the vantage of those in attendance without the intercession of Murrow as commentator. This form invites a different sort of cognitive response. Lacking the guiding commentary of Murrow, the viewer-subject will likely naturally draw more upon an understanding of the conventions of social behavior and the conventions of depiction found in film stylistics. Both sets of codes will become crucial to understanding "An Argument in Indianapolis."

As for the conventions of film style, students of cinema have long recognized that certain properties of film stylistics may shape the responses of an audience.[23] One important element of film style has to do with the depiction of physical setting or space, and clues within the scene may suggest associations important to textual themes. In "An Argument in Indianapolis," for instance, the Legion meeting hall has a minimum of depth clues. Partly because of the physical setting of the room (and partly the lighting), when the Legionnaires are presented, their image seems flat and uninteresting. They appear but in two dimensions. Moreover, the arrangement of the meeting hall itself has an exaggerated formality, even a martial quality: in the only view of the entire room, an extreme wide shot, members sit in straight and uniform rows, the leaders at an elevated dais in the front. In contrast, the Civil Liberties group is shown only in close shots, and the group members' arrangement within the space seems random, unplanned. Also, an American flag is prominent in the ACLU meeting, and in certain shots the speakers are framed in front of the flags, by implication sharing in the ethical appeal. While the flag is also prominent in the Legion meeting, its use is very different. There the flag is carried as part of a soldierly ceremony accompanied by shoulder arms, pomp, and military convention.

Another element of the mise-en-scène that serves to contrast the groups is costume. While the members of the Civil Liberties group are attired in sports coats, suits, and ties, the Legion, as befitting its military heritage, is martial in appearance. The hats that each member wears recall the military origins of the organization.

Another important element of film style often marked by film analysts is the lighting. The amount, direction, and quality of lighting can affect the way a viewer is likely to interpret a series of images. In both meetings the lighting is "hard," giving both groups a distinctness and clarity. But there are striking differences: in the Legion meeting the light is directed solely from the front. The absence of back or fill lights adds to the sense of flatness in the visualizations of the Legionnaires. But in the ACLU meeting, the lighting is more even and modeled; front and back lights work together to lend a sense of depth and fullness to the Civil Liberties group that contrasts with the stark depiction of the Legion.[24]

Moreover, in dominant tonal scale and brightness the two meeting places differ strikingly and present an ideal contrast for black-and-white television. As noted, the parish hall of the church is bright, well lit, and seemingly spacious, while the Legion hall is dark and cavernous, cramped. The different setting and the very different quality of light make it easy to tell which meeting is which as the text cross-cuts between them and perhaps also suggest how a viewer is to characterize the meetings.

As important as the elements of film style are for a developing sense of the opposing organizations, so is the behavior and actions of the members themselves. This may be illustrated by looking at the remainder of the "debate" segment. Arthur Garfield Hayes, an engaging speaker and the national counsel of the ACLU, is introduced: "There is only one thing that I know of on which President Eisenhower and ex-President Truman seem to agree," he says, "and that is on the good work done by the American Civil Liberties Union."

There is laughter in the room and we cut to a shot of a young couple listening intently, smiling. Behind them is an elderly woman. A cut to the Legion meeting: another Legionnaire is at the podium; he attempts to read his prepared statement, though he does so with great difficulty and stumbling.

Mr. Commander, in my hand I have a clipping taken from the *Nation* magazine of June 28, 1952. This clipping is an advertisement of the American Civil Liberties Union, which asks the reader to join them in fighting the Smith and McCarran Act. I believe that any organization that would advertise such a fact cannot have the interest of the United States at heart. And I think Commander Amos is right in exposing them in Indiana.[25]

As the speaker mentions Amos's name, we cut to a shocking, extreme close-up of the commander. From the camera angle, he looms above us against the dark background, nodding at the mention of his name. Back to Hayes: he stands before the light gray backdrop of the Civil Liberties Union meeting, framed by the American flag. His remarks return us to the theme of "disagreement," echoing and amplifying those of Father Goosens earlier: "What is the matter with a controversial subject?" he demands. "Controversy is as American as the Rocky Mountains or the Fourth of July." To the Legion meeting—another Legionnaire who can hardly read. He chastises the ACLU for defending a union leader accused of "following the Communist party line." "An organization which gives aid and comfort" to such a person, he declares, stumbling, "does not belong in Indiana."

Then, a final Civil Liberties speaker addresses the camera. His demeanor, too, is congenial. He reminds us that the concept of civil liberties is sacred to an American way of life. Furthermore, he says, disagreement is vital and important in "the court of public opinion," for it is only through controversy that "freedom and truth will become victors."

Once again, in the middle of his statement, *See It Now* shows still more shots of the audience at the Civil Liberties meeting. This time, the camera concentrates upon a youngish man who listens intently, nodding agreement with the speaker's words. This is contrasted with the final speakers at the Legion meeting. Quite formally, appropriate with military procedure, Amos recognizes a Legionnaire who stands, salutes, and advances. The speaker reads a resolution condemning the American Civil Liberties group and forcefully demands that a "unanimous vote of confidence" be given Commander Amos "for exposing the ACLU in Indiana." Another Legionnaire salutes, is recognized, and stiffly marches to the lectern. The effect is comical—this Legionnaire's hat is askew, his glasses reflect in the light.

Quite dramatically, he pauses and then with great pomposity says: "I, Orin Nailan, of the Ninth District, school supplies salesman, take great pleasure in seconding this motion."

Because it focuses on the behavior of the members of the two groups, the effect is to render the representatives of the Legion as, if not seriocomic, then clearly inappropriate when contrasted to the members of the Civil Liberties group. And as their words and actions are compared, a viewer likewise develops a sense of the essential nature of the motives and character of both organizations. Even the tactic of the close-up shots of the audience members at the ACLU meeting (these become more and more frequent as the text unfolds) has no analog among shot choices at the Legion meeting. This, too, subtly identifies auditor with the Civil Liberties group. After all, those at the Union meeting are diverse, attractive, attentive; in their diversity they contrast with the Legion, whose members, with their military garb and formality, seem to be of one cloth.

I have quoted so much of this "debate" segment because I think it is important to resolving the question of the text's claim to "impartiality." In this case, even though the text may well give "equal screen time" in the "debate" and lets "the participants involved" speak, it is difficult to watch "An Argument in Indianapolis" and not apprehend, without a word from Murrow, without any overt "argument" by an "impartial" *See It Now*, that the Civil Liberties Union is a group that deserves our approbation. As we watch, we are invited to sympathize with the "good folks" of the Civil Liberties Union and to dissociate from the Legionnaires. We are clearly asked, in this "impartial" text, to side with those who value controversy over conformity, to deny those who would deny disagreement.

This attitude is emphasized in the final segment of "An Argument in Indianapolis," which begins with Murrow's reintroduction of Father Goosens. The newsman's tone is ironic, hinting at the strange and ironic days of the era of McCarthyism. "The Legion had its say and its resolution, and the Civil Liberties Union had their meeting," Murrow says. A pause. "Indianapolis is still there and the controversy is everywhere."

We see Father Goosens once more. He explains why he thinks "someone has to take a stand." "When the climate is such that so many people are so quick . . . to deny to others the right to peaceful assembly and free speech—then somebody certainly has . . . to prove to them that they are, in their activities, actually un-American."

Goosens argues that those who stay in the middle, those who want to avoid any and all controversy, are those who deserve our disapproval for their apathy. "It's up to us, I think, to lead the way, because we know that the freedoms—the American freedoms—are all based upon the rights which God has given us. And if the church and religion do not uphold those basic principles which come from God, then who will?"

With Goosens's question lingering in the air, the text cuts quickly back to Murrow in the *See It Now* studio. "That," he says, "was the argument in Indianapolis last week." He looks down. "Good night and good luck!"

The final words of Father Goosens are suggestive: to begin with, he proposes that a shared cultural tradition be held as the benchmark to judge the conflict between the American Civil Liberties Union and the American Legion. And as an audience has been invited to identify with those who celebrate disagreement and controversy, so, through Goosens's words, are they also prompted to recognize that only through conflict and the clash of ideas can the truth emerge. In the coda delivered by Father Goosens, the proposal is tendered that disagreement is not conspiracy and that conformity is deadening to the American spirit.

At the outset of this analysis I noted the claim of impartiality asserted by the text and subsequently verified by the majority of media critics. But clearly, a more sophisticated response to "An Argument in Indianapolis" demands that we look past the simple claims of "impartiality" as a species of "mathematical precision" and understand the clues within this text that so obviously invite ideological judgment. Furthermore, we must relate the way in which the participants in the controversy are depicted with our judgment of them, and finally, the conflict in Indianapolis must be analyzed as it pits the liberal celebration of controversy against the conformity of McCarthyism. In that "argument," *See It Now* is clearly partisan. I shall return to this significant point shortly.

## Response to the Telecast

Any persistent doubts about the increasingly formidable power of television as a force in public discourse were dispelled with the broadcast of *See It Now*'s "An Argument in Indianapolis." The conclusion seemed inevitable: Talbott's reversal of the Air Force board of review, announced on *See It Now* five weeks after Murrow and Friendly had brought the Radulovich story to national attention, revealed the potency of the medium. As Friendly said later, "The appearance of Air Force Secretary Talbott confirmed the power and the impact of television reporting."[26]

The decision in the Radulovich case was applauded by the public and the press. *Newsweek* called it a "week of triumph" for *See It Now* and noted the "satisfaction" that Murrow and Friendly must have enjoyed, "opening . . . with a film of the Air Force announcing that Lieutenant Milo J. Radulovich would not lose his commission."[27]

The handling of the controversy in Indianapolis received admiring reviews as well: it was hailed as a "powerful documentary" tracing the "embattled steps" of the small group of citizens seeking a place to meet. By the end of the program, *Newsweek* admitted, it was almost impossible not take sides either with the American Legion or with the ACLU and Reverend Goosens. But the average viewer would have a hard time "escaping the sincerity of Goosens's reasons."[28] Others observed that "An Argument in Indianapolis" derived its timelessness from its focus on the Bill of Rights.[29] And indeed, the Pentagon reversal cast *See It Now* in an unusual role—it now seemed clear to most reviewers that, with the Radulovich telecast and then "An Argument in Indianapolis," the *See It Now* makers were engaged in a campaign to counter assaults on basic freedoms: "Murrow's rating will undoubtedly continue to climb if he keeps on covering such controversies. To many, he has become a good deal more important than a TV performer. As one admirer put it: 'Ed Murrow and Fred Friendly have become the eyes of conscience.'"[30]

In the wake of the broadcasts, *See It Now* was awarded the Sidney Hillman Foundation Award for both "An Argument in Indianapolis" and the Radulovich program. And in its annual review of the television medium, *Variety* said that these two broadcasts more than anything else had made television better in 1953 than in the previous year.[31] But despite the growing reputation of the series, despite the heady praise for its producers, not everyone considered "An Argument in Indianapolis" constructive or even "fair."[32] Though Murrow would defy critics to "point out where I took sides," concern over the equity of the program has been a continuing source of argument.[33] In looking at the text, "An Argument in Indianapolis" reads as clearly partial—a finding that runs counter to the claim of impartiality explicit in the text and to its evaluation in more traditional academic critiques. But in contrast to those orthodox perspectives, a concentration upon the stylistic elements in the text's visualizations and attention to "how" the representatives of the opposing philosophies are depicted there, reveals that "sides were taken" in "An Argument in Indianapolis." To better explain how this might work, an examination of the model of depiction found in the rhetorical tradition can frame a sense of how depiction functions as an instrument of attitude change. Afterward we will be in position not only to explicate how depiction works in this visual text but also subsequently to mount a critique of the traditional grounds for determining "partiality."

## Rhetorical Depiction

In his essay "Rhetorical Depiction," Michael Osborn reconsiders the rhetorical tactic of depiction and proposes depiction as nothing less than the "key to synchronic, multiple, simultaneous meanings in rhetoric."[34] Osborn traces the use of visualizations or "strategic pictures" back to the classical teachers of oratory who recognized the presentational power of vivid depiction to thrust its subject matter forward for the attention of an audience in a way that seemed to those teachers to give an almost irrestible potency to the striking and carefully wrought image.[35]

Osborn finds that depiction serves at least five distinct rhetorical functions: presentation, intensification, identification, implementation, and reaffirmation. Accordingly, Osborn says, a "modern theory of depiction" is called for, one that recognizes the connections between visualization and magnification, visualization and deliberation, visualization and demonstration.[36] Clearly the most problematic of these connections is the last—the connection to forensic discourse and to the enthymematic form. Osborn argues that "even forensic rhetoric, which depends more on enthymeme, connects ultimately if indirectly with the theory of depiction. Depiction . . . can be instrumental in the formation and maintenance of basic premises that ground enthymemic [sic] demonstration."[37] I suggest that "Argument in Indianapolis" furnishes a test case for this conclusion and, in considering how an audience is prompted to evaluate the characters and the motives of those involved in the dispute over the meeting hall, suggests the question of precisely "how" this grounding of forensic discourse might happen. For instance, how does an audience arrive at a decision about "character" by way of external visualization? An implicit connection between image and ethos, I believe, lurks in Osborn's assumptions about forensic depiction and needs to be drawn out, not to overturn his argument, but to complicate it and to add to an understanding of depiction in See It Now.

Adopting the strategy that drives Osborn's seminal essay, a return to classical authors seems warranted as a way to begin to link image and ethos. If we return not to Greek rhetoricians but rather to the Roman rhetorics, however, we gain a view of depiction as considerably more than a way of making discourse "vivid and vivacious." In the Latin forensic rhetorics the "motives" with which someone acted became of utmost importance. And for Cicero, for instance, depiction had a clear argumentative purpose. In court cases, Cicero said, "the pertinent fact is the purpose with which anyone performs an act, not what success he attains."[38] Depiction became in judicial oratory a way of showing the connection between the attributes of people and their actions—a connection, in short, between character and motive—in such a way as to inform a judgment of the person or the act. The Roman orators learned to use the topic of "attributes of persons or actions" to fashion descriptions of the actions of their clients in such a way that the attributes of their character could be as easily ascertained as they are in real life—"according to the habits of ordinary people and the beliefs of the audience."[39]

This often overlooked link between attribute, character, and action has been revived in current rhetorics, and it is pivotal to the "New Rhetoric" of Chaim Perelman. For Perelman, listeners reason from an account of an act to the attributes of a person's character and so reconstruct the character of a person as revealed in action. In other words, a person is known and judged by acts committed. "The person, considered as support for a series of qualities, the author of a series of acts and judgments, and the object of a series of appraisals, is a durable being, around whom is grouped a whole series of phenomena to which he gives cohesion and significance."[40]

That is, this "fixing" of character involves a simplifying reduction of the person. Perelman recognizes that often this simplified "persona" becomes a shorthand for the person and is used in argument because it is "easier to manage."[41] In other words, person is "summed up" by a "persona" constituted of a limited number of selected attributes and qualities.[42]

Depiction, then, has a constructive argumentative function in this realm: auditors may well ascertain attributes of character, depending upon the actions described by the rhetor, and judgment is elicited through the comparison of that persona with culturally accepted standards of propriety or with social experience of the cultural norms of how people ought to behave or through comparison with the actions of others in the same situation. In this way, the connection between symbols and social control, and the relationship between visualization and judgment of character that occupies Osborn's essay is made concrete.[43]

*Verbal and Visual*

But clearly *See It Now* is much more than verbal discourse. And while depiction, traditionally considered, pivots upon the striking image, it does not refer explicitly to visual texts. Yet depiction is central to "An Argument in Indianapolis," both to shift perspective and to prompt judgment; and attribution-depiction works within it in a strikingly similar fashion to the way it seems to work in the verbal forensic argument of the ancient Romans.

To begin with, the rhetor's act of "describing" in verbal forms is taken over in the documentary text by the raw and powerful photographic image. Any photograph or film appears as a record, in a literal sense, of the "facts," and attests that the events "really happened." Film footage has a specific way of passing itself off as an aspect of "nature," through its claim to be an aspect of reality—the "literal visual-transcription of the 'real world.'"[44] We believe that the "camera doesn't lie," and so we assent to the power of the image as "uncoded," as the "denotated analogon of reality."[45] But for this denoted image to be used as an instrument of attitude change, it must be "written" or "inflected" and thus must take on interpretative significance.[46] Roland Barthes suggests one way in which this may happen. In two essays, "The Photographic Message" and subsequently "The Rhetoric of the Image," Barthes contends that there are, in addition to the denoted image, other messages at work in the photograph.

First, there is what he calls the "linguistic" message. This message involves either spoken or written language that serves to extend or to delimit the potential meanings of what Barthes considers the virtually polysemous denotative image. In this case, watching the parallel meetings in "An Argument in Indianapolis," auditors might begin to construct personae that sum up or characterize each organization partly on the basis of what the representatives of each group say (that is, upon standard linguistic denotation) and partly on the basis of what they imply (standard linguistic connotation). Qualities of character are attributed to those seen in the documentary in line with standards of shared knowledge of what people mean when they speak and what their motives are.[47] This is no different from the "decoding" that we do when we "read" everyday subjects and occasions in an expressive way: these codes are part of the cultural stock of knowledge that is used to understand a set of bodily cues and conversational markers as index of character. In sum, we likely use the same linguistic messages whether we come face to face with a living subject or encounter a visual transcription of it.

But significance at the linguistic level does not exhaust the photographic message. In "An Argument in Indianapolis" there is also a curious stylistic treatment of the two groups realized in the striking differences in mise-en-scène and lighting. As film scholars have noted, in the visual text, elements of film style help to constitute physical denotation and contribute to thematic messages as well.

In Barthes's terms this contribution is the result of another order of "visual" message—a "connotated" message—found in the art or treatment of the photograph or the profilmic event. For Barthes, the "style" of the visual transcription is an "imposing" of another level of meaning on the image.[48] These connotative codes permit the image to signify, in addition to its denotative reference, other, implied meanings.[49] In this way, layers of conventional signification are added to what we take as the natural image, what Barthes describes as indexical and "uncoded."[50]

In "An Argument in Indianapolis" this plane of photographic connotation, laid over the ontological power of the natural image, has a special persuasive potency. One preferred message in "An Argument in Indianapolis" extends beyond the events surrounding the hiring of a hall to encompass a perspective on the groups and an attitude toward the personae depicted in the text. Auditors are coaxed to link the antagonists in Indianapolis with a set of associations that are fostered in the text and predispose ethical judgment.

One way to trace the associations that lie at the heart of this *See It Now* text is to determine which of them are linked with which of the groups. Once sets of terms have been "clustered" together with other terms, they may be lined up into "equations." Finally, when considered from this dramatic perspective, the program can be made to disclose its implicit symbolic appeal.[51]

A cluster analysis of "An Argument in Indianapolis" reveals that the depiction of the Civil Liberties Union is associated with the descriptors light, directness, friendliness, typicality, and diversity. The Legion, on the other hand, is consistently depicted by reference to darkness, obliqueness, menace, conformity, and regimentation. Thus there are, on the basis of a reading within this text, a number of general equations. The Civil Liberties Union is light, openness, complexity, controversy, patriotism, and plurality. The American Legion is dark, hidden, simple, conformist, singular, monolithic, and authoritarian.

Whether consciously or unconsciously, in "An Argument in Indianapolis," *See It Now* associates terms chiefly negative in force with the Legion, and consciously or unconsciously, antitheses of these come to be associated with the Civil Liberties group. Thus *See It Now* portrays the ACLU as an organization that celebrates diversity and plurality, a group that rejects formality and regimentation and is representative of the American heritage of civil rights and of the constructive value of conflict.

Moreover, in dramatic terms, the two groups are clearly antagonists—the one associated with light, openness, plurality, diversity; the other associated with darkness, authoritarian-ness, regimentation, and conformity. This text activates judgment, not just by what is said, or who says it, but also through the connotative messages woven through the text's visualizations or depictions and through the power inscribed within the agonistic drama it symbolizes. Such depiction also draws upon our store of cultural archetypes and commonplaces, and these are activated by the way the text stylizes the groups. The associations of this contrast in tonality are conventional: the openness and sincerity of the Civil Liberties group gains a strong psychological appeal when the meeting draws upon archetypes of light and brightness; the Legion a reverse psychological revulsion. Such archetypal power of light and dark images has long been recognized by poets, playwrights, and orators and has been used by them to elicit predictable emotional and cognitive response.[52]

Furthermore, this symbolic plane is crucial in closing the gap between the text's depiction and its theme and message. We may say that "An Argument in Indianapolis" works by visually elaborating the desired connotations on the uncoded and denotated indexical image or that, in the style of its presentation, *See It Now* "inflects" the image so that its connotations elicit our disapprobation for the Legion, our approval of the Civil Liberties Union seen as "characters" upon a wider dramatistic stage.


*Bias Reconsidered*

At this point, the utility of traditional conceptions of the grounds of "partiality" for assessing visual forms seems fatally attenuated. That is, as we have found within this *See It Now* text, elements of the visual form—depictions not marked as partisan verbally—direct our attention and control our interpretation of the program. And a dramatistic vocabulary clearly discloses what the academic terminology cannot. Impartiality is destroyed by negative associations linked to the Legion as they are set in dramatic development with an antithetical cluster of positive associations linked to the Civil Liberties group. Therefore, we may say that the grounds for justifying a claim to impartiality must take into account not just a statistical assessment of the amount of screen time given to opposing sides but also the connoted and conventional associations that are "brushed" upon the surface of the denoted and natural image.

This depiction in dramatic terms of the contrast between the Civil Liberties Union and the American Legion also speaks to the conflict between two antagonistic ideological views. Instead of an impartial and mathematically precise presentation of two competing sides, this two-sidedness, when symbolized in agonistic terms, becomes a way of weighting public discourse through dramatic conflict.

## Microcosm of a Movement

In his study of *See It Now,* Michael Murray worked out the connections between the American Legion as it is portrayed here and the McCarthyism movement. Murray called "An Argument in Indianapolis" the "microcosm of a movement" and recognized within it the "ideological structuring of the McCarthy movement."[53] Murray argues that, in addition to being generally considered supporters of the Wisconsin senator, the tactics of the American Legion as depicted in "An Argument in Indianapolis" were "in keeping with the dictates of the McCarthy movement," and he identifies four specific methods that were shared by McCarthyism and by the American Legion in the Indianapolis dispute.[54]

The first method, "multiple untruth," is a combination of truth and half-truth; for example, Murray cites the manner in which the Legion Commander continually stresses the ACLU's defense of accused subversives as "proof" of the organization's Communist inclinations. Second, Murray notes that the Legion and McCarthyism share an "abuse of documentation." In this case, the Legion cites the advertisement in which the ACLU called for a repeal of the Smith-McCarran Act as documented "proof" of leftist tendencies. The third characteristic that Murray finds shared by the Legion and the McCarthyism is the use of "insinuation and innuendo." Such abuse can most clearly be seen in the Legion's contention that it possesses "documentary evidence . . . that the speaker for the Union, Arthur Garfield Hayes, had subscribed to, and been a member of, organizations listed as subversive." As Murray notes, this evidence is never revealed in the program. One final method, frequently used by the McCarthyites and graphically depicted in "An Argument in Indianapolis," is what Murray calls "slander amalgam," that is, the practice of slurring distinctions between alleged Communists and genuine espionage agents and then attacking one's enemies by placing them among the bona fide conspirators. Murray points to the Legion's charge that the Civil Liberties group's defense of an accused labor leader reflected the organization's total and complete association with Communist offenders. And we may add to Murray's methods another equally explicit association. Watching closely, there is, in the statements of the Legion members, a striking stylistic similarity with the oratorical style of Senator Joseph McCarthy himself. The phrasing and diction, and the pacing and intonation of the Legion speakers, sound as if the senator himself had been making the charges against the ACLU.

In sum, content, tactics, and style all reveal similarities between the Legion and McCarthyism. By suggesting that the Legion and McCarthyism share attributes, *See It Now* prompts its audience to view the Legion as representative of McCarthyism, standing metonymically as a part for the whole. As both share in the ideology of a closed society, so viewers are warranted in drawing a clear inference: just as they are invited to deny the tactics of the Legion, so are they invited to universalize judgment from the particular case and to deny McCarthyism.

## Plurality and the Value of Disagreement

But we cannot close this consideration of "An Argument in Indianapolis" without explicating the final developments in the theme of controversy and disagreement or without developing the suggestion that "An Argument in Indianapolis" may be read as an informal disquisition upon the nature and value of conflict itself. I suggested several times that "An Argument in Indianapolis" sought to resolve the debate between those who represent the value of constructive conflict and those who would silence controversy and still debate. On the one hand, resolution is suggested in the statements of Father Goosens, in Hayes's observation that "controversy is as American as the Fourth of July," and in the depictions and the associations attributed to the groups—the view of the Legion as conforming, formal, and impersonal, while the Civil Liberties Union membership is treated as plural, relaxed, and as individuals.

But more intriguing still is the curious paradox of the program: by presenting the dispute at all, *See It Now* warrants the notion of disagreement and so justifies the idea of controversy as beneficial. That is, *See It Now* implicitly takes disagreement as not only acceptable but the only way "both sides" of an issue can be judged. In even allowing the Civil Liberties Union to have its say, *See It Now* implicitly joins its own perspective with that of the ACLU in the argument over the value of controversy. Plurality is thus celebrated as natural, nonthreatening, an important "right."

Moreover, the program's celebration of controversy over conformity is an elaborate justification of *See It Now* itself. While not partisan toward any political party or faction, *See It Now* may well be biased in favor of the tradition of American pluralism and for the preservation of a systematic ideology of tolerance—biased that is, precisely, in favor of the ideology that McCarthyism and its representative, the Legion, attacked.[55]

Perhaps, this is not so surprising: in a way, pluralism and disagreement, change and dynamism, and the sifting and setting of side against side constitute the epistemological form of the television documentary itself.[56] Thus, a sense of national unity (personified by Murrow) in the particular (the monitors that call in all parts of the diverse land) is a myth instantiated within the form of the *See It Now* text. Television is continually celebrated as making possible the direct link between antagonists ("See it Now," the bank of monitors, the debate) and as resting within the tradition of the impartial airing of conflicting ideas.

Thus, it is remarkable and striking that *See It Now* uses the symbolism of the infant medium of television—its fictional transparency, and the openness that is the fabricated illusion of the medium, as "argument" against McCarthyism and the uniformity of ideas.[57] Considered this way, part of the argument against McCarthyism is in the very form of the *See It Now* program and in the myth it fosters—that of the open and free exchange of ideas. Clearly, one of the great metathemes of the *See It Now* series on McCarthyism is the motif that controversy is valuable—that disagreement is "American"—that unity arises solely from diversity and plurality. *See It Now* seeks to rescue precisely this liberal heritage from the conformity of the era of McCarthyism.

In a number of ways, then, in "An Argument in Indianapolis," we have found a supposed "impartial" text that, through depiction, casts McCarthyism in an unbecoming light. And we have peeled back layers of signification from the bare denoted image, disclosing the persuasive dimensions of the documentary text.

But this disclosure leads to a larger concern—one with an ethical dimension. That is, how can a text be at one and the same time "natural" and "conventional"? Or again, how can the *See It Now* text be considered "objective" and simultaneously "invested" with suasory meaning?[58]

In the next chapter, I shall address more directly the "philosophy of objectivity" and the claims of the objective visual text, because there, questions of objectivity and the relation between reportage and argument in the television documentary surface directly before us.

Ironically, on the same night as the telecast of "An Argument in Indianapolis," the dangers of McCarthyism presented themselves even more graphically. Thirty minutes after *See It Now* signed off, Murrow and Friendly watched Sen. Joseph McCarthy in his own nationwide address.[59]

In his speech, McCarthy lashed out at former president Harry Truman, condemning him for deceit and appeasement and charging that his administration had been "crawling with communists." The senator countered Truman's widely publicized definition of "McCarthyism" by proposing the concept "Trumanism," which he defined as "placing your political party above the interests of the country." Then McCarthy turned to the Eisenhower administration. He denounced the Republican administration for doing little more than the Democrats in excising "communists and fellow travelers" from government. He lamented the "greatest failure of my party," what he characterized as "delivering our Chinese friends to Communist hands."[60]

McCarthy, it seemed, would not hesitate to bring down both the Eisenhower administration or even the Republican party in his zealous pursuit of the subversive in the nation's government and psyche. Perhaps that conclusion impressed itself on the *See It Now* coproducers. After McCarthy's speech, Murrow asked Friendly about the film library that *See It Now* had been compiling on the senator, and the two decided to review the footage available in the files—with the idea of putting together a *See It Now* program on McCarthy himself.[61]

For a complex of reasons, then, November 24, 1953, stands as a watershed. Whatever their motivations—whether they were buoyed by the Air Force reversal of the Radulovich case, awed by the senator's performance on nationwide television, spurred by McCarthy's personal threat against Murrow, convinced of the value of disagreement, or whatever—the *See It Now* rhetors had reached a momentous decision. Having used television to show the effects of McCarthyism indirectly, in a way providing "background" on its potential dangers and having achieved an impressive victory, they would now turn their television weapon directly on the junior senator from Wisconsin, the namesake of the era and the movement, to illuminate his practices.

6

# Argument and the News Documentary: "A Report on Senator Joseph R. McCarthy"

It is March 9, 1954, 10:30 P.M. EST, a Tuesday evening. Following the usual opening credits, Edward R. Murrow appears suddenly on the screen. "Good evening," he says. "Tonight *See It Now* devotes its entire half hour to a report on Senator Joseph R. McCarthy told mainly in his own words and pictures. Because a report on Senator McCarthy is by definition controversial, we want to say exactly what we mean to say."[1] Thus, with grim seriousness, *See It Now* begins one of the most controversial and influential telecasts in television history, and what followed that evening, by all standards, remains one of the most provocative documents in American public discourse. One commentator has argued that it is "the most important single broadcast in television"; another observed that the "Report on Senator McCarthy" marked the moment at which "television came of age."[2] Recent appraisals agree: the "Report on Senator McCarthy" is regarded as "TV documentary at its best" and as the most famous of the *See It Now* series.[3]

It was, as Erik Barnouw has said, perhaps inevitable that *See It Now* should take up the subject of Joseph R. McCarthy himself.[4] After all, following "The Case of Milo Radulovich" and "An Argument in Indianapolis," the program found itself in the middle of public debate over McCarthyism. But the "Report on Senator McCarthy" is not the most typical, not the most polished in terms of style or format, and certainly not the best understood of the series.[5]

In *Documentary in American Television*, William Bluem laments that "the program on McCarthy [has] suffered from too much heat and too little light."[6] Most of the heat, to be sure, comes from a preoccupation with the telecast's "fairness" or its "objectivity."

## The Question of Fairness

A continuing source of controversy has been the methods of the "Report on Senator McCarthy." Following its telecast, some reviewers called it a partisan attack on the senator, and most considered it a "flawed" documentary because it violated standards of impartiality. The respected critic Gilbert Seldes, for instance, has argued that the program was clearly an attack on the senator, no matter what it claimed to be. Seldes likened the program to "the summing up of a judge who marshals evidence."[7] Another critic disparaged the program because Murrow "used the senator's own statements as a weapon of editorial attacks."[8] While others saw the broadcast as setting a "dangerous precedent," one reviewer went so far as to say that the program was unfair to McCarthy precisely because it relied on pictures rather than on a spoken text.[9]

Contemporary accounts have also been preoccupied with the question of "fairness." In these, too, "A Report on Senator McCarthy" is often cited as a failure. For instance, one study concludes that the program slighted the senator in its form and its content and so was unfair; another, on the basis of interviews with the principals, asserts that Murrow and Friendly never intended to be "objective."[10]

But such appraisals fail to satisfy. To applaud the "Report on Senator McCarthy" as a courageous "journalistic report" or to denigrate it as an "unfair" attack is to miss subtleties of the text. Furthermore, to rehearse this traditional debate is to overlook more vital issues concerning visual texts that are raised by the *See It Now* broadcast.

### Reportage and Argument

From the study of "An Argument in Indianapolis," it seems clear that the way a subject is depicted is as important an index of a television news documentary's impartiality as is what is said either by participants or by a commentator or narration. We may pursue this question, however, to determine how the very form of the television news documentary itself—its structure—complicates simplistic assumptions about the relationship between objectivity and reportage.

Furthermore, it may be that the unsatisfactory quality of the existing critiques of "Report on Senator McCarthy" reflects a confusion in classification of the program. Trained in apprehending the program in terms of journalistic categories formed around rather empiricist notions of bias and objectivity, these critics are incapable of recognizing the "Report on Senator McCarthy" as anything but a "flawed report." But if we kick away the standard classification of the text as "journalistic report," and read instead the visual and verbal dynamics of the text itself, it becomes clear that the program quickly exhausts both senses of the bifurcated form of the television news documentary—it is far from mere "objective report" and equally far from "biased attack." The "Report on Senator McCarthy" works in several ways at once—it invokes the conventions of journalistic objectivity and reportage yet exploits them for argumentative effect. As we adopt this perspective, our expectations of the text and our analytic categories will shift. Ultimately, the rhetorical act of accusation renders questions of conventional journalistic fairness beside the point.[11]

In this chapter, then, I will focus on the ways in which reportage and argument move together across the "Report on Senator McCarthy." As we will see, this telecast illustrates one way in which the television documentary discourse situates itself between the genre of the objective news report and the genre of public argument. This undertaking does indeed involve "objectivity," but rather than being the goal of the text, objectivity is used as a fabricated strategy of appeal.

## An Industry Under Direct Attack

Direct and indirect pressure on the newly born television industry was a fundamental tactic of the McCarthyite movement.[12] But during the first week of March 1954, the entire industry found itself under a direct frontal assault as Senator McCarthy demanded that the networks give him free time to answer what he perceived as "attacks" by the Democratic party. The networks refused and "as never before, an unrehearsed and spontaneous American political drama [broke] on the national scene in the broadcast media."[13] The circumstances that came together in March 1954, however, and contributed to "A Report on Senator McCarthy" had their direct origin some six months earlier.

During the fall of 1953, the McCarthy subcommittee was continuing its probe of the army, and soon McCarthy discovered the "case" of Maj. Irving Peress, an army dentist stationed at Camp Kilmer,

New Jersey. The "Fifth Amendment dentist," as the senator called him, had refused to answer some questions on an army form concerning membership in organizations labeled as subversive but was routinely promoted while awaiting discharge. In late January 1954, Peress was summoned before the McCarthy subcommittee. After the major had taken the Fifth Amendment in response to questions in executive session, McCarthy appeared triumphantly before the assembled press. "Who promoted Peress?" he demanded.[14]

The senator concluded that General Ralph Zwicker, commander of Camp Kilmer and a decorated war hero, had been responsible for the promotion. In mid-February, McCarthy lost his temper with Zwicker during televised hearings. The senator called the general "not fit to wear the uniform" because he had refused to answer questions about the promotion of Peress, and McCarthy berated him for not agreeing that the person who had promoted Peress should be removed from the military. The general, McCarthy announced, "did not have the brains of a five-year-old."[15]

The transcript of Zwicker's testimony was soon published, and with it editorial opinion briefly turned against McCarthy. Emboldened, Secretary of the Army Robert T. Stevens called for a "showdown" with the senator over his treatment of army officers. But behind the scenes, Republican party officials fashioned a "compromise" that obliged the army to furnish military witnesses to McCarthy and to supply the loyalty board officials who had presided over the Peress incident.[16] The press labeled the agreement a "sellout" to McCarthy—"the Army's retreat."

With the army dispute dominating the news, and with relations between the senator and his own party apparently worsening, in early March, McCarthy appeared once again before the media. He grimly told of the "threat" of infiltration and depicted Eisenhower as "slow" to act in eliminating "subversives" from the armed services.

In this supercharged atmosphere, Democrat Adlai Stevenson chastised the Republicans, claiming that, in refusing to deal with McCarthy, Eisenhower had shown a lack of leadership. "It seems to me," Stevenson said, in a March 6 television address, "that a political party divided against itself, half McCarthy and half Eisenhower, cannot produce national unity."[17]

McCarthy was incensed. Just as in the Truman controversy four months earlier, the senator demanded free and equal time over all television networks to reply to Stevenson. The networks, feeling the pressure, delayed—they hoped for a compromise. On March 7, the Republican party offered them a way out by requesting that time be given to the Republican National Committee rather than to the senator from Wisconsin. CBS and NBC, the two major networks, both quickly agreed to provide the free time to the party. And when the Republicans appointed Vice-President Richard Nixon to respond officially to Stevenson's charges, it was apparent that the senator and his party were on opposing sides. But McCarthy was adamant. He threatened to "drag" the networks before the Federal Communications Commission or sue them in the courts. He branded the decision "dishonest" and "immoral" and announced that he would delegate no one to answer "the lengthy and vicious attack on me personally." The networks, McCarthy said ominously, "will grant me free time or learn what the law is. I guarantee that."[18] But the only offer of "free time" came from an old McCarthy ally: the senator was quickly scheduled on the nationally syndicated radio program of Fulton Lewis, Jr., for the evening of March 11.

### See It Now's Decisions

This course of events, quite naturally, had an unsettling effect on Murrow and Friendly directly. Throughout the winter of 1953–1954, the question before them was not whether to produce a program on Senator McCarthy but when to produce it for maximum effectiveness.[19] As McCarthy threatened the broadcasting industry, the producers worried over whether CBS or See It Now itself would become the object of the next investigation. Tension increased steadily as everyone realized that another week's delay increased the risk that McCarthy might strike first with his twenty-year-old exposé of Murrow's alleged "Communist past."[20] But each week, Murrow reviewed the McCarthy footage available in the See It Now files and decided to wait.

In late February, not long after the Zwicker testimony, Murrow and Friendly decided to proceed with the program on McCarthy. Staff work continued around the clock through the next six days. Everyone knew that some means had to be found to give the film footage a powerful impact.[21] Murrow and Friendly faced a crucial rhetorical problem—how to give significance to the raw film clips of documentary footage. Friendly later confessed to thinking at the time that the existing film footage was "thin" and contained no "new" material.[22] A few of the staff members expressed reservations because they felt "the material was not as dramatic or as cohesive as the Radulovich or Indianapolis programs." Joe Wershba has said that "the reporters didn't think the program was strong. The film was neutral, simply a photographic record of McCarthy in action that, by itself, would merely reinforce the belief of the senator's supporters in his greatness."[23]

It seemed that in this program much depended upon Murrow's conclusion. When the staff asked what he would say in his "tail piece," Murrow replied that, when one individual is allowed to terrorize the country, then the entire nation is responsible.[24] "If none of us ever read a book that was 'dangerous,'" he said, "or had a friend who was 'different' or joined an organization that advocated 'change,' we would all be just the kind of people Joe McCarthy wants."[25]

Shortly before the telecast Friendly made a special request for advertising funds to make sure "people would watch."[26] But as with "The Case of Milo Radulovich," his request was turned down by the advertising department. And again, Murrow and Friendly used their own funds to purchase an advertisement in the *New York Times*. The ad read simply: "Tonight at 10:30 on *See It Now* a report on Senator Joseph R. McCarthy. Fred W. Friendly and Edward R. Murrow, co-producers."[27]

By Tuesday evening, the program was nearly complete, and the crew gathered for rehearsal. But the final "mix" ran longer than anticipated, and it was almost nine o'clock before all the film was in the studio; the crew finished the hectic final run-through only fifteen minutes before air time. At 10:29, in the thirty seconds between network and local commercials, Friendly leaned over and whispered to Murrow: "This is going to be a tough one." Murrow agreed. "Yes, and after this one they're all going to be tough."

Suddenly it was 10:30. On cue from the stage manager, Murrow looked up into the camera. He began: "Good evening." At that moment, Friendly found his right hand shaking so much that when he tried to start his stopwatch, he missed the button completely.[28]

## Textual Analysis

The "Report on Senator McCarthy" divides easily into three clear sections. The first juxtaposes selections from McCarthy's public statements and concludes with Murrow's quotations from newspaper editorials concerning the senator. The second begins with examination of what *See It Now* calls the "two staples" of McCarthy's political career. The last and briefest section, the only one clearly presented as nonobjective, is Murrow's final comment.

Each section is quite distinct in tactics, tenor, and style. According to the traditional classification of the "Report on Senator McCarthy" as "journalistic report," the program may be considered "flawed," as it has traditionally been, since these dramatic shifts are impossible to reconcile. By examining links between the sections, however, I will trace shifts in their appeal to the viewer and will take a fresh approach to assessing the bias of the text.

*Section 1: The "Objective" Text*

The first section commences after Murrow's grim promise of "a report on Senator McCarthy told in his own words and pictures." This opening develops the reference points for analysis. "A report on Senator McCarthy is by definition controversial. If the Senator feels that we have done violence to his words or pictures—and desires, so to speak, to answer for himself—an opportunity will be afforded him on this program." Murrow's opening grounds the text in expectations of journalistic objectivity. For instance, when he calls the program a "report," he draws upon expectations of fairness anticipated in the news discourse and developed in previous *See It Now* programs. And since the telecast will consist of the "words and pictures" of Senator McCarthy, this, too, tends to reinforce expectations of journalistic objectivity. But the acknowledgment of "controversy," the offer of equal time to McCarthy, the mention that "violence" might be done, are unusual in the news documentary. Taken together, they tease expectations regarding what is to follow.

Our working thesis tonight is this quotation—"If this fight against Communism is made a fight between America's two great political parties, the American people know that one of these parties will be destroyed and the Republic cannot endure very long as a one-party system." We applaud that statement. And we think Senator McCarthy ought to. After all he said it seventeen months ago in Milwaukee.

Murrow turns, looks up at the monitor screen on the control panel beside him: MILWAUKEE OCTOBER 3, 1952. The camera begins the familiar slow zoom. When the graphic completely fills the screen, it holds for a split second and then cuts to the senator for the first time.

McCarthy is speaking from behind a podium, the camera's vantage slightly below; he is framed in the familiar "head-and-shoulders shot" of the newsreel. The senator's face is wildly animated; he shouts his words. In grandiloquent style, he emphasizes with a flourish, his finger wagging in the air, "If this fight against Communism is made a fight between political parties," the senator intones—a repetition of the very same words that Murrow had read only moments before.

Back to Murrow in the studio. The framing is wider than before and reveals more of the small control room. "But on February 4th, 1954, Senator McCarthy spoke of *one* party's treason," Murrow says and reaches for the controls of a large tape recorder in front of him. The camera moves slightly down, and the focus is on the recorder's slowly revolving tape reels. "There were no cameras present," Murrow explains.

McCarthy's words are matter-of-fact. There have been "twenty years of treason," he claims, "and the hard fact is, the hard fact is that those who wear the label 'Democrat,' wear it with the stain of an historic betrayal." Murrow reaches forward and turns off the recorder. The program's pacing is rapid, the language pushed forward by coordinate conjunctions: "And seventeen months ago candidate Eisenhower met Senator McCarthy in Green Bay, Wisconsin, and he laid down some of the ground rules on how he would meet communism, if elected."

On the monitor, the date: "OCTOBER 3, 1952," and place, "GREEN BAY, WIS." Again, the camera zooms slightly into the monitor and cuts to Eisenhower. He, too, is conventionally framed as in most news film—head-on in medium shot, standing on the rear platform of a railroad car. The candidate "pledges" to "see that subversion and disloyalty is [*sic*] kept out of the Executive Department." That is the president's "responsibility," Eisenhower says. "But," Murrow announces, in voice-over, "that same night in Milwaukee, Senator McCarthy stated what he would do." Quickly, a cut to a close shot of McCarthy: it is another portion of the same Milwaukee speech seen just before.

How should we interpret these first moments? Clearly, *See It Now* unfolds by juxtaposing statements from the public record with other public statements. But these first statements are, importantly, for the most part presented as news film, and as this public content is stylized within the familiar conventions of the documentary news form, the text invites the audience to see it as unbiased—confirming its status as neutral reportage.

## Objectivity as Rhetorical Form

Traditionally considered, questions of fairness and objectivity fall within the domain of journalistic ethics. The goals of the news professional include objectivity and maintaining the distinction between reporting the "facts" and interpreting them. Objectivity is associated with news-gathering practice and the verification of "facts" through appropriate procedures.[29] But the assumption of "fact" as equivalent to "thing" in the world comes laden with potential problems. In this paradigm, questions of facticity are settled by reference to data outside a discourse, and fairness is evaluated solely by the comparison of the content of discourse to independently verifiable evidence.

Such a distinction between bias and objectivity may sometimes be useful, but it does not advance us very far in explaining the "Report on Senator McCarthy" or other visual texts. Indeed, it is tempting to yield to the argument that pictures are a "simple" natural process of recognition, as if news and documentaries could capture reality without imposing their own rules. In the last chapter, we noted the likely origins of a desire to regard them in this way: the denoted natural image stands as an index of the "real," of that preexisting neutral structure that lies beyond question and beyond interpretation.

But Ernst Gombrich has made it forever impossible for us to treat any sort of representation as showing us the "actual" world. In *Art and Illusion*, Gombrich argues persuasively that "representational," whether applied to drawings, photographs, or news film, must refer to codes, conventions, and social schemata, identified as representational by members of a specific culture.[30]

So although documentary presents itself as the representation of actuality, it is the product of rhetorical agents—artful fabrications that seek to obscure the marks of construction. These we interpret as signs and symbols structured by a set of conventions.[31] That is to say, objectivity consists only partly of traditional content or verification issues and also includes formal or stylistic issues and what some have called the "shared common sense" of the world.[32] Objectivity, in this view, becomes a question of the rhetorical strategies of the discourse itself. And so, in seeming tautology, auditors may be strongly compelled to take a text as objective if it satisfies the conventions of objectivity.

So far, only a few analysts have begun to regard news film and the television text modeled as such a visual system. Still, Gaye Tuchman in her work has made the case that assent to journalistic "objectivity" encompasses not only the traditional content issues but also both formal issues and what she calls "inter-organizational relationships," that is, a "shared common sense" of the world.[33]

Tuchman found that journalists use "rituals of objectivity" as strategies to avoid charges of bias and unfairness and that television news film claims "actuality" by carefully honoring temporal and spatial visual conventions. By adhering to convention, Tuchman says, news can claim to present facts and not interpretations.

For example, temporal convention demands that news film use a standard filming speed that presents actions neither speeded up nor slowed down.[34] Spatial convention requires a standard set of framings and shot distances. As long as the television text uses film of individuals seen "head-on" with the standard "head-and-shoulders" framing, Tuchman argues, the program avoids any overt appeal to dramatic convention and to charges of bias.[35]

Tuchman found another set of "rituals of objectivity," that involve the form of journalistic discourse and also sustain the claim of impartiality. This set includes both the presentation of conflicting views or competing explanations within the single news story and the copious use of direct quotation by the journalist. Because such quotes are "said by somebody," sets of conflicting statements become, from the practicing journalist's view, "facts." As a result, through direct quotation the news discourse can claim to be simply reporting the "facts."

Tuchman found a final formal strategy of journalistic objectivity in an analysis of the structure of news discourse itself. A news report may claim nonbias when it clearly identifies "analysis" or "comment" sections, Tuchman argues. Such marking off makes permissible some "nonobjective" comment because that comment is so clearly separate from the "objective" sections.[36]

If we take Tuchman's lead and reconsider "objectivity," we clearly interpret it in a more sophisticated fashion than through a sort of traditional and simplistic content analysis. Objectivity, in this approach, becomes a question of the rhetorical strategies of the discourse itself. By shifting the basis of objectivity from a concern with the intentions of the human maker to a concern with the form, we treat objectivity as partly a formal strategy, and we thereby open the question to textual analysis.

There is a match between the characteristics of the initial section of "A Report on Senator McCarthy" and Tuchman's conventions of news objectivity. To begin with, except for Murrow's linking commentary, its content consists of eight filmed sequences of McCarthy speaking at various public and private functions, plus one lengthy sequence in which he engages in committee activities, one where he questions Reed Harris, and one audiotape of a speech from Charleston, West Virginia. This is supplemented by film statements of Dwight Eisenhower and Secretary of the Army Robert Stevens. Moreover, all the footage, relying upon sound-on-film and avoiding excessive voice-over commentary, appears as standard news footage. Furthermore, each of the film segments is introduced with a repeated device—a graphic noting the specific location and the date of the event.

In this fashion, the "Report on Senator McCarthy," builds through the presentation of the visual transcription of McCarthy's "own" words. And since they are simply presenting the "words and pictures" of the senator, the *See It Now* rhetors can appear to be adhering to this convention of objectivity as well. As Murrow notes, somewhat disingenuously: "After all, [McCarthy] said it."

Finally, in this text, as in all *See It Now* telecasts, Murrow's final statement is marked as editorial opinion. By contrast, then, *See It Now* encourages its audience to assume that the remainder of the program will be free of overt opinion. And as long as a viewer expects opinion to be confined to the "nonobjective" final section, *See It Now* retains credibility for the "objective" sections that precede.

In sum, as Tuchman says, "the claim to actuality and actual representation [is] a claim to facticity," and through its honoring of news film conventions, this *See It Now* program seeks our certification of its "objectivity."[37] By its adherence to the conventions of the documentary news program, the text and its makers may claim to offer open access to the "real." Stylistically mimicking news discourse, the text seeks assent that it is not opinion, not attack, but is presenting just the facts—without manipulation—disavowing overt attempts to shift sensibilities.

*Crossing the Conventions of "Objectivity"*

But another appeal operates simultaneously in this first section of "A Report on Senator McCarthy." Beneath the adherence to strategic conventions of objectivity, there is an ever more obvious flouting of these conventions. *See It Now* marshals sarcasm and satire against the ethos of Joe McCarthy to suggest an increasingly negative view. It is noticeable first in Murrow's commentary, which introduces the first McCarthy speech. Its tone is biting: the senator "ought" to agree, Murrow allows; "after all," he said it. Or: "that same night, the junior senator said what he would do if elected."

Even the curious tactic of quoting McCarthy's own words seems to undercut his ethos. The effect is deflating. Coming right after Murrow has calmly read the very same words, the senator's presentation appears, in comparison, highly overwrought. Consistently, McCarthy seems wild and inappropriate by contrast with the urbane, correct Murrow. Quotations of the senator's own words further emphasize the clear contradictions and inconsistencies in the senator's juxtaposed statements.

The visualizations, too, begin to challenge the conventions of the standard news discourse. For instance, in the second McCarthy speech segment there is a controversial tactic. When McCarthy finishes, instead of cutting in what would be conventionally recognized as the "right" place (when the senator pauses), *See It Now* lingers on the senator for a moment longer. It is a deadly, revealing moment. McCarthy pauses, he looks about, his eyes seem to bulge. Nervously, he licks his lips, purses them, licks them again. The closeup microphone catches loud smacking as he opens and closes his mouth.

The subverting of convention becomes more defined in the segment of McCarthy that follows Eisenhower's campaign speech. Seen above and behind the podium, McCarthy talks about his earlier meeting with Eisenhower. "I spent about half-an-hour with the General last night. While I can't report that we agreed entirely on everything, I can report that when I left the meeting with the General, I had the same feeling as when I went in. And that is: that he is a great American, will make a great President."

In delivering the second sentence, McCarthy laughs, as if anticipating his own words. It is an almost fanatical laugh, touched with a giggle of nervousness, as if he can hardly be sure what he will say next. He stops for the crowd reaction; three seconds, four—we can faintly hear the enthusiastic response: "Pour it on, Joe. Pour it on!" yells someone in the auditorium. But the sensitive microphones instead only emphasize the senator's breathy giggle, which continues, rising in pitch, unnerving. Magnified by the sound track, McCarthy's laugh is eerie, even chilling. But then there is a jump, instituted in the editing, to another point in the same speech. Although he has just praised Eisenhower, McCarthy promises to "continue to call them as I see them, regardless of who happens to be President." The juxtaposition of the two statements, once again, makes McCarthy appear to contradict himself in the space of several sentences.

Clearly, for all its mimicry of the conventions of journalistic objectivity, the text is at the same time working to defeat those expectations. Despite the overt appeal to "objectivity," it is difficult to watch the early parts of the "Report on Senator McCarthy" without the sense that we are encouraged to take the senator as disreputable.

The next sequence highlights this tension. As Murrow speaks, the program shows McCarthy at a committee hearing. "But on *one thing* the senator has been consistent," Murrow says.

Often operating as a one-man committee, he has traveled far, interviewed many, terrorized some; accused civilian and military leaders of the past administration of a great conspiracy to turn over the country to communism; investigated and substantially demoralized the present State Department; made varying charges of espionage, interrogated a varied assortment of what he calls "Fifth Amendment Communists."

Here, the undercutting of McCarthy is quite remarkable, given that the text began by claiming to be a "report." *See It Now* extends an invitation to read beneath the expectation attached to the form of this program and to sense the sarcastic force of Murrow's remarks: "on one thing" he has been "consistent," "substantially," "a great conspiracy," "varying charges," "what he calls Fifth Amendment Communists." But what is especially striking and unexpected here are the visualizations. There is a progression of five closer and ever closer framings of McCarthy, ending with an extreme close-up that frames him from eyebrow to lips—an edited sequence that clearly exceeds the constraints of news documentary.

As this sort of treatment continues, taking new forms, "Report on Senator McCarthy" presents a puzzle: the sarcasm of Murrow's commentary becomes unavoidable; the visualizations begin to counter the conventions of news film; the editing and camera angles more and more defy conventions of distance and framing. Through its stylistic strategies, *See It Now* reveals the residues of another form.

Watching "A Report on Senator McCarthy," the audience is implicitly invited to compare its features with expectations for the television news documentary—expectations that the text purports to engage. But there are also an increasing number of alternative cues: the generic subversions, conventional surprises; clues in Murrow's commentary, in the visualizations—in other words, expectations are overturned. As the text increasingly subverts generic conventions, as it becomes more a suspect text of indirection, the program suggests a rejection of its literal meaning and a search for an alternative interpretation. To reconcile the ambiguity within the first section of the text, the audience is permitted to replace the overt yet increasingly impertinent interpretation—"this is a report"—with an alternative interpretation that brings back into line what is found in the text and what is surmised of its makers. I suggest there are similar features—the violation of generic constraints, and the invitation to recast the text's meaning in another form, the rhetorical figure of irony.

## Generic Expectations and the Rhetoric of Irony

Irony has, since the time of the ancients, been considered a prime means of helping auditors change their minds. For both Aristotle and Quintilian, irony was closely allied with satire, derision, and contempt.[38] Contemporary theorists of argumentation recognize the same instrumental effect. Perelman and Olbrechts-Tyteca suggest that irony is one way of making one's subject "laughable" and of disarming one's adversary.[39]

The ancient teachers of oratory also recognized that irony is distinct from other forms of argumentation because of the role it confers on the audience. Because irony is by definition indirect expression, the ironist depends upon the audience's foreknowledge.[40] Quintilian defined irony as "saying something quite contrary to what is meant. One can censure with pretended praise or praise under the appearance of censure." Irony, he said, could be "understood either from the mode of delivery, the character of the speaker, or the nature of the subject. If any of these be at variance with the words, it is apparent that the intention is different from the expression."[41] Irony, then, depends upon an auditor's recognition that the text is ironic, which implies knowledge of the conventions of genre and an intuition regarding the rhetor's intent.[42]

The residues of irony show clearly in the next sequence of "A Report on Senator McCarthy." It opens with Murrow in the control room. "Some," he says, have accused the senator of using the "bullwhip and the smear," but there was a time when the "senator and his friends said that he had been bullwhipped and smeared." Murrow turns and looks at the monitor. The vantage shifts: "MILWAUKEE DEC. 11, 1951." Then a wide shot of a banquet meeting. An unidentified speaker is at the rostrum with McCarthy to his left. The speaker pays sentimental tribute, listing the senator's accomplishments, then claiming that the senator's enemies "damn" and brush him with the "vilest smears." The speaker finishes his tribute by dramatically plucking a flower from a nearby vase; he turns and presents it to the senator with the words, "So in our hearts our love for you lies unrevealed."

The effect is comical, incongruous, almost sophomoric. In replying, McCarthy delivers his answer with hesitant and often dramatic pauses. The senator wipes his eye and laments "the past eighteen or nineteen months, when we've been bullwhipped and damned," and confesses that "I didn't think that I could be touched very deeply." He finishes quickly. "Frankly, my heart is so full I can't thank you," and he rushes to sit again.

How could we understand this sequence if we took the program as "straight"? Here, after all, we see the senator praised. But once we square this sequence with our developing ironic reading of the program, we are "in on the joke." We understand that the praise is brittle and that the accolades are delivered by fools, and we take a perspective that is morally and intellectually superior to that of the senator and "his friends."[43]

In the next sequence, the program sustains its clear invitation to be read ironically. In introducing it, Murrow continues the undercutting of McCarthy and once more parodies McCarthy's words from a preceding sequence. "But in Philadelphia, on Washington's Birthday, 1954," Murrow says, "his heart was so full he *could* talk. He reviewed some of the testimony of the General Zwicker hearing and proved he hadn't abused him." Clearly, Murrow's words cannot be taken literally. The program invites a reinterpretation at the expense of Joe McCarthy.

The sequence begins with a focus upon a wall-sized mural of George Washington comforting his bedraggled soldiers in the winter of Valley Forge. In implied contrast, the frame pans down: McCarthy stands beneath the mural, reading from the transcript of his questioning of army general Zwicker. McCarthy dramatizes the exchange, his haughty tone revealing an obvious enjoyment of his own performance. "Are you enjoying this 'abuse' of the General?" he asks, laughing. Complete with gestures, he acts out both Zwicker's part and his own. "Shall we go on with that for a while?" McCarthy asks his approving audience. "I hate to impose on your time, but this is the real meat of the 'abuse.'"

Overall, McCarthy's behavior seems inappropriate, and his melodramatic performance and haughty tone suggest disdain and contempt. But the visual images again dominate. The sequence alternates between wide shots of the senator at the lectern and head-and-shoulder shots. As he looks from beneath thick eyebrows, our attention is caught by a slash of hair across his forehead. From McCarthy's thinning scalp, it curls down almost scarlike. The effect is difficult to explain precisely, but the image prompts us to perceive Joseph R. McCarthy as ill groomed and unkempt.[44]

Finally, to cap the performance, McCarthy's feeling of persecution is clearly revealed: "And wait until you hear the bleeding hearts scream and cry about our methods of trying to drag the truth from those who know, or should know, who covered up a Fifth Amendment Communist major. But they say, 'Oh, it's all right to uncover them, but don't get rough doing it, McCarthy.'" As he says the last sentence, he reaches up and smooths his hair. And once more, the camera stays on the senator before we cut away. As in the earlier footage from Milwaukee, McCarthy is in unconventional and extreme close-up. He shakes his head, disgustedly. He looks up and gazes chillingly into the camera. His eyes cold and unresponsive, he looks around the room and purses his lips. He licks them, the tongue darting in and out quickly. He shakes his head again.[45]

Once acknowledged, the irony at the center of the "Report on Senator McCarthy"—its tension between reportorial objectivity and the rhetoric of public argument—offers a potential for drawing an audience in. Instead of attending to McCarthy's words in their original context, we are invited to give them an ironic alternative reading: instead of accepting "proof" that Zwicker was not abused, we are invited to understand that, in appearance and action, the senator has exceeded the bounds of appropriateness and decorum. He is a ruffian, a barbarian, and the text disarms predispositions toward Joe McCarthy by portraying the man in a negative and ever more ridiculous light.

In sum, the early sequences of "A Report on Senator McCarthy" invite its audience to apply conventions of the television news documentary to a text that uses those expectations ironically. But the process of irony, in this first section, is more complicated than a mere negation of the text's literal, "neutral" presentation of McCarthy and a substitution of its opposite—say, that the man is debased or his supporters foolish. Instead, the persuasive potency of irony itself prompts a cognitive and affective transformation of our sense of text, rhetor, and subject.[46]

First, we adjust our image of the makers of *See It Now.* Once we have recognized them as ironists, we are invited to perceive them as clever and witty to have fashioned this ironic textual "game" for our decoding. Furthermore, we are invited to conclude that if *See It Now* is "right" in its irony, then it may also be right in its implied negative judgment of McCarthy.

In addition, as Wayne Booth has argued, because irony cloaks what it means and requires reconstruction, the ironic text invites a kind of self-persuasion. Though each audience member who "gets" the irony cannot fail to reconstruct the message in a form that tells against McCarthy, each will reconstruct it according to his or her own estimate of the senator. Each will be likely to assume, too, that the makers of *See It Now* see it the same way. In this way, each adds to a negative judgment of McCarthy, however mild, the strength of pleasure in joining with the *See It Now* text.[47]

While this *See It Now* is built from the raw material of McCarthy's own words and actions, the text ironically redirects the connotations in the McCarthy footage.[48] The depiction of the public man as inconsistent and uncouth is built from "objective" news film—it is laid over footage that we take as "fact." This ironic layering of another sense over "objective" footage partly depends upon our assent to the "actuality" of what we see.

If we consider only its content, the program may sustain itself as reportage. But considering its rhetorical action—how it works ironically to undermine the ethos of the senator, how it invites participation in "judging" McCarthy—"A Report on Senator McCarthy" clearly exhibits features of another genre of argumentative discourse, the public accusation.[49] In sum, the first section of the "Report on Senator McCarthy" works by exploiting expectations of the news report against expectations of the rhetorical accusation and uses the trope of irony to lever itself from objectivity into argument.[50]

## The Ironic Text

The final parts of the first section of "A Report on Senator McCarthy" now move more quickly. There follow a series of press conference statements, each dealing with the Zwicker controversy. Again, Murrow's narration is satiric, biting. "But two days later, Secretary Stevens and the senator had lunch, agreed on a memorandum of understanding, disagreed on what the small type said." Murrow speaks over a medium shot of an obviously nervous army secretary Stevens. He stands and delivers his short statement in head-and-shoulders newsfilmlike frame. Then Murrow describes Eisenhower's "nonresponse" to McCarthy over scenes of the president at his press conference.

McCarthy's statement follows and is clearly provocative. Seen before a bank of microphones, the senator addresses the assembled press corps. "Apparently the President and I now agree on the necessity of getting rid of Communists. We apparently disagree only on how we should handle those who protect Communists." A cut: the camera moves in for an extreme close-up of McCarthy. "When the shouting and the tumult dies, the American people and the President will realize that this unprecedented mud-slinging by the extreme left-wing elements of press and radio was caused solely because another Fifth Amendment Communist was finally dug out of the dark recesses and exposed to public view."

But once we have recognized the irony in the text, it is difficult to read this statement as "straight." Instead, a viewer is prompted to reject McCarthy's prediction and to reframe it in line with the developing judgment being formulated about the man. Seen this way, the statement may be taken as evidence of his paranoia and his fatal sense of persecution and martyrdom, his willingness to oppose the president of his own party.

Quickly, the text relocates back to the control room studio. As the camera moves around behind him, Murrow says, "Of the 50 largest circulation newspapers in the country, these are the left-wing papers that criticized [McCarthy]. These are the ones which supported him." He reaches down and taps two stacks of newspapers on the desk before him. The stack of papers supporting McCarthy is one-third the size of the other, seemingly evidence that a majority opposes the senator and his tactics in the Zwicker affair. Then Murrow takes up copies of the newspapers in front of him and quotes from them, the camera position reading over his shoulder. First, among the "so-called left-wing press" he quotes the *Chicago Tribune*, "McCarthy will better serve his cause if he learns to distinguish the role of investigator from the role of avenging angel."[51]

Murrow reads others. The *New York Times:* "The unwarranted interference of a demagogue." The *New York Herald Tribune:* "McCarthyism involves assaults on basic Republican concepts." The *Milwaukee Journal:* "The line must be drawn and defended, or McCarthy will become the government." The *Washington Evening Star:* "It was a bad day for everyone who resents and detests the bully-boy tactics which McCarthy so often employs."

Such quotations of opinion allow *See It Now* to editorialize yet still retain its claim of objectivity. After all, here the program is merely quoting fact, namely newspaper reactions to the Zwicker incident. But this segment also hints, in its parody of the "so-called left-wing papers," at the strategy of refutation that will ground the second section. In coaxing its audience to join its ironic stance and to assent to its progressively more negative depiction of Joseph R. McCarthy, *See It Now* solicits a reaction crucial for response to what follows.

*Section 2: From Ironic Report to Direct Refutation*

The second section of the "Report on Senator McCarthy" begins with another parody of a McCarthy quotation. Murrow lays aside the last of the newspapers and pauses. The monitor shows McCarthy, who claims to be shocked at Stevens's refusal to allow officers to testify before his committee. "As I read his statement," McCarthy says with a haughty smile, "I thought of that quotation 'Upon what meat doth this, our Caesar, feed?'"

In a curious turn, the second section takes another tack. Murrow wonders aloud, "Upon what meat doth Senator McCarthy feed?" and announces that *See It Now* will submit samples of "two staples of McCarthy's diet," what Murrow calls "the investigation—protected by immunity—and the half-truth." The program shifts its tone and tactics, and the text becomes clearly adversarial.

Again Murrow looks up at the monitor, "First, the half-truth." A graphic—CHICAGO OCT. 27, 1952—and a section of McCarthy's speech attacking Democratic nominee Adlai Stevenson on the eve of the 1952 election. What follows is a remarkable and chilling sequence of McCarthy in action, and as before, what is presented is news film of the speech.

"I perform this unpleasant task," McCarthy begins, "because the American people are entitled to have the coldly documented history of this man who wants to be your president." Then, quite self-consciously, McCarthy deliberately mixes the name of Adlai Stevenson with Alger Hiss and plays the "mistake" for comic effect. He laughs and affects ignorance.

McCarthy waves a photostat, "one of those documents which never was supposed to see the light of day." It is, he claims, a memorandum from Hiss, "a convicted traitor," recommending that Stevenson attend a postwar diplomatic conference. "Why? Why [does] Hiss . . . find that Adlai Stevenson is the man [he] wants representing [him] at this conference?" McCarthy asks dramatically. "I don't know. Perhaps Adlai knows."

*See It Now* cuts to Murrow, who looks up grimly. "Senator McCarthy didn't permit his audience to hear the entire paragraph." The camera pulls back as he picks up a paperbound book. This, Murrow says, is the official record of the Congressional hearing; "anyone can buy it for two dollars." Murrow turns to a marked page and reads a more simple explanation: Stevenson was recommended for the conference because of his position as assistant to the secretary of the navy. Murrow scowls and takes up his script again. His anger is noticeable, disdain crackling in his voice: "We read from this documented record, not in defense of Mr. Stevenson, but in defense of truth."

The next sequence reveals the second "staple" of the senator's diet, "a sample of an investigation." Murrow fills in the background. A "civil servant," Reed Harris, then director of the Voice of America, was summoned and questioned by Senator McCarthy "about a book he had written in *1932.*" Murrow's voice rises in seeming disbelief. He looks at the monitor: WASHINGTON, MARCH 3, 1953. What follows is the longest single sequence in the program—a remarkable exhibition of McCarthy's tactics in committee hearings: bullying, then ignoring witnesses, distorting answers.

The senator asks about Harris's book. The witness explains that in the 1930s there was "no awareness" of the Communist threat. But while the voice-track carries Harris's explanation, the visuals show Senator McCarthy. He leans out of, then back into, the picture; he talks to someone behind him; listens to Roy Cohn, seated to his right. Impatiently, he glances back in the direction of Harris, then leans over and whispers again to Cohn, completely ignoring Harris's answers.

"Did the Civil Liberties Union provide you with an attorney at that time?" McCarthy demands at one point. Harris responds that he received many offers of attorneys. "The question," McCarthy sneers, "is did the Civil Liberties Union supply you with an attorney?" When Harris hesitates, McCarthy demands a yes or no answer: "The answer is yes?" he urges. "You know the Civil Liberties Union has been listed as 'a front for and doing the work of' the Communist Party?"

Finally, a cut back to Murrow. What had been gained in this testimony, he sarcastically asks. "Senator McCarthy succeeded in proving that Reed Harris had once written a bad book, which the American people had proved twenty-two years ago by not buying it, which is what they eventually do with all bad ideas." And once more, the text offers a refutation of McCarthy charges through counterevidence. "The Attorney General's list does not and has never listed the ACLU as subversive, nor does the FBI or any other federal government agency," Murrow claims.

"A Report on Senator McCarthy" has radically shifted from the indirect and the ironic tenor that characterized the first section. In its second section, the format is of confrontation. For each of McCarthy's charges, the program provides an alternative explanation; for each claim, a refutation. Furthermore, the text here is clearly accusing Joseph McCarthy, unambiguously charging him with distortion and misuse of his office.

The relationship between the program's second section and the first raises some problems of interpretation. But other commentators sense no difficulty. Most consider it as wildly unfair, out of keeping with a news documentary, and, as such, conclusive evidence of the defectiveness of the "Report on Senator McCarthy." But let us recall the question of generic classification. Once we have grounds for considering "A Report on Senator McCarthy" an act of rhetorical accusation, then our expectations of the text and our analytic categories shift. As accusation, requiring evidence and invoking argument, the program begs the question of conventional journalistic fairness. Its purpose becomes precisely to put a coloration on its subject through the selection and the arrangement of its evidence. Ultimately, it seeks to move an audience to its point of view.

Standards of fairness, then, are a function of the genre of discourse.[52] A "fair" accusation demands a clear setting forth of charges and the arranging of evidence in support of those charges. The "fair" accusation must present itself as justified in its charges. Moreover, in alleging specific wrongs, the accusation provides the accused with a clear set of charges and so furnishes the basis for defense.[53] The "Report on Senator McCarthy" begins as ironic discourse. But irony, with its indirection, cannot be "fair" accusation. The new argumentative tack of the program is best understood as meeting the rhetorical requirements of accusation itself. The genre demands a shift from the ironic undercutting of McCarthy's ethos to a direct confrontation.

In view of the rhetorical problem facing the *See It Now* rhetors, this shift is not surprising. Recognizing the psychological makeup of their audience, the filmmakers first present the negative persona of McCarthy. Words and images undercut the man, while irony prompts the audience to join *See It Now* in a satiric perspective. Once *See It Now* has invited its audience to share in disapprobation of McCarthy, once it has them "on its side," then it may take the next step: to confront the senator directly, to charge him with misdeeds, to refute his claims. Once a viewer has been convinced by the seeming "objective" evidence of McCarthy's self-contradiction, and has perceived him as almost "laughable," then the viewer may more readily assent to Murrow's contradiction of him. In short, building upon expectations of the television news report, acceptance of the direct confrontation of the second section depends upon assent to the irony of the first. But at the same time, the conventional news film certifies charges against the senator and justifies the accusation that follows.

## Section 3: Mortification and Redemption

The final and perhaps most famous section, Murrow's "editorial," begins with a swift transition—a short segment showing a grinning McCarthy quoting Shakespeare. Back to Murrow: he pauses, then shifts in his chair and looks up at the camera. "Had [the senator] looked three lines earlier in Shakespeare's Caesar, he would have found this line, which is not altogether inappropriate: 'The fault, dear Brutus, is not in our stars, but in ourselves.'" As the camera focuses steadily on him, Murrow looks up and presses his point: "We will not be driven by fear into an age of unreason, if we dig deep in our history and our doctrine, and remember that we are not descended from fearful men—not from men who feared to write, to speak, to associate and to defend causes that were, for the moment, unpopular."

We must find in the "timeless sense" of who we are, Murrow says, the antidote for the urgent, the dangerous, the unstable present. "We can deny our heritage and our history, but we cannot escape responsibility for the result. There is no way for a citizen of a republic to abdicate his responsibilities." But in Murrow's view, McCarthy's actions are not the cause of the present situation. "He didn't create this situation of fear; he merely exploited it—and rather successfully." A pause. "Cassius was right," Murrow concludes, "the fault, dear Brutus, is not in our stars, but in ourselves."

In this *See It Now* text McCarthyism comes to have less to do with Joseph McCarthy than with our own culpability. Since we have rejected our past, we stand responsible for McCarthy's potency in the present. And so, the final move of this increasingly complex text is an invitation to participate in an act of mortification.

In the works of Kenneth Burke, the ritual cycle of guilt-victimage-redemption is detached from its specifically religious significance. When it is used in this secular sense, the cycle attains both explanatory power and universal appeal. In Burke's view, the ritual cycle strives for completion. Mortification or guilt demands purification to rid ourselves of the pollution that prompts that guilt.[54]

Burke's vocabulary indicates one way the discourse invites our participation against McCarthyism. From this perspective, the textual appeal of mortification is a masterstroke. By seeing the guilt as ours and by participating in shared mortification, we also share in the need to purge ourselves of our failings. And so, if Burke is right, the appeal of "A Report on Senator McCarthy" is finally to the completion of the ritual cycle—an identification of our salvation.

Thus, instead of a direct call for outright action against McCarthyism, the text fabricates a much subtler strategy. Purification can come only through penance, and penance is served by embracing our heritage, by speaking out. Seen in this way, the "Report on Senator McCarthy" is self-reflexive; it is both argument and action. For not only does it invite us to take action, it is an action. And as it invites us to speak out, by speaking out itself, *See It Now* models our contrition.[55] *See It Now*'s "Report on Senator McCarthy" stands as an enactment of its argument.

## Response to the Telecast

Murrow's challenge, that this was "no time to keep silent," was taken literally by many who watched the "Report on Senator McCarthy." Broadcast in thirty-six cities, the program had a 61.5 coverage, and 2,394,000 homes—approximately 9.2 percent of homes with television receivers—were watching.[56] When it was over, switchboards at the network and at local affiliates were swamped with the "greatest flood of calls in television history."[57] CBS reported it received more than 12,000 telephone calls in the twenty-four hours after the broadcast, and those praising the telecast outnumbered those who were critical by fifteen to one. At CBS affiliates across the country the ratio was much the same.[58] Over 3,200 complimentary telegrams arrived, along with fewer than 250 negative responses.[59]

Press response was equally enthusiastic.[60] *Newsweek* said that "no political show so damning [had] ever been done."[61] The *New York Herald Tribune* described the "Report" as "a sober and realistic appraisal of McCarthyism and the climate in which it flourishes."[62] And one trade journal called it the greatest feat of journalistic enterprise in modern times.[63] *Variety* declared that "all TV" was proud of the show: "Murrow has now attacked head-on the one-man-myth and pointed up its factual inconsistencies and dubious logic."[64] *New York Times* columnist Jack Gould devoted two columns to praise the program in the following week.[65] He congratulated CBS and ALCOA and called the program "crusading journalism of high responsibility and genuine courage . . . for TV, so often plagued by timidity and hesitation," he said, "the program was a milestone that reflected enlightened citizenship."[66] Gould would also recognize the call for action in the telecast. It was "an indictment of those who wish the problems posed by the senator's tactics would just go away and leave them alone." He said, "One could hardly help react to the Murrow challenge." John Crosby of the *New York Herald Tribune* agreed: "At least I can never recall any other time when a network . . . has told its listeners to straighten up and act like free men with the clear implication they are not now doing so."[67] Some of the highest praise came in a *St. Louis Post Dispatch* editorial that set the telecast in the context of a national crisis: "No one needs to fear television and radio so long as demagogues are matched and more by honest men who care about the fate of their country."[68]

But the praise was not universal. Jack O'Brian in the *New York Journal-American* labeled Murrow, a "pompous portsider," called the program an "unwarranted, unprecedented attack," and insisted that CBS had attempted to prevent the *See It Now* McCarthy broadcast from being aired by threatening Murrow with dismissal.[69] Also, Murrow received a quantity of hate mail, some of it addressed to "Red" Murrow.[70] In response to threats, CBS protected the Murrow family, and Murrow's young son was watched continually.[71] As for Senator McCarthy, he told the press that he had retired early in the evening and so had not seen the *See It Now* program.[72]

Historical assessment has been divided over the program's direct impact on the senator himself. Some have seen it as the decisive moment at which opinion turned against McCarthy, but others contend that, while he was "badly cut up" by the Murrow broadcast, the senator and his cause were hardly destroyed by it.[73] *See It Now's* producers tended to agree with this perspective. Friendly later remarked that the program was hardly the "decisive blow" against Senator McCarthy's power, and Murrow called the program "late."[74]

However, what seemed most impressive was *See It Now's* ability to generate reaction among its viewers, because in those days such potential had not been established. According to television writer Jack Gould, everyone was surprised at the response to "A Report on Senator McCarthy." No one really thought that television had such "reach," he said; Murrow said nothing that some newspapers have not said for some time, Gould commented, but in the end, the program was "significant" because it was "on television."[75]

Gould's is an interesting conclusion not just because it refers to the medium as a means for the dissemination of information or as a way of reaching a wide cross section of audience beyond the major metropolitan areas, nor because it refers to the institutional decisions involved in the attack on McCarthyism. Instead I will consider its implications for the television documentary both as it relates to the text's ideological dimensions and as a form of persuasive appeal used in the defense of the medium itself.

## Documentary Form Versus McCarthyism

Television documentary may have been the best medium to confront McCarthyism directly. In seeking to explain the phenomenon of McCarthyism, some historians have argued that one source of Joseph McCarthy's appeal to the American public was precisely his intuitive understanding of the power of documentation. McCarthyism could succeed, this argument goes, because Americans are obsessed with fact-fetishism and are as a result especially susceptible to the rhetor, like McCarthy, who claims to have proof or evidence in the form of documents, copies, or photostats.[76]

*See It Now* plays upon the very same appeal to facticity. In its appeal to the power of the "real world" through the denoted natural image, the television documentary also exploits attitudes toward "documentation" and "facts." Presenting words and pictures, certifying their time and place, the program also uses raw material from the public record. And so, strikingly, this television documentary, in using film of the senator as evidence against him, likewise turns McCarthy's own rhetoric of documentation against him.

In addition, the potency of the documentary form may reside

partially in this ability to shift interpretation as it removes action from its original context. Furthermore, this capacity, once articulated, suggests that irony is embodied in the very form of See It Now itself. Erving Goffman's analytic paradigm, frame analysis, suggests one way in which this effect may work. In Goffman's terminology, the See It Now text takes events from one frame and reinserts them into an alternative frame. In other words, the "Report on Senator McCarthy" works by shifting a strip of the "factual record of experience" (the photographic image) from its original frame to another frame—the See It Now text. An audience sees the words and the actions of Senator McCarthy selected and presented out of their normal context, and within this alternative frame, the meaning and significance of the film segments are "rekeyed" and understood differently.[77]

For example, in the primary frame of, say, reviewing the whole of Senator McCarthy's remarks in Milwaukee, we might focus upon his descriptions of his meeting with Eisenhower, listen to his plans about the upcoming election, and take the oration as a successful, if partisan, election year address. But in the frame of the See It Now text, we are invited to read this same film "evidence" in a different way, and we respond according to the ironic tenor of the program. Within this ironic textual frame, we reground the film segment and may then focus upon the way that the senator contradicts himself; we may watch the movements of his jaw and denounce his actions as scandalous.

The documentary key, then, sometimes suppresses original meanings as it removes action from its original context. In this program, See It Now uses the medium to permit access to a variety of "factual" clips of McCarthy in action, within a peculiar vantage. The medium itself permits us to move easily through time and across space, encouraging us to take a "godlike" perspective. As we possess a vision simultaneous in time and comprehensive in scope, we are thus made to recall previous acts and words of Joe McCarthy that are mocked by acts and words of the present. The form of the See It Now text presents a form of dramatic irony: the spectacle of a persona (McCarthy) ignorant of his true situation. We assume the part of observer and/or superior being, taking in "all things at one glance" and finding in such an ironic vantage the potential for a transforming perspective.[78]

Clearly, Goffman's notion of framing and reframing itself partakes of irony in important aspects. We are simultaneously aware of both the original and the new framing. And in rekeying a strip of experience, we understand that the experience is modeled upon the original but is somehow "different." That is to say, we know that the content is reframed, and we revel in its rekeying, yet at the same time we recognize that its original meanings have been perverted. Only an intended audience of surprising sophistication can sustain both readings at once.[79]

The reason is partly the way irony works upon an audience. Irony always presupposes that supplementary information is available about facts or norms, and its use depends upon a community's shared knowledge. A rhetor could not successfully use irony if an audience was ignorant of the rhetor's actual views or the requirements of genre. As Booth argues, irony is nearly impossible for an audience to recognize when the viewpoints of the ironist and his intended audience are extremely far apart.[80]

Because irony in discourse depends so much upon a shared knowledge, the ironic text defines its ideal auditors quite precisely. It is possible to sense in the ironic appeal of "A Report on Senator McCarthy" that *See It Now* possessed a definition of the specific audience to which it was appealing. The audience imagined by Murrow and Friendly was one that could be expected to understand the conventions of television documentary, the proper code of behavior in the political sphere, and the expected attitudes of Murrow.

So it may be that being "on television" did more than heighten the importance of "A Report on Senator McCarthy." Perhaps television documentary most of all possessed the potential to accuse Senator McCarthy and effectively to undermine the base of persuasive appeal, that unquestioning assent to "facts," upon which Joe McCarthy and McCarthyism stood. For the *See It Now* rhetors, perhaps, the particular mode of the visual documentary form itself—its appeal to "facticity" and "objectivity," its reframing of film footage, its implicit ironic tenor—lent significance and coloration to the "neutral, photographic record of McCarthy in action," inviting its audience to participate in an act of public accusation.

## The Role of Irony

*See It Now*'s "Report on Senator McCarthy" is a complex and sophisticated television discourse. I have argued for a reading of the text "against" its traditional classification as a "news report" and have instead insisted that "A Report on Senator McCarthy" more properly belongs to another genre—the public accusation. Furthermore, it is clear that the program subversively uses the conventions of one genre to prepare for assent to ends belonging properly in another. It solicits assent to the "objectivity" of reportage and the journalistic discourse as a source of appeal to disarm reservations and to coax the audience to another point of view. And to appreciate the subtlety and sophistication in this text is to free the way for a critical reappraisal of this controversial and important public discourse.

Once we read "A Report on Senator McCarthy" as ironic argument rather than as "flawed news report," concerns about inconsistencies in the text and problems with its interpretation are relieved. Once we have acknowledged the accusatory intent of "A Report on Senator McCarthy," the sarcastic and satiric tenor of Murrow's commentary is explicable. The emphasis in the text upon the character of McCarthy is rationalized. Also, the curious subverting of the generic visual conventions of the news report, while out of place in the objective news documentary, are rendered quite compatible within the generic conventions of the public accusation.

By viewing the trope of irony as central to an understanding of the program, we may solve another long-standing critical problem with "A Report on Senator McCarthy," the uneasy transitions between the three sections of the program, which are difficult to explain by conventional analysis. That is, finally, once we have acknowledged the irony in "A Report on Senator McCarthy," then we can reconcile the indirect and satiric first section as a necessary prelude to the direct confrontation of the second.

As it unfolds, *See It Now* constructs its audience, pulling together those who grasp its ironic tenor. But in addition, once it has been read as ironic, *See It Now* can employ the trope to enlist viewer support. Viewers might more readily join in challenging Joe McCarthy after having persuaded themselves, through participation in the irony of the first section, that the refutation is warranted. And irony also functions to tie Murrow's final comment to the other two sections. Auditors are invited to espouse, in the call to mortification, a surprising perspective that interprets McCarthyism as "our" fault.

Thus, irony in this *See It Now* text resonates on a number of levels. Its shared sense of guilt implicates all of the potential audience, while its linking and unifying of the three-part construction invites a reconfiguration of McCarthyism. The trope of irony is the engine that drives the textual strategies of appeal and defines "A Report on Senator McCarthy" as a response to the excesses of its era.

## Irony, Mortification, and Ideology

So far, we have chiefly considered irony as a local and finite rhetorical figure. But in the end, we can consider irony enlarged or in a slightly different key and can recognize its close kinship with mortification. Indeed, rhetorical irony also partakes of a more global and infinite sense. This is first hinted by Quintilian, for example, who says that irony may be on two levels: first at the level of words, as in "that excellent man, Marcus." This level Quintilian calls the "trope of irony." But he also recognizes that irony may be extended to the whole; that is, an entire discourse or dialogue might be ironic—what Quintilian calls the "figure of irony."[81]

In "Four Master Tropes," Burke discusses irony not as a figure of speech but as a figure of thought, as a way of seeing the world or of locating the "truth."[82] For Burke, because the ironic perspective encourages us to adopt both literal and alternative readings at once—because irony "uses" this plurality of viewpoints—irony is the "perspective of perspectives." "True irony is based on a sense of fundamental kinship with the enemy, as one needs him, is indebted to him, is not merely outside him as an observer, but contains him within, being consubstantial with him."[83]

I suggest that the "Report on Senator McCarthy" represents the ironic as a response to the world and so summarizes a way of coming to know that world. That is to say, the "Report on Senator McCarthy" is concerned as much with epistemology as with politics or morals. It is fair to say that Senator McCarthy was abhorrent to pluralist sensibilities in part because he challenged a central tenet in his drive for conformity.[84] See It Now invites us to perceive Mc-Carthyism as at once outside and within us, and to accede to the appeal of mortification in this text is to acknowledge McCarthyism as our dark side. To counter it, Murrow argues, we must encompass it. To undermine it, we must acknowledge it and take it in. In this suggestion, See It Now's discourse turns upon itself, ironically rekeying McCarthyism in tune with a well-rehearsed sense of pluralist guilt.

Such mortification is precisely the ironic perspective—a pluralism that can encompass even such an anathema as McCarthyism, recognizing it as one of a number of possible perspectives. In this way, the ironic mortification at the center of See It Now circumscribes the text within the ideology of liberal pluralism—quite apart from the overt and visible content of the program.

I have noted that the "Report on Senator McCarthy" is strangely reflexive and introspective for an ostensibly "journalistic" or "objective" text. Edwin Black has observed that such a discursive tone marks the discourses of liberal politics to a greater degree than is usually suspected. As Black has indicated, the discourses of liberal pluralism are frequently animated by an attention to an inward turning, an epistemological self-centering that is really less "political" than it appears.[85]

Moreover, Black's argument also illuminates the operation of irony as we have seen it in "A Report on Senator McCarthy." Our explication seems to mark the trope of irony as central to liberal pluralism. Just as the pluralist sensitivity works through liberal discourse seeking to encompass all elements through mortification, so too may irony function as figure of thought and speech to characterize such discourses. Thus, *See It Now's* answer to McCarthyism is an ironic answer and the "Report on Senator McCarthy" a pluralist response. In the end, questions of fairness and objectivity fall away. In the end, we understand the "Report on Senator McCarthy" as an ironic defense of plurality, a rehearsal of liberal epistemology.

## Irony and the News Documentary

This analysis of "A Report on Senator McCarthy" also suggests a relation between reportage and argument that does not entail the traditional bifurcation. In this news documentary, television seeks its warrant in the "real world" and draws a persuasive potency from that given, neutral structure which we expect to find in the "objective facts." But the trope of irony invites a reading against the overt and surface signification of the words and images and coaxes into being a second level of meaning, one that overlays the "objective" and "factual" content. Encouraging an ironic reading, *See It Now* is able to infuse the genre of journalistic discourse with alternative meanings and so positions itself between objectivity and accusation.

Thus the "Report on Senator McCarthy" may represent a hybrid of two genres. The result permits auditors to participate, depending upon their recognition of the ironic tension between reportage and argument. Moreover, the mix of generic convention furnishes a "protection" of sorts against the direct attacks of McCarthy by seeming to satisfy the constraints of "fairness."

Finally, the analysis suggests that this hybrid depends directly upon our assumed knowledge of the conventions of other genres for its effect and that the form plays expectations off one another. This conclusion seems compatible with certain assumptions regarding the generic perspective as it has developed in the literature of speech communication.[86] But our analysis also indicates that generic expectations may be less constraint in the television medium than a source of inventive and suasive potential. Certainly, we approach this *See It Now* text expecting a news documentary distinguished by its journalistic objectivity. But this program subtly exploits our agreement to its purported objectivity. And precisely because we are disarmed by its claim to be a natural representation of fact and event, *See It Now* gains the capacity to layer over those representations a second-level message—one that prompts a judgment of McCarthyism. Turning this the other way round is to say that the *See It Now* documentary's potential to reshape our view of the world resides in the way that its second-level message is "naturalized" by our expectations of the news discourse. The hidden rhetoric of irony saturates the objective discourse of journalism with meanings while at the same time disguising this connection.

Before the evening of March 11, 1954, was over, what *See It Now* had said about Senator McCarthy had been driven from the front page headlines. That night, the army charged McCarthy and his assistant, Roy Cohn, with demanding special treatment for a former committee counsel. The report was a bombshell. And by the time McCarthy appeared on Fulton Lewis's radio program that evening to respond to the earlier attack made by Democrat Adlai Stevenson, the junior senator was under fire from all sides.

# 7

# Naturalism and Television Documentary: "Annie Lee Moss Before the McCarthy Committee"

Tuesday evening, March 16—it is only one short week after the broadcast of *See It Now*'s "Report on Senator McCarthy," and Edward R. Murrow again faces the cameras in CBS Studio 41. This time he announces the second consecutive *See It Now* installment on the senator from Wisconsin: "Good evening. On 'See It Now,' we occasionally use the phrase 'the little picture.' Tonight we bring you a little picture of a little woman, Mrs. Annie Lee Moss, and the due process of law."[1]

This *See It Now* telecast, "Annie Lee Moss Before the McCarthy Committee," as it came to be known, is a most unusual program. It is remarkable for its origin, for its form and style, and for its ability to elicit from its audience a reaction that seems to run against Senator McCarthy and the abuse of congressional hearings on which the McCarthyites relied. First, the producers of "Moss" claim that it was not preplanned or part of a conscious strategy to follow the "Report on Senator McCarthy" with another telecast on the same subject the very next week. Instead, the decision seems to have combined coincidence, spontaneity, and serendipity. Fred Friendly later confessed that "if someone had suggested a week earlier that we might run two McCarthy broadcasts on successive weeks, we would have scoffed."[2] And yet, even without conscious design, and though the program may well have been overshadowed by the political revelations of the week and the furor in the wake of *See It Now*'s "McCarthy " telecast, "Annie Lee Moss Before the McCarthy Committee" may be the most powerful of the four *See It Now* McCarthyism programs that I have examined.

Stylistically, "Moss" differs from the other telecasts: it is made up almost entirely of an edited visual transcription of Mrs. Moss's testimony in answer to charges that she was a member of the Communist party while she worked as a secret code machine operator for the army Signal Corps. Unlike the earlier programs (and especially "A Report on Senator McCarthy"), it does not depend upon Murrow's voice-over or on-camera commentary to guide its audience and to persuade a viewer to adopt a specific argumentative solution. While Murrow does add short comments over the film at two points for clarification or to introduce speakers, in this text Murrow is nearly absent, and for the most part, the audience is "there" watching the McCarthy committee in session.

But the program's singular form apparently did not weaken its affective power. Reviewers called it "nearly as devastating an indictment as the previous show (on McCarthy)"[3] and recognized that the "power of television saved Annie Lee Moss. . . . To millions she seemed to be telling the truth."[4] Murrow, himself, would later label the program "possibly the most unpremeditatedly analytical report ever telecast by *See It Now*."[5]

Murrow's comment indicates the common thread that runs through reactions to the program and one that warrants exploration. It is interesting and perhaps curious that, for all its seemingly "negative" depiction of the McCarthyites, there was apparently never any controversy over the "objectivity" or the bias of the "Moss" telecast. In the case of this program, quite unlike the "Report on Senator McCarthy," the question of "fairness" seems hardly to have been mentioned.[6] Many have seemed naturally drawn to compare "Annie Lee Moss Before the McCarthy Committee" with the earlier "Report." Columnist Marya Mannes sums up what might be a general reaction: where the earlier "Report on Senator McCarthy" was an "unfair and biased attack," Mannes concedes that, in the "shocking" procedure used against Annie Lee Moss, which Mannes had seen with her own eyes, the senator had, in fact, "convicted himself."[7] Even critic Gilbert Seldes, who passionately objected to the March 9 program, accepted "Annie Lee Moss Before the McCarthy Committee" as "fair." "This was a report," he said, "picked up by the cameras on the spot—condensed and edited, no doubt, but retaining the essentials of the original event."[8]

Such unanimity with respect to a potentially controversial telecast is intriguing and at first, puzzling. Clearly, one partial explanation may have to do with the textual shifting of relative importance away from the voice-over commentary and toward the visualizations of the observing camera. In a way, one could say that the strategy of this text is to absent its maker and to rely upon the camera itself—to let us "see with our own eyes."[9] This naive assumption of "seeing is believing" might cast the "Moss" program, while "devastating" to the McCarthyites, as nevertheless a text that plays "fair," that does not "manipulate" or "bias" its story. But this simple answer glosses over basic assumptions. Quite obviously, once the controlling perspective of the voice-over narrator has been eliminated, the potential for other problems increases. This chapter will explain how "Annie Lee Moss Before the McCarthy Committee" "means." In answering the question of meaning, I will analyze the "Moss" text in relation to the actual historical events in the committee room, in relation to other documentary texts, and in relation to other, even fictional, discursive forms.

## Direct and Indirect Address

In his work on documentary and ethnographic film, Bill Nichols specifies some of the pitfalls that await the documentary text that diminish the importance of the controlling and guiding perspective of the narrator or commentator. In both *Ideology and the Image* and his later work *Representing Reality*, Nichols divides the genre of documentary into categories on the basis of what he identifies as the basic modes of address in documentary. Nichols calls the two most typical of these modes "direct address" and "indirect address," and for Nichols, a documentary text falls into one or the other category, depending on whether the viewer is explicitly acknowledged as the subject to whom the film is "spoken."[10]

To take one example, the category of direct address, in which the viewer is specifically acknowledged as a viewing subject and is addressed either by a narrator or by characters in an interview situation, Nichols calls "expository cinema." This, Nichols argues, is the "classic" format of documentary, including, we might add, the other *See It Now* programs on McCarthyism (a possible exception to the "debate" segment of "Argument in Indianapolis"). In this classic expository direct address mode, a narrator (either on camera or off) addresses the audience—talks to them directly—and frames the thesis of the text. For Nichols, "direct address documentaries," or the "expository" genre, is characterized by a narrator guiding the "argument" of the text. Such texts, Nichol says, are therefore usually characterized by the "diachronic march of cause/effect, premise/conclusion, problem/solution."[11] Moreover, the expository form takes this characteristic style precisely because it is organized around the verbal commentary directed toward a viewer. Visualizations serve, for the most part, Nichols argues, as "illustration" in such texts. Furthermore, viewers of expository documentary likely hold a commonsensical expectation that "the world" they see will be organized according to the establishment of a particular suasive intent on the part of the producers.[12]

In contrast, the indirect form, the form of "Annie Lee Moss Before the McCarthy Committee," is quite different; here, Nichols says, the viewer is never fully acknowledged as subject and instead watches social actors in their roles. Nichols calls this form "observational" documentary. The indirect, observational text organizes itself around what Nichols terms "the depiction of the everyday" rather than an argument that offers a "solution to a puzzle or problem" as is characteristically found in the expository form.[13] But the observational mode is seldom the form of television documentaries because, Nichols suggests, it "runs the risk of incomprehensibility (lacking the guiding hand of the narrator)."[14]

Precisely because such indirect discourse lacks this guide, Nichols argues that the "thesis" of an "observational" documentary text is often difficult to ascertain. The implication is in part that the observational mode has a very close kinship with fictional discourses. Viewers not only "look in on and overhear social actors" but also use expectations and codes of action taken from the everyday to identify, define, and judge the activities and intentions of the actors depicted in the text.[15] Thus while the observational documentary conveys the sense of affording unmediated and unobstructed access to the world—access similar to that promised by the fictional film—Nichols argues that this "strength" might paradoxically "weaken" its function as a discourse of persuasion:

As we pursue the study of documentary into the realm of indirect address, the strategies of rhetoric begin to recede into the background. Instead of advancing arguments, films now observe situations and events. . . . the film makers no longer speak to us directly. Like the narrative or poetic film maker, the observational film maker is mute.[16]

It seems clear then, that, though we might quarrel with Nichols's division of the documentary genre, his taxonomy has the potential usefulness of focusing attention upon the expectations of audiences, upon the relationship of documentary and fiction, and upon the commonsense assumption that "argumentation" is problematic in the "indirect" or "observational documentary."[17] The question implicit in Nichols's analysis, which might be tested by a rhetorical analysis, may be framed thus: does the indirect television documentary "argue"?

Clearly, we have a set of interrelated problems here: a discourse that presents itself as an unmediated transcript of an event in the world, a documentary style capable of giving viewers the sense of "observing" the event, and recorded responses to the text that take completely antithetical interpretations of that event. On the one hand, this documentary is seen as "unbiased report"; on the other, sometimes even to the same viewer, it appears as "devastating argument." More specifically, then, how does this "observational" *See It Now* text seem both to sustain its claim as "fair report" and to function as argument and make clear its "thesis"?

"Annie Lee Moss Before the McCarthy Committee," as a paradigm case of an "indirect documentary," represents a subgenre whose grounds for evaluation and standards for judgment approach those usually reserved for discourses more properly considered poetic. Indeed, the observational documentary may add a new dimension to Aristotelian genres of discourse. In "Annie Lee Moss Before the McCarthy Committee" we can see the tension in the "indirect" television documentary that seems to stretch the boundaries of "argument."

One potentially useful analytic approach involves focusing upon the paradigms used for assigning meaning to this documentary text. Theories that explicate these paradigms are, of course, grouped under the critical rubric of "intertextuality." The theory of intertextuality proposes that any one text is necessarily read in relationship to others and that a range of textual knowledge is brought to bear upon it. These intertextual knowledges preorient the reader to exploit the text by activating it in certain ways, that is, by making some meanings rather than others.[18] According to Roland Barthes, such textual relations are so pervasive that our culture consists of a complex web of intertextuality, in which all texts finally refer only to each other.[19]

This chapter examines "Annie Lee Moss" according to three dominant intertextual relationships: text and history, text and genre, and text and myth.

## The Story of "A Little Woman"

"Annie Lee Moss Before the McCarthy Committee" had its origins in the month before the telecast. At the time Sen. Joseph McCarthy was embroiled with Secretary of the Army Robert H. Stevens over the Peress case and the treatment of Gen. Ralph Zwicker. The senator threatened new and startling revelations of Communist infiltration into the army Signal Corps.[20] He promised that he would soon expose a civilian employee whose job was encoding and decoding "top secret" messages and who was listed by the Federal Bureau of Investigation (FBI) as a member of the Communist party. Such revelations would prove, McCarthy said, that the army hid "known Communists" in sensitive positions.[21]

On February 23, the employee was revealed to be Mrs. Annie Lee Moss. On that day, a former undercover agent for the FBI in the Communist party, Mrs. Mary Stalcup Markward, testified that she knew Annie Lee Moss from party membership roles and that Moss had been a party member for over ten years. While conceding that she had never met Moss and that she could not identify her by sight, Markward said that Moss's employment record and address matched the data available to her in the early 1940s.[22]

The charges were denied by Mrs. Moss, who said that she "had never been inside a code room in my life." The army also disputed the charges and said that Moss merely operated a code machine transmitting coded messages and knew nothing of the codes themselves. Even some of the Democratic members of the McCarthy committee had doubts, and after Mackward's testimony some raised the possibility that the Annie Lee Moss in question might not be the same person currently employed by the army.[23]

But McCarthy waved objections aside and assured everyone that there was no mistake; the Annie Lee Moss, a Pentagon cafeteria worker named as a Communist in 1945, was the same woman who today was an army "code clerk" handling "topmost secrets" for the Signal Corps. McCarthy added ominously that, if Mrs. Moss continued to deny her Communist ties, she would "run the risk of indictment for perjury" when appearing before him.[24]

"Relishing the thought of the humiliation he was about to inflict upon the Army, and attempting to smother headlines produced by the Zwicker testimony,"[25] McCarthy called the investigation a further sign of an immense conspiracy: "I am not interested in this woman as a person at all. Who in the military, knowing that this lady was a Communist, promoted her from a waitress to a code clerk? The information we have is that she has no special ability as a decoding clerk. We know that she has been handling classified material despite the statement issued by the military last night."[26]

Finally, on March 11, Mrs. Moss was called before the McCarthy committee. But the testimony did not result in shocking revelations as planned. Instead, after McCarthy had hastily excused himself from the hearing, his assistant and committee counsel, Roy Cohn, became the target of the Democratic members, who challenged him to produce the evidence against Moss.[27]

Even as the Moss hearing was in process, other events were quickly driving the story from the front pages. On the evening of March 11, Senator McCarthy spoke on the nationally syndicated radio program of Fulton Lewis, Jr., and fought back at his critics, including *See It Now.*[28] In response to Adlai Stevenson, the senator described Stevenson's attitude as equivalent to saying that, if people could not agree on how to clean a barn, then it must be "perfectly clean." He quoted Lincoln in answer to Republican senator Ralph Flanders's argument that the danger to the United States is greater from without than from within. But McCarthy's strongest words were reserved for Murrow. "If I may say, Fulton, I have a little difficulty answering the specific attacks . . . because I never listened to the extreme left-wing bleeding-heart elements of radio or television," McCarthy began.[29] As expected, he relied upon the "exposé" from his files, claiming to "have in my hand" a copy of the Pittsburgh newspaper asserting that Murrow was directly connected with the Communist apparatus; Murrow had, he alleged, served in 1933 on a committee planning a summer session at Moscow University, "a school where the violent overthrow of an existing social order is taught." "This may explain," he concluded, "why Edward R. Murrow, week after week, feels he must smear Senator McCarthy. . . . maybe he is worried about the exposure of his friends—I don't know."[30]

Fifteen minutes after the senator's broadcast, Murrow, on his own nightly news program, reported McCarthy's remarks. His voice breaking as he spoke he responded to McCarthy's characterization of him: "I may be a bleeding heart, being not quite sure of what it means. As for being left-wing, that is political shorthand; but if the senator means I am somewhat to the left of his position and of Louis XIV, he is correct."[31]

But all other events of the week were overshadowed by the major news story of the day: the same evening as the Moss testimony and the Lewis broadcast, the Eisenhower administration dropped a bombshell of its own. The army released a report charging that McCarthy and Cohn had used improper pressures in seeking to win favors for their protégé G. David Schine, scion of a leading hotel empire, who had been drafted as an army private. Reports that Private Schine was a "privileged character" receiving frequent weekend and evening passes and infrequent "K.P." had leaked out of the army grapevine along with rumors that Cohn was constantly on the phone to General Zwicker, the Fort Dix commandant.[32] Since February, the army had quietly been documenting the extraordinary pressures brought to bear on behalf of the new inductee: demands that Schine be given a direct commission, that he be assigned to duty in Washington or New York, and that he be awarded passes for "committee work" and allowed to live off base. When told that Private Schine would probably get an overseas assignment, Cohn was reported to have threatened to "wreck the Army" and to see that Secretary Stevens was "through." McCarthy was depicted in a dual role: telling Stevens that Schine was a "pest" and a "nuisance" but in Cohn's presence supporting his demand for special favors. The effect of the report's release was immediate: "The Army report, obviously bearing the full authority of the Administration, was the most devastating attack ever launched against McCarthy. . . . Even a slight acquaintance with the report produced disgust at the irrational and wholly irresponsible use of congressional authority on behalf of one Army draftee."[33]

Meanwhile, telegrams flew between the *See It Now* offices and those of Senator McCarthy. When *See It Now* renewed its earlier offer to give the senator time for reply to the "Report" program, at first McCarthy designated someone else to answer in his place, but Murrow said the invitation was "not subject to transfer." McCarthy finally asked to appear April 6 and, in a press statement, rehashed his charges: "Normally I would not waste the time to merely prove that a radio and TV commentator who attacks me is lying. However, if I am correct in my position that you have consciously served the communist cause, then it is very important for your listeners to have the clear-cut documented facts."[34]

*See It Now* accepted McCarthy's offer and Murrow responded that neither "ignorance nor youth" were acceptable excuses for his service on the council of the Moscow summer institute. Instead, Murrow explained that he had served on the council as an officer of the Institute of International Education, and identified the other members of the committee.[35] "It was and is a rather distinguished list," he said. "I believed nineteen years ago and I believe today that mature American graduate students and professors can engage in conversation, controversy, and the clash of ideas with Communists anywhere under peacetime conditions without becoming contaminated or converted." And Murrow ended with a direct challenge to McCarthy: that the "record would soon show" who had served the Communists—"You or I."[36]

But the winds had clearly changed since the *See It Now* telecast on McCarthy merely a week before. There was applause for dissenting Democrats in the next day's McCarthy committee hearings. There was laughter in the public reaction to Murrow's broadcast quip about "Louis XIV" after McCarthy labeled him "extreme left-wing."[37] President Eisenhower publicly praised Senator Flanders's charges about McCarthy in the Senate chamber. A new Gallup poll showed McCarthy's approval rating had dropped four points, down to 46 percent, since its all-time high in January-February of 1954. And that Sunday, March 14, the *New York Times* "Week in Review" reported the developments in an eight-column story headlined "Turn of the Tide? McCarthy on the Defensive."[38]

### The "Unanticipated" Telecast

Meanwhile, in the *See It Now* offices, the staff was poring over the film of the Annie Lee Moss testimony. Reporter Joe Wershba had pushed for *See It Now* coverage of the Moss hearing because he felt that Moss would be overwhelmed and muted by the awesome power of the McCarthy committee and might submit to the accusations.[39] Friendly recalled that "we did not know what we'd do with any more McCarthy film, but we decided that this was no time to stop,"[40] and so, forty-eight hours after "A Report on Senator McCarthy," he had assigned Wershba and cameraman Charles Mack to the hearing.

As soon as the Moss session was completed, Wershba and Mack called New York, enthusiastically describing the film of the hearing as better than "anything we had used on the broadcast two days before."[41] The raw footage was rushed to Murrow and Friendly in New York. By Thursday, the decision was made to use the Moss film, and "Annie Lee Moss Before the McCarthy Committee" was scheduled for the following Tuesday, March 16. The short turnaround time was possible, Friendly said, because Mack, with one tripod camera and a small hand-held camera, had virtually edited a program while filming the hearing, and so the Moss broadcast was easy to put on.[42]

In a way, the Moss hearing was a stroke of luck for the *See It Now* rhetors, allowing them both to continue the momentum established by the "Report on Senator McCarthy" and to save a revealing "small story" that was in danger of being lost in the currents of the week's major news. In another way, however, this telecast more than the other three reveals the potency of "observational" documentary.

## Textual Analysis

"Annie Lee Moss Before the McCarthy Committee" begins with the usual *See It Now* opening segment: the imperative to "stand by" and the evocation of "live television" that introduces the telecasts.[43] Before us, we see a pair of monitors, on one: STAND BY SENATE CAUCUS ROOM 318. And on the other, STAND BY WASHINGTON. When the camera pans and we first see him, Murrow greets us with a large smile. He begins with an unusually jaunty "good evening."

Permit me to read what has been said in substance on this program before. This program is a weekly document for television, both live and on film, and is not designed to present hard, fast-breaking news. I and my co-editor, Fred Friendly, have been delegated the responsibility for its content. Never has our sponsor, the Aluminum Company of America attempted to pass upon subject matter or to influence the selection of material. *See It Now* operates under the broadcasting policies set by CBS.

Oddly, then, this telecast opens with a reflexivity curious even by the conventions of *See It Now*. Such introspection might suggest the increasing pressure upon Murrow and Friendly in the preceding week, and the emphasis upon personal authorship is clear. Certainly, it was not unusual for the series to draw upon the personal ethos of Murrow himself for persuasive appeal.

But the careful self-definition of *See It Now* by its own makers is particularly noteworthy: in its own terms, the program is portrayed as nonpartisan, "a document"—that is, unbiased, "objective," and operating under the policies set by the broadcasting institution. It is interesting how the rhetors equivocate: they avoid conferring responsibility on CBS and ALCOA, and yet at the same time they invoke the ethos of the broadcasting industry in the way they carefully describe *See It Now* as operating within the "policies" of that medium.

The self-referential tone continues: "Last week we made a report on Senator Joseph R. McCarthy. We labeled it as by definition, controversial. In accordance with CBS policy of fairness and equality, we offered the senator time to reply tonight, or a week from tonight. He suggested the date of April 6, and we accepted; and he now says he will appear on that date."

As we have seen, the week after the "Report on Senator McCarthy" featured the exchange of charge and countercharge between Murrow and the senator. Thus, the self-reflexivity of the text is appropriate: during an overwrought week, *See It Now* itself had become, not just the medium for "a weekly document for television," but also the object of news coverage. As the *See It Now* program has "become" news, so it reports the developments around its own story.

Moreover, such self-reflexivity here reminds us of the controversy of the previous program and provides both a background and a frame for our response toward "Annie Lee Moss Before the McCarthy Committee." Thus, in its self-referentiality, *See It Now* implicitly suggests a frame for our interpretation of this text. The program insinuates itself as a continuation of the widely publicized, ongoing dispute.

Murrow shifts in his chair. He smiles broadly once more and announces the subject of this week's program: the "little picture of a little woman." For *See It Now*, Mrs. Moss is a "little" woman in both senses of the word. Slight in stature, she is also a small figure trapped in the drama of a national dispute; knowing "little" about "Senator McCarthy, General Zwicker . . . , or . . . the argument in Washington," Annie Lee Moss is to be portrayed as the simple and unwilling participant in a serious contest of political gamesmanship.

But Moss's story will also take as its theme the "due process of law." *See It Now* thus reveals that this telecast will address some of the same issues that animated "The Case of Milo Radulovich" but five months earlier. In the earlier telecast too, the rhetors used a "small story" to depict in miniature the anguish of an individual before the power of the bureaucracy. As previously noted, the figure of Milo Radulovich assumed rhetorical potency when seen as a representation of both a particular, albeit thoroughly typical, citizen and a generalized, universal "hero."[44]

In contrast to the earlier portrait, the introduction to this program portrays Annie Lee Moss as knowing "little about the argument in Washington," as the "little woman," possessing a certain artless nature, the innocent who speaks frankly and without guile. Annie Lee Moss assumes the part of the crude, unsophisticated yet honest rustic, innocently drawn into the game of the more sophisticated. Still, she is the innocent who retains the potential to undo the game precisely because of her lack of pretension. In other words, the text treats the unaffected sincerity of Annie Lee Moss as a sign of her apparent childlike honesty and innocence.

A cursory examination discloses that "Annie Lee Moss Before the McCarthy Committee" divides conveniently into three distinct sections: the first is Murrow's introduction and narration of the events leading up to the Moss hearing; the second and most lengthy, the coverage of the hearing itself; and the third, a section of a speech by President Dwight Eisenhower. The first of these divisions holds evidence of another, a second, principal motif of the program.

Murrow begins by reading the narrative of events leading up to the Moss hearing. The recitation is familiar: Stevens and McCarthy were locked in "total controversy" when McCarthy announced some more "news for the country and the Army and Secretary Stevens." "Senator McCarthy charged . . . that the Army now employs a woman in its code room who was and still may be an active Communist."

Next Murrow adopts a strategy used often on *See It Now*—he quotes from the official record of the testimony of Mary Stalcup Markward, the FBI undercover agent who charged Moss with being a Communist party member.

"I recall, sir, that I had a woman by the name of Annie Lee Moss on the list of card-carrying, dues-paying members of the North East Club; and at that period in the history of the Communist Party, detailed lists were kept." Chairman: "Was Annie Lee Moss a member of the Communist Party?" Mrs. Markward: "She was."

Scarcely looking up, Murrow continues.

. . . the Army suspended Mrs. Moss. Finally, last Thursday, March 11, Mrs. Annie Lee Moss was called before the committee again, and this is what our cameraman, Charles Mack, saw through his camera.

As Murrow reads the last two sentences, the program cuts to a view over his shoulder and we see once more the pair of monitors on the control panel before him. There is a slight tightening on the graphic SENATE CAUCUS ROOM 318; then on the monitor, we see senators entering the meeting room. There is another cut: Senator McCarthy sits at the table and, rapping a gavel, calls the hearing to order.

We have, then, through familiar conventions and transitions, found ourselves relocated from our position with Murrow in the control room and are now placed in the position of observers in the caucus room. And from this point on, "Annie Lee Moss Before the McCarthy Committee" unfolds differently from any of the other programs on McCarthyism. It uses the form of "indirect" or "observational" documentary and replaces the guiding narration of Murrow with evidence that we see "with our own eyes." Consequently, by combining its portrayal of Annie Lee Moss and the persuasive power of its "indirect" form, "Annie Lee Moss Before the McCarthy Committee" weaves a compelling tapestry. But far from being simple observation, through its choice of visualizations and behind its studied look of "naturalism," the text reveals its argumentative intent and subtle power to direct the viewer's response.

*An Object of Identification*

From the first glimpse of the hearing room, Annie Lee Moss is centered as an object of audience identification. When seen for the first time, the framing confirms Murrow's description of a "little" woman: slight in stature, Moss is a bespectacled, middle-aged black woman. She wears a white hat and a cloth coat that she keeps buttoned tightly throughout her appearance. Her attorney sits behind and to her right. She seems small and indeed nearly lost in the bustle of activity around her.

The first questions for her are formalities: the spelling of her name, her address. The *See It Now* camera pans from Cohn and McCarthy at the Senate table to Moss facing them; other senators are arrayed along the long conference table. The camera technique of the text is often unpolished: at times it is unsteady or shaky, and sometimes other people walk between the lens and the principals.

McCarthy repeats the testimony of his informant that Mrs. Moss's name was on the membership list of the Communist party. "Can you shed any light on that?" he asks.

"No, sir," she says. "I don't even know what the dues are or where they were paid." And you say you never attended any Communist meetings or paid any money to the Communist party? McCarthy asks. "That's right," Moss responds. "Have you ever handled coded messages?" asks Cohn; the camera cuts back to Moss. Moss shakes her head: "Receive and transmit the messages. That's all I had to do. And the code room—I have never been into the code room in my life."

Quietly, consistently, methodically, Annie Lee Moss denies being a Communist, denies ever seeing a Communist card, denies attending any meeting. Her plain openness disarms; she does not try to evade any questions, she simply does not know. And yet something in the demeanor of Annie Lee Moss invites sympathy. Perhaps it is partly her homely appearance, partly too her seeming ignorance of how to act in such a setting: for instance, with great exaggeration, she leans toward the microphone with each answer, and periodically McCarthy politely asks her not to get too close.

The alternating questions of Cohn and McCarthy fail to shake Mrs. Moss's story. With straightforward responses, she continues to deny any suggestion of "Communist" activities:

COHN: Have you ever subscribed to the *Daily Worker?*
MRS. MOSS: No, sir. I didn't subscribe to the *Daily Worker,* and I wouldn't pay for it.
MCCARTHY: You say that you never have been a member of the Communist party?
MRS. MOSS: No, sir. I have not.

To the obviously increasing frustration of her questioners, Mrs. Moss denies having discussed communism with anyone. When questioned about buying the *Daily Worker* from "Rob Hall," whom Cohn calls "one of the leading Communists in the District of Columbia," Mrs. Moss admits that "Robert Hall" once came by her rooming house. But on that occasion, her husband told Hall never to come back with that "communist paper." Moss confesses that she knows "Robert Hall" by sight but does not know him personally.

When *See It Now*'s cameras pull back for a wide shot of the entire hearing room, the scene is certainly grim: McCarthy and Cohn take turns questioning the small woman before them, and Moss, speaking softly, surrounded by spectators, is sometimes barely visible behind the table crowded with microphones. Surrounded by the glare of national attention, Annie Lee Moss is simple, humble, earnest. Perhaps partly because of her denials, and yet partly too because of her demeanor, there may well be a slow movement within the text that asks a viewer to gauge Moss's actions and appearance against codes of everyday action. This comparison might implicitly result in an ever so slight shift of presumption about the guilt of Annie Lee Moss.[45]

Suddenly, Senator McCarthy takes the floor to announce: "I'm afraid I am going to have to excuse myself. I've got rather an important appointment tonight which I have got to work on right now."[46] The camera follows as the senator leaves the room and the Moss hearing. He will not return. And just as suddenly, the tenor of the hearing changes; where McCarthy and Cohn had failed to undermine Annie Lee Moss, now the questioning falls to other senators, and they, especially the committee's Democrats, are more sympathetic toward her.

Immediately, confusion arises over the conflicting testimony about "Rob Hall." Senator Stuart Symington, who has taken over the questioning, tries to clear up the discrepancy and asks Moss once more about "Mr. Hall."

And here, for the first time since his introduction, Murrow intrudes into the text. His voice-over explanation contains important information: "Mr. Cohn wanted to know about Mrs. Moss's connection with Rob Hall, an alleged Communist leader in Washington; but this Rob Hall was known to be a white man."

The *See It Now* camera swings back to the committee counsel; Cohn seems confused. "We assume that that is the same Rob Hall," he says. "If there is another one, or anything like that . . . ," but he is cut off by Symington.

"Now, let's get this information, counsel," he commands. "Is the Robert Hall that you know a colored man?" he asks Moss.

"Yes, sir," she responds. "Yes. I am pretty sure that he is colored. . . . The man that I have in mind as Robert Hall was a man about my complexion."

"Then," Symington smiles, "it's fair to say that you didn't think he was a white man?" He turns to the recorder: "I would like to put in the record . . . that Robert Hall of the *Daily Worker* is a white man."

As Symington leans back, satisfied, Senator John McClellan, sitting to his left, says quite audibly into his open microphone, "If one's black and the other's white, they're different."

This exchange is a pivotal one. To begin with, we witness Senator Symington exposing the misinformation and shoddy investigation of Cohn and his staff. Once it is clear that Annie Lee Moss's inquisitors have potentially made serious mistakes, this itself functions as a sign confirming a developing disposition about the possible innocence of Mrs. Moss. But this sequence is significant for another reason that marks it as a fulcrum in the text. The climax occurs quietly, when Symington asks Annie Lee Moss if it was possible for her to confuse Rob Hall, since he had a complexion like her own. Answering "no, sir," Mrs. Moss laughs nervously. The effect of this strange and out-of-place laugh releases the tension, and Symington has to smile in response.

But interestingly, the *See It Now* text shows us at this moment a close shot of a very glum Roy Cohn. Suffering this setback rudely, his hand covering his mouth, Cohn stares malevolently at Moss. While laughter engages the room, Cohn is impassive. He shifts his cold stare to Symington, then back again to Moss. As Cohn is shut out of the humor, as he is dissociated from the others present, he is also dissociated from the viewer. And as shall be clear soon, the *See It Now* camera will return over and over to quiet close-ups of Roy Cohn and to the empty chair of the senator from Wisconsin.

Afterward even the tenor of the remaining questions seems changed; their sharpness is blunted, their tone simpler and more sympathetic. Childlike in their simplicity, they emphasize the childlike demeanor of Annie Lee Moss. Indeed, a curious change has clearly taken place among the senators at the hearing; through their reaction as well, we find the text suggesting the guiltlessness of Annie Lee Moss. For example, Symington sympathetically asks Annie Lee Moss about her job status. She has been suspended, she says, by the Department of the Army until "this thing is over."

Once more the visualizations are curious; once more, instead of focusing upon Annie Lee Moss, or even upon Symington, the *See It Now* camera again shows us Roy Cohn. He watches in chagrin, occasionally scratching his ear. These lingering and repetitive shots of Cohn are a curious choice of visualization at this point.

Yet I think, in this remarkable sequence, the text reveals one of the reactions it demands from its audience. Clearly, simple pity for

Annie Lee Moss is here superseded by another appeal. Indeed, if the impetus for the shot choice were to enlist sympathy for Moss, we could reasonably expect *See It Now* to focus on her during the description of her plight. Yet, in upsetting our expectations, and instead turning our attention to Cohn, *See It Now* indicates that it is the counsel, the surrogate of McCarthyism, who is to be the focus of viewer reaction. In short, by focusing upon Cohn, the text reveals that the response it seeks from its viewer is more resentment of Cohn and McCarthy than sympathy for Annie Lee Moss. Thus, we are subtly directed through the visualizations of the text to hold them responsible and view the text as insisting that its thesis has to do not with Annie Lee Moss but rather with McCarthyism.

When Symington asks the reasons for Mrs. Moss's dismissal, the camera focuses once more on him and then cuts to Moss. Here Murrow enters for the second time, again in voice-over, again explaining, his tone incredulous. "This woman, under suspicion because of charges made by Senator McCarthy and Roy Cohn, alleged to have examined and corrected secret and encoded overseas messages, attempted to read the uncoded words of her suspension notice."

Murrow's voice drops out, and we hear Moss read haltingly; finally her lawyer has to help her. Clearly, Annie Lee Moss can hardly read. And now, just as clearly, the attempted casting of her as a dangerous spy hidden away within the Signal Corps seems completely implausible.

We cut to Symington, who listens with a friendly smile. He asks gently: "Did you read that the very best you could?" Moss answers: "Yes sir, I did." And then, she breaks into an embarrassed giggle. Now, once more, the others join her. In a wide shot, we watch four of the senators grin, laugh, and look down. Symington too, consumed by laughter, cannot continue with his questioning. Again, the humor releases the tension, undermines the charges against Moss, and potentially enlists sympathy on her side against those who accuse her.

Kindly, Symington asks Moss if she had ever talked to a Communist in her life? Not that I know of, says Annie Lee Moss. "Did you ever hear of Karl Marx?" Symington asks playfully, the straight man. "Who's that?" Mrs. Moss asks, genuinely puzzled. There is a roar of laughter in the usually sedate Senate hearing room. "I'll pass the question," Symington says. The senators on either side of him are laughing openly. Symington asks Annie Lee Moss if she considers herself a good American. "Would you ever do anything to hurt your country?" "No, sir," Moss says emphatically. "Have you ever talked to anybody about espionage?" At the witness table, there is consternation; Annie Lee Moss looks puzzled and turns to her attorney. The counsel begins a lengthy and inaudible explanation that ends with the recognizable word "spies." Annie Lee Moss swivels in her chair, leans to the microphone, and says loudly, "No, sir." No one has ever asked her for information and if someone had, she says, she would have reported it. "I certainly would have."

By now, it would seem quite difficult to sustain, given what the text has revealed, that Annie Lee Moss is the dangerous Communist whom McCarthy had promised to expose. It has been slowly revealed that she cannot read; she does not know Karl Marx or even understand what espionage is.


## A Model for Reaction

I mentioned earlier that one indication of a shift in sensibilities toward Annie Lee Moss is the shift in the tone of the questions directed to her. In parallel fashion, another marker or cue to the same desired reaction comes by way of the visualizations. For instance, throughout the Symington questioning, the *See It Now* camera remains for the most part, not on the witness, Annie Lee Moss, but instead on the senators themselves. The audience watches their reactions to the questions and to the answers of Annie Lee Moss. Sitting on either side of Symington, they are animated and clearly enjoying the naïveté of Annie Lee Moss. And as the text unfolds, an aura of the seriocomic attaches itself to the proceedings; the charges against Annie Lee Moss are rendered "silly." In a way, through the senators' reactions, we might be prompted to recognize the irony of the situation. Thus, through its visualizations, through its focusing upon the senators rather than the witness, and upon the somber visage of Cohn in moments of general laughter, the text solicits reaction to Annie Lee Moss, to her predicament, to her accusers, and, by implication, to McCarthyism.

The use of the "observing" camera as a way to suggest a reading against the text is exemplified in the next exchange. Symington questions Annie Lee Moss about her losing her job.

SYMINGTON: What are you living on now? Have you got any savings?
MRS. MOSS: No, sir.
SYMINGTON: You haven't?
MRS. MOSS: No, sir.
SYMINGTON: If you don't get work pretty soon, what are you going to do?
MRS. MOSS: I am going down to the Welfare.

But most remarkably, the *See It Now* cameras focus throughout this exchange upon the empty chair of Senator McCarthy. Clearly the inference to be made is that the senator, even in his absence, has caused the economic destruction of Annie Lee Moss. And equally clearly, the text reveals a sense of pure visual argument. In the linking of these shots, and without a word of commentary from Murrow, *See It Now* levels a devastating editorial upon the effects of McCarthyism on the common man. This inference arises from the juxtaposition of the empty chair as an image with the committee hearing on the sound track.

The creation of this inference as symbolic action is remarkably similar to a phenomenon of visual style recognized and discussed by film theorists. Drawing upon the writings of influential Soviet film-maker Sergei Eisenstein, the editing together of two seemingly contradictory segments of film draws upon the predilection of film viewers to connect or to eliminate the inconsistency in the images and in doing so to read the two images as comment upon one another. This process, called "intellectual montage" by Eisenstein, appears in examples such as the cross-cutting between a factory owner and a wolf. Such seemingly inexplicable juxtapositions serve to comment on some aspect of the story or argument by asking the viewer to sort through the possible meanings.[47] According to this interpretive approach, one likely preferred reading of the "Moss" montage is a negative commentary on the senator.

But "Annie Lee Moss Before the McCarthy Committee" also features a stirring statement on behalf of due process of law. Soon after Mrs. Moss's assertion "I never heard of [Communism] until 1948," and amid the ensuing laughter, an obviously disgusted Cohn concludes his questioning, saying that he has no further questions for Mrs. Moss.

But I will say this: We have the testimony of Mrs. Markward, the undercover agent of the FBI, stating that Annie Lee Moss was a member—a dues-paying member of the Communist party. . . . We have corroboration of that testimony by another witness who was called before the committee and gave a sworn statement to the effect that she also knew Mrs. Moss as a member of the Northeast Club of the Communist party.

Another senator asks to be recognized, and the camera pans to include him in the shot. As the senator begins, Murrow quietly introduces him in voice-over: "Senator McClellan of Arkansas." McClellan, to judge from his tone of voice and his posture, is clearly agitated and disturbed:

We are making statements against a witness who has come and submitted to cross-examination. She has already lost her job . . . because of this action. If she's a Communist, I want her exposed, but to make these statements that we have got corroborating evidence that she is a Communist—under these circumstances I think she is entitled to have it produced here in her presence and let the public know about it and let her know about it. I don't like to try people by hearsay evidence. I like to get the witnesses here and try 'em by testimony under oath.

The caucus room rings with loud applause. When the temporary chairman agrees that Cohn's comments should be stricken from the record, McClellan objects. He is clearly angry, his voice rising, his hand cutting the air in emphasis. Seen in medium shot, he gazes coldly in the direction of Cohn:

You can't strike these statements made by counsel here. . . . you cannot strike that from the press nor from the public mind, once it's planted there. That is—that is the evil of it. I don't think it's fair . . . to a citizen of this country to bring them up here and cross-examine them, and then, when they get through, say, "we have got something—the FBI's got something on you that condemns you." . . . It's not sworn testimony. It's convicting people by rumor, and hearsay, and innuendo.

McClellan is interrupted again and again by loud applause. And once more, *See It Now* is able to include in "Annie Lee Moss Before the McCarthy Committee" a partisan statement without seeming itself to take sides. The strategy of this text is to use the persuasive potency of the "objective" camera to efface itself from the argument.

But the text presents another revelation before it concludes the Moss hearing. As the applause dies, Senator Symington resumes the questioning. He establishes that Annie Lee Moss has never met her primary accuser, Mrs. Mary Markward.

Almost as an afterthought, he asks: "Do you know anybody else in this town named Moss? Are there any Mosses in Washington besides you?" "Yes, sir," Mrs. Moss answers innocently, "there's three Annie Lee Mosses."

The response is startling: "What was that?" someone says. "Will you state that again?" asks another. The senators whom we see on either side of Symington at the committee table lean forward; one puts on his glasses. "There's three Annie Lee Mosses. And when I went to get a real-estate license I had an awful lot of trouble then," says the witness calmly.

Once more, the visualizations are remarkable. The *See It Now* camera directs our focus to Roy Cohn, whose reaction is surprise, almost consternation. In an extreme close-up, Cohn starts, and he too leans toward the witness after her revelation; someone whispers in his ear but is waved away by the suddenly intent counsel. His brow furrows, and he stares blankly at Annie Lee Moss.

We cut to a close shot of Senator Symington, who offers the fitting coda to the horrific comedy we have just witnessed. "I want to say something to you—and I may be sticking my neck out . . . , but I have been listening to you testify this afternoon, and I think you are telling the truth. . . . If you are not taken back in the Army, you come around and see me, and I am going to see that you get a job."

To raucous applause, Moss thanks the senator. But most important are the shots that end this middle section of "Annie Lee Moss Before the McCarthy Committee." Once more, as at critical moments in the hearing, the *See It Now* cameras focus on those who accuse Annie Lee Moss; here the text shows us an extreme close-up of Roy Cohn. He sits, glaring alternately at Symington and at Annie Lee Moss, his hand covering his mouth. But then the masterstroke of visual inference: the *See It Now* camera pans to the left, and we hold, once again, on the empty chair of Joe McCarthy.

We cut back to Murrow in the control room. He looks up into the camera at us. His remarks are simple: "You will notice that neither Senator McClellan, nor Senator Symington, nor this reporter know or claim that Mrs. Moss was or is a Communist. Their claim was simply that she had the right to meet her accusers face to face."

The argument is thus set in the terms Murrow described in opening: a "little picture" about due process of law. After a short commercial break, *See It Now* returns.


*Text as "Nonargument"*

"We'd like to run something else from the record," Murrow says. He turns and looks at the left-hand monitor beside him. We zoom into it: WASHINGTON. "President Eisenhower, in November of 1953, talking about the right of every man to look his accuser in the eye."

The program cuts to its final section: a lengthy portion of an Eisenhower speech.[48] The president is not usually a moving speaker, but on this night, his sentiments are inspiring. Eisenhower describes the code of the West under which he was raised as a boy in Abilene, Kansas, and concludes:

In this country, if someone dislikes you or accuses you, he must come up in front. . . . He cannot assassinate you or your character from behind without suffering the penalties which an outraged citizenry will inflict. If we are going to continue to be proud that we are Americans, there must be no weakening of the codes by which we have lived. By the right to meet your accuser face to face—if you have one. . . . By your right to speak your mind and be protected in it. Ladies and gentlemen, the things that make us proud to be Americans are of the soul and the spirit.

We cut quickly back to Murrow who ends "Annie Lee Moss Before the McCarthy Committee" without additional comment: "November 1953, the thirty-fourth president of the United States speaking rather eloquently about due process of law. Good night and good luck!"

What is interesting in this *See It Now* text is the way in which it has seemingly removed itself from any kind of overt argumentative claim. Through its adherence to naturalism and the observing camera, it seems to be merely presenting evidence, to be recording what took place at the hearing and in Eisenhower's speech. The explicit claim of the *See It Now* documentary is that it took no editorial stand.

Yet we have noted how, in the text, subtle but clear suggestions are made about the guiltlessness of Annie Lee Moss, about the complicity of those who accuse her. Through the juxtaposition and antithesis of the concluding two sections of the program, the text clearly sets the dispute in terms of opposed positions. And though Murrow claims that *See It Now* is, in this case, merely presenting items "from the record," we implicitly realize that much more is operating in this "indirect" documentary text.

## Response to the Telecast

Perhaps because of the week-long controversy between McCarthy and Murrow, "Annie Lee Moss Before the McCarthy Committee" had by far the largest single audience of any of the *See It Now* programs on McCarthyism, and it produced another spate of letters and telephone calls. The program had a 59.6 percent coverage, with 3.3 million homes viewing the telecast—over 12.5 percent of American homes equipped with television receivers.[49] Again, the favorable comments far outweighed the unfavorable, running nine to one in Murrow's favor.[50]

By "rescuing" the "small story" of Annie Lee Moss from the tide of the week's harrowing events and the revelations about McCarthy, Cohn, Schine, and the army, *See It Now*'s version, the televised version of Mrs. Moss's testimony became the actuality of what happened, and for many, a developing sense of McCarthy's reprehensible tactics was seemingly reinforced by the program.[51] Apparently, this *See It Now* touched a shared concern among Americans, even among those who considered themselves satisfied with Senator Mc-Carthy overall. In the Gallup poll of early March 1954, while the senator still had an exceptionally high "approval" rating, with 46 percent of those surveyed professing a favorable opinion of him, there was clearly a more mixed view of his tactics. Those surveyed disapproved of his methods by a margin of 47 percent to 38 percent. The most frequently mentioned objections were "he goes too far," "he is too tough," and "he uses methods like the Gestapo."[52] The Moss testimony may well have confirmed such opinions for those who watched.

No doubt, the appearance and demeanor of Annie Lee Moss herself had a powerful effect. Columnist John Crosby described Mrs. Moss as an "earnest, humble, scared Negro woman . . . , the most dangerous woman in America." According to Crosby, her physical presence before the McCarthy committee and the "aroma of decency" that filled the room when the Democratic senators sprang to defend her constitutional rights damaged McCarthyism. "The American people fought a revolution to defend, among other things, the right of Annie Lee Moss to earn a living, and Senator McCarthy now decided she has no such right. It's about time McCarthy was labeled for what he is—a subversive who is trying to undermine the very cornerstone of this country."[53]

The entire Moss episode, as one historian characterizes it, "contributed to the alienation of subcommittee Democrats, blackened Cohn's reputation as an investigator, and helped shatter [McCarthy's] nationwide popularity." And as it was presented to a wide audience by *See It Now*, the episode became an "unmitigated disaster" for the senator.[54]

But to observers within the television industry, the Moss program was also successful for a wholly different reason: "as a technically more adept use of the television medium without the intrusion of a commentator to make its point about a fair trial and due process."[55] In retrospect, Fred Friendly considered "Annie Lee Moss Before the McCarthy Committee" "one of the best broadcasts ever done by anyone." He also confessed, "if we had done it first, we might never have done the McCarthy show."[56] This time, even the executive management at CBS noted the "superiority" of the Annie Lee Moss program to the "Report on Senator McCarthy" one week before. As Friendly recalled it, "[They] congratulated us, saying it was much better than the one on March 9, and that we should have used Mrs. Moss on last week's program: 'In this one you let him hang himself.'"[57]

## Intertextuality and Sources of Persuasive Potential

The seemingly incompatible readings reported by viewers at the time of the broadcast of "Annie Lee Moss" may be explained as a function of three sources of appeal within the text—functions interwoven and interdependent. First, we read the program as one that apparently offers unmediated access to the "real" Moss hearing. Second, in attempting to "frame" the text in order to understand it, we are invited to interpret the text in line with archetypal narrative and myth forms. Finally, I contend that we read "Annie Lee Moss Before the McCarthy Committee" in the context of the earlier *See It Now* programs and so are inclined to take it as further evidence against McCarthyism in a manner partially calibrated beforehand through those earlier texts. That is, the program uses foreknowledge of the conventions of documentary referentiality, conventions of documentary indirect address, and conventions of what we may call "proletarian discourse" to attempt a shift in our perception of Mrs. Annie Lee Moss and of her situation. Each of these intertextual relationships merits further consideration.

*Access to the "Real"*

At one level of intertextual relationship, "Annie Lee Moss" prepares its readers to acknowledge the link between documentary discourse and history by three distinct strategies: it contextualizes the program around the ongoing news narrative concerning the McCarthy-Moss story, it grounds the event as an unmediated transcription of the McCarthy hearing by drawing upon assumptions about the relationship of documentary discourse and the real, and it uses the conventions of indirect documentary to invite viewers to accept its claim of neutral observation.

The decision by *See It Now* to do the Moss story was inspired by the desire to "save" a story from the rush of other news events during the third week of March 1954. In doing so, *See It Now* deliberately set out to make explicit the connections between the Moss hearing and these events in the news. So, for instance, the program begins by redirecting attention to the ongoing news narrative concerning the McCarthy charges and Moss's denials. "Annie Lee Moss" incorporates this news discourse, in part by referring directly to the controversy in Murrow's reading of the transcript, but also by adding Eisenhower's statement at the end. The *See It Now* rhetors could, with some assurance, expect their audience to be familiar with at least the outlines of these sensational events, for the stories were the subject of a widely publicized confrontation in the news several days before the broadcast.

Thus at the level of its explicit discursive argument, "Annie Lee Moss" refers to the text of the news narrative. In dealing with a topic that has passed through news, the program immediately grounds the issue in the terrain in which it originated. The viewer is consequently reminded that, though the parameters of "Annie Lee Moss" will frame and organize the topic throughout the program, the topic has its origin in the ongoing political debate outside the media. Thus, in part, the text's relation to the topic is validated by substantiating that the topic already has a discursive life outside the program.[58]

But *See It Now* activates its intertextual relationship with history in another way. Visual footage in an "observational" documentary relies upon its indexical relationship with the profilmic event, and "Annie Lee Moss Before the McCarthy Committee" works therefore by fashioning a world that we treat as an index of the real. This sense of verisimilitude rests upon an audience's commonsense assumption that the text supplies a visual record of events that transpired before the camera, and a viewer might well assent to the photographic component of the documentary footage, assuming that "what we see is what there was." The observational documentary text, in other words, gives the appearance of matching the event like a template.[59] Thus, we are invited to believe that our access to the profilmic event is complete. Most significantly, the text is fashioned to minimize the signs of this construction. In this instance the highly naturalistic visual style attests to the authenticity of the documentary record and does so by foregrounding the conventions of such recording (for example, the shaky camera work; the slightly out-of-focus shots; the loping camera pans and awkward zooms, the sometimes grainy and poorly lit shots; and, in the audio, muffled and sometimes unclear words).[60]

A second assumption is vital to our acceptance of the observational evidence. The ideal audience member must accept that what occurred in the presence of the camera would have occurred in its absence as well and that there was no influence by the rhetors upon the profilmic event. In short, we must as viewers believe that we are seeing what we would have seen as observers if the camera had not been there.[61] Indeed, the documentary text distinguishes itself from the fiction film in its way of celebrating the idea that the action we see before the camera is not directed or motivated by the documentary's makers.[62] Thus, there is in the relationship between observational text and the historical event an interaction between textual or generic form and style, on the one hand, and, on the other, the expectations of an audience. Relying upon the assumption and shared acceptance of these implicit claims in the observational documentary, Murrow can disarmingly and innocently announce in his introduction: "This is what our cameraman saw through his camera."

These shared assumptions about the indirect documentary clearly shape the readings given to television texts. For instance, in their early investigation of the relationship between politics and television, Kurt and Gladys Lang noted a parallel set of popular assumptions about the televisual rendering of public events. The public readily assumes, the Langs found, first, that television permits the viewer to be "there" and that this allows direct participation in public affairs; second, that the camera does not "lie," and so one does not depend on the interpretations of others; last, that audiences get a fuller picture from TV than is conveyed by other media and that watching an event over TV is better than "being there."[63]

While we may question some of these assumptions, what is of interest is that they have a considerable potency precisely because people have come to believe that these effects exist. The Langs concluded that viewers believe they have "seen for themselves" and seem unaware that they have been influenced by the style of coverage.[64] Thus, the very "observational" style itself disarms our potential objections in that we believe we are seeing a "slice of life," not a tampered version. "Annie Lee Moss" offers a "reading" of itself as a "slice of life" in part because it draws upon the codes of the observational documentary discourse and explicitly incorporates news stories about an historical event. But the appeal of "Annie Lee Moss Before the McCarthy Committee" is more subtle and more complex, I believe; it affords the viewer more than merely "unmediated" access to the "real." Instead, this text seems to situate the historical person, Annie Lee Moss, so that we identify with her. Furthermore, how that identification is furthered is part and parcel of the indirect documentary style.

To begin with, it may be helpful to contrast the use of the film image in this text with the way in which it is utilized in the more controversial and allegedly more "biased" "Report on Senator McCarthy." Both rely upon the force of the filmic image to supply visual "evidence" and upon our assent to the reality of the image and the "actuality" of what we see. But there is a great difference. In the earlier report, the text introduces short segments of the senator's public and private statements, and the program advances in argumentative blocks. Emphasizing the "evidentiary" function of documentary film footage, the "Report on Senator McCarthy" presents its footage in order to support the development of an inferential argumentative structure discrediting the senator. For example, Murrow says that McCarthy engages in half-truths, presents recorded evidence, and then refutes McCarthy by countering with the "whole truth."[65]

The "Report on Senator McCarthy" has an order or mode of arrangement more temporal than spatial. Consequently we watch it with the clear understanding that what we are seeing temporally precedes our perception. In "McCarthy" there is no pretense that we are watching a "live" program. The medium is celebrated not as permitting us to "be there" but as the proof that "this happened," that "he said this," that "he was there."[66]

But "Annie Lee Moss Before the McCarthy Committee" uses its film footage in a different way: while also relying upon assumptions about the "actuality" of what we see (it promotes the conventions of "vérité" documentary for purposes of emphasis), it presents that actuality to us in a way that makes the events seem contemporaneous; in other words, this text uses what Barthes calls the "being there" sense of the film image. The text is organized more spatially than temporally, and its "reality" is certified by concrete place and setting. In "Annie Lee Moss," the events seemingly happen "now," and so we accede to the feeling of "being there," watching and listening as the events unfold.

This difference suggests two distinct cognitive operations within nonfiction television and indicates that the "actuality" they promote may be read in at least two different ways—ways that have the potential for working quite differently upon a viewing audience.[67] In the "Report on Senator McCarthy," the strategy is to dissociate us from Joseph McCarthy, and the text positions us temporally after the events have taken place and spatially removed and distanced from what we see in the text. But in "Annie Lee Moss Before the McCarthy Committee," as one of the salient strategies is to encourage us to identify with Annie Lee Moss, so we find ourselves positioned in time concurrent with the "actuality" we witness.[68]

Thus the formal arrangement and the position established for us in each of the texts parallels the reactions its rhetors demand, and we "see" our response suggested by properties of the form itself. One source of the power of "Annie Lee Moss Before the McCarthy Committee," then, is the identification with Mrs. Moss that is fostered in our "position of seeing," a subjectivity that is implicit in the observational text.

*Symbolic Action and Conventional Plot Line*

A second intertextual relationship that provides a frame for interpretation of "Annie Lee Moss Before the McCarthy Committee" is its symbolic aspect—the connection between this text and preexisting myth or literary discourse. Indeed, this *See It Now* text functions at the intersection of two distinct sets of generic conventions. On the one hand, this program is squarely within the tradition of what is often called "the common man or proletariat documentary."[69] William Bluem traces the generic antecedents of this genre to the crusade against human suffering begun in the early 1900s by photographers Jacob Riis and Lewis Hine ("Carolina Cotton Mill" and "Americans at Work," 1932). The genre reached its apotheosis in the photography units of the Rural Resettlement Administration and the Farm Security Administration in the 1930s.[70] Works such as the classic study of the rural South, *You Have Seen Their Faces*, published by Erskine Caldwell and Margaret Bourke-White in 1937, and those of Dorothea Lange (*In a Camp of Migratory Pea Pickers*, 1936, and *American Exodus*, 1939) and Walker Evans and James Agee (*Let Us Now Praise Famous Men*, 1942) have left us with a graphic view of the reality of American life during the Great Depression. These "proletarian documentary" texts may be characterized, William Stott argues, by their portrayal of a simple person, often from the lower socioeconomic classes, and their casting of social problems in terms of the effects on that "common man."[71] Thus, the story of displaced, economically stricken, innocent individuals caught in forces beyond their control is a recurrent motif in American culture, even showing up in important works of literature by John Steinbeck, Theodore Dreiser, Sinclair Lewis, and Thomas Wolfe.

*See It Now*'s "angle" in its coverage of McCarthyism across all four of these broadcasts embodies conventions of the "common man myth." The stories presented in the series talk of the larger issues of McCarthyism in terms of the "small picture." This both enhances our sense of identification with the common man who is the ostensible subject of the text and also vivifies complex and often abstract issues in terms that are relevant for the audience. The issues of McCarthyism serve as the backdrop against which the individual is foregrounded.[72] This strategy figures not only in "Annie Lee Moss Before the McCarthy Committee" but also, as we have seen, in the portrayals of Milo Radulovich, of the ACLU in Indianapolis, and of Reed Harris in "Report on Senator McCarthy."

Such strategic revelation of McCarthyism's effects on the common man highlights the effects of McCarthyism's excesses and their meaning in human terms. This "humanizing" may be explicable in terms of the intent of the *See It Now* rhetors—in trying to "get the issue across," a strategy of depiction and a focus upon the feelings of those directly involved has, we might surmise, significant persuasive potential.[73]

But there may be even more at work here. So far, I have noted that the "observational" text creates a sense of verisimilitude that guarantees a unity and coherence to the events we see visualized. In other words, the certificate of verisimilitude is the imaginary time and space that the text constructs.[74] But such a fabricated, verisimilar "reality" is a common feature of narrative film as well. In an aside, while discussing the nature of the observational or indirect mode of presentation, Bill Nichols notes that the indirect genre is also the principal mode of narrative film. Both genres, observational documentary and narrative, foster a self-enclosed, a "fictional" plane of reality—what Nichols calls a diegesis.[75] Nichols does not pursue his idea, but the suggestion is intriguing. In reading "Annie Lee Moss Before the McCarthy Committee," are we subtly invited to invoke the similarity between the observational documentary genre and the fictional narrative film and so to invest nonfiction with an appealing and dramatic fictional significance?

In a way, precisely because of its indirect form, where we are neither addressed nor guided by a commentator, the Moss text is open-ended and so, like a fictional text, has the potential of offering a number of different readings.[76] "Annie Lee Moss" unfolds as classic narrative, revealing recurrent characters, consistent point of view, temporal development, and closure. I believe, furthermore, that this narrative intertextuality of "Moss" offers its readers several potential means of interpretation. First, the use of diegetic narrative to present the "story" of the Moss hearing prompts the reader to engage in a process that is both rule governed and reductive. Readers make sense of this text in the same way that they make sense of other narratives: by applying a series of strategies to simplify it—by highlighting, ignoring, making symbolic, and otherwise patterning the text.[77] This narrative structure thus has the potential to engage its readers by likely compelling them to participate in the story—both in decoding its narrative construction and in attaching significance to it.

As we have seen, "Annie Lee Moss Before the McCarthy Committee" in agonistic terms clearly pits the innocent and unassuming Mrs. Moss against the active "evil" of Joe McCarthy and Roy Cohn. Moss's Democratic defenders, who spring to her rescue, round out the drama. Naturally, we assign parts as we watch. We are prompted through the visual rhetoric to cast Cohn and McCarthy as villains, Annie Lee Moss becomes the innocent, and the Democratic senators act as the "good guys."

In doing so, we have the opportunity to prefer an interpretation of "Annie Lee Moss Before the McCarthy Committee" that is in line with commonplace stories we already know and share. This tale has a heroine and villains, it has the "rescue" of the innocent, and it shows the bully getting what was coming to him. Thus the veri-similar world of the indirect documentary text begins to diminish the distance between its nonfiction status and its more dramatistic interpretation. The actuality of the Annie Lee Moss hearing, once it is translated and rekeyed as part of the documentary text, begins to draw part of its significance from the dramatistic and mythic fictions that we spin around it as we seek to understand it in the context of our own experience.[78]

A similar link between dramatic or mythic conventions and television news has been recognized by students of the media and its relation to culture. They argue that both television and newspapers are "essentially melodramatic accounts of current events." Both depict events as actions that carry forward an implicit and simplistic line of dramatic action. And both are alike in using the same themes, formulas, and symbols in constructing the lines of melodramatic action that endow events with meaning and identity.[79] Others suggest that in the mass-mediated version of reality, organizations, bureaucracies, and movements are all reduced to personifications.[80] Moreover, such conventional plot lines, stories, and personifications are reflected in other popular culture texts.[81]

The mythic forms and story lines of the news and documentaries are not inconsonant with the mythic forms represented in the adventure stories and westerns. "Good" and "evil" are rather clearly placed in conflict. . . . There is a continuity between the prime-time news and prime-time programming. . . . The mythic structure of both is harmonious.[82]

In sum, as we watch, we continually search for "frames" that would anchor our interpretation. It may be that one of the frames most easily available within our discursive repertoire is the archetypal stories or myths that resonate in our shared cultural heritage. There is some warrant, then, in concluding that we are invited to think of the Moss text in terms of archetypal symbolic frames, and so the observational documentary layers a signification drawn from conventions of "story" or "myth" over the nonfiction film footage. Indeed, we may say that "Annie Lee Moss Before the McCarthy Committee" represents a blending of rhetorical forms and conventions. It imposes an order on the real that is a function of alternation between conventions of the nonfiction "reality" and a symbolic reading that promises a resolution paralleling that of other stories.[83]

The text represents an intersection of two sorts of signifying codes: the one, based on our assent to the indexical relation of image and world, an acknowledgment of the ontological potency of the observational text; the other, based on the mythic and dramatic, drawn from a cultural stock of characters and inviting us to read the text as melodrama, as the acting out of an allegory or parable.

Thus, in "Annie Lee Moss Before the McCarthy Committee," the manner of realization is distinctly fictional, while the message is not. Charles Affron has suggested that once such alternation has occurred, the "nonfiction becomes more or less informed with presentations essential to dramatic texts, and its veracity becomes more or less a function of artistry and expressivity."[84] Part of the assumption of the "actuality" of the historical event is thus the "artistic" manner of its transformation. In this way, it seems also clear that the relationship between the historical event and the narrative is salient. It is widely agreed that narrative, as part of a universal mode of human consciousness, appears in both fictional and nonfictional discourses. But we have already noted that the sign is "tied" more closely to the referent in nonfictional texts. As the program encodes the historical situation in structures borrowed at least in part from the symbolic or the imaginative, reading may be suspended between intertextual relations. That is, as readers encounter the essentially traumatic image on the screen, where we have been previously reading as we would a fictional narrative film, using the expectations we have learned from that genre, suddenly we are confronted with the realization that we are watching "real" events and hardship. The images resist a simple one-directional reading. The reader is potentially caught between the desire to respond on a level different from that of fictional films and an inability to experience the predicament as Mrs. Annie Lee Moss was experiencing it.[85]

*The Context of Preceding Telecasts*

A third intertextual relationship assists in our explication of "Annie Lee Moss Before the McCarthy Committee," a relationship that draws upon the context of the program. Coming one week after the *See It Now* "Report on Senator McCarthy," and after several other *See It Now* programs having to do with aspects of McCarthyism, an ideal viewer might approach this program with an understanding of *See It Now*'s predisposition toward the issue. In this regard, Michael Murray's suggestion that the *See It Now* series of programs on McCarthyism ought to be analyzed as a persuasive campaign seems worthwhile. Certainly, Murray is right—when we see the programs as a series, linkages and connections are inevitably forged between the programs, and we can develop a sense of the interrelationships between each of the telecasts.[86]

Thus, I suggest that an ideal viewer intuitively *knows* how to interpret the remarks of Senator Symington or the seemingly incongruous remarks from President Eisenhower partly because this viewer feels she knows the intent of the *See It Now* rhetors on the basis of her experience of the earlier telecasts. Thus this text is rendered coherent partly also because it positions itself to be read in line with the programs that preceded it. Murrow and Friendly fashion a "campaign" that adopts a coherent and consistent attitude toward McCarthyism, and reaction to each of the texts as they come in sequence is part and parcel of its position in the campaign.

When taken as a whole, *See It Now*'s series reveals a graded development in its exposure of the dangers of McCarthyism. In "The Case of Milo Radulovich" we were presented with only the "victim" of the attitudes that characterize the era. In that program, the forces responsible for the lieutenant's plight were literally and figuratively silent. Instead, the response was more social and individual; the issue was seen less as an ideological conflict and more as an example of a bizarre and unfamiliar turn of events cast within the small-town milieu of personal knowledge and familiarity.

"Argument in Indianapolis," however, moved the issue onto another plane. In that program the unreasoning "fear" of anything "different" or "controversial" is central. Here, in the contrast between the American Legion and the Civil Liberties Union developed by way of a stunning visual depiction, McCarthyism connects to ideological conflict. The two-sidedness of that *See It Now* text weighted the dispute in dramatic terms, and the disreputable tactics of the Legion represent a metonymic reduction of the similar disreputable tactics of McCarthyism.

The next program, "A Report on Senator McCarthy," was a figurative journey into the heart of the darkness of McCarthyism and displayed the "enemy" himself in the person of its most polished practitioner. Just as "guilt by association" and "fear of controversy" were elements of the McCarthyite movement in America, so too was the senator himself, the namesake of the movement, also an issue. Thus, *See It Now* directly attacked the doubtful actions and logic of the senator.

"Annie Lee Moss Before the McCarthy Committee" again shows us the "victim" of the ideology. As in "Radulovich," we focus upon the unwitting citizen caught in issues outside her control, understanding, or influence. But here there is a great difference. Having worked through the series of programs, we have been prepared to understand that Moss's accusers, unlike Radulovich's, are now identifiable and, moreover, that they can be explicitly named and shown. At the end of the series of *See It Now* programs on McCarthyism, an ideal viewer has been given a perspective on history that sees the "common man" victimized by an ideology now clearly identified, an ideology now clearly depicted as thoroughly evil.

The paradigms likely used to assign meaning to "Annie Lee Moss Before the McCarthy Committee" are a multidimensional textual web of genre, history, and myth. Each dimension offers potential interpretive advantages. On one dimension "Annie Lee Moss Before the McCarthy Committee" may be read in the context of the other *See It Now* programs on McCarthyism. In a way, it can be taken as continuing the argument from the previous week: Annie Lee Moss is more evidence of the dangerous and destructive power of the junior senator from Wisconsin.

If we consider another dimension, certain readings are emphasized when the program can be contrasted with traditional television documentary. The indirect or observational form of "Annie Lee Moss Before the McCarthy Committee"—a form that rejects external narration and instead lets the subjects reveal themselves through their activities, filmed by the unobtrusive *See It Now* camera—gives the appearance of objectivity. While upon reflection we clearly know objectivity to be problematic simply because of the editing and structuring by which the text is constructed, nevertheless the chief difference between the direct and the indirect documentary forms is "the latter's acceptance of life's complexity, ambiguity, and lack of closure." Thus, the indirect documentary, with its very structure more closely resembling reality, gains a power by mimicking that world and so calls upon us to participate in making sense of it in a way that is much more active than that entailed by the direct form.[87] This indirect observational form seems to leave more room for our response and subsequent action.

Finally, a third textual dimension of "Annie Lee Moss Before the McCarthy Committee" is its mode of presentation. That is, because its "indirect" style offers less overt guidance for understanding, the audience must "make sense" of the text by bringing to it what we know of other programs and of other genres. This treatment by itself may evoke different sorts of responses. Because it mimics reality through its verisimilar structure, and because it seemingly describes what and how, not why, the indirect form of "Annie Lee Moss Before the McCarthy Committee" seems to be a pretheoretical mode of expression difficult to analyze and refute in ordinary ways. Thus the indirect form of the text can perhaps briefly override immediate defenses and introduce perspectives that would be rejected outright if presented in other ways. Also, because after seeing the indirect presentation an audience can push beyond it to find a thesis, the very act of hermeneutic completion prompts us to seek out less obvious meanings and to complete our persuasion ourselves.[88]

This case study suggests that the observational documentary text claims a privileged link to the historical situation. It uses our experience of understanding and decoding narrative. It engages our foreknowledge of the signifying power of myth and spectacle—it is, in short, quintessentially intertextual. But at the very same moment, "Annie Lee Moss" exploits these potential levels of intertextuality to assist in the rather local project of transforming a viewer's perspective on historical exigence. And we may be warranted, then, in concluding that in this case intertextuality may well account for the function of the discrete text as a discourse set in a specific time and place.[89]

Clearly, in these latter features, our discussion seems to channel us in the direction of inquiry into the relationship of the visual documentary with the fiction film—into the problematic intertextuality of poetic and rhetoric. That is, "Annie Lee Moss Before the McCarthy Committee" operates at the juncture of argument and poetics and seems to draw upon the conventions of both to shift sensibilities. In a word, this documentary text shares elements with texts that are usually interpreted according to terms generated in poetics, and yet the documentary is also inextricably bound by the nature of the photographic image to a concretized historical moment. That we have found such a blurring of lines between discursive categories suggests that a similar tempering of the standards of critical response may be warranted.

# Conclusion: Documentary as Rhetoric? Fiction? Ideology?

In his seminal essay "Documentary Theory and Practice" (1976), Bill Nichols lamented that the examination of the formal structures of documentary, its codes and units, had "scarcely begun."[1] But since 1976 there has been a steady flood of new critical work in the field, inaugurated in many ways by Nichols's own scholarship. The best of these efforts reads documentary in terms of the spate of challenging interpretive methodologies developed in the seventies: semiotic/structuralist analysis; psychoanalytic approaches; formal(ist) analysis; ideological analysis; oral history; and the ethnographies of audience.[2]

My own approach to these four CBS *See It Now* documentaries, however, has been at one and the same time both radical and thoroughly traditional. I have assumed that close examination of the forms and historical circumstances of these programs can help in understanding the representational conventions of media imagery and language and the relationship of mediated public discourse to the societies within which they are set.[3] As Roger Silverstone puts it in a striking phrase: "the semiotics of the television documentary can reveal the sociology of the society which helps to 'make' the documentary."[4] In short, I attempted to understand these discourses *rhetorically:* to read them so as to explain how they are structured and organized and to examine the kind of potential meanings that these forms and devices might produce in an audience set in a particular situation and historical context.

My rhetorical approach is radical, I believe, in part because it refuses to reify the documentary discourse: it implicitly insists that the text is "more" than a structure of signification, that the text is also an "action" in the world—a form of power and performance—with implications, meaning, and results in history. Rhetoric as an interpretive paradigm takes the perspective that discourse is not solely devices or strategies but also act and activity, ultimately "inseparable from the wider social relations between writers and readers, orators and audiences and largely unintelligible outside of the social purposes and conditions in which they are embedded."[5] But my rhetorical approach is clearly traditional as well, because it takes as a given that television texts (like all texts) are strategies for "managing meaning"—not aesthetic objects separate from other considerations—and in this way it seeks to return interpretation to its ancient foundations. My approach seeks to understand discourses in terms of concrete performance, not as theoretical examples to be endlessly deconstructed—not as exercises in interpretive dexterity. To read "rhetorically" and to do so fully, then, is to understand two senses of the term, to understand that "rhetorical" includes both textuality and the relationship between discourse, audience, and world.

In the course of this book we have considered the specific ways that rhetoric might solve the problems involved in understanding these television documentary texts. But the most important question has yet gone unanswered in explicit terms. What does rhetorical analysis permit us to do with these television documentaries and with the genre of television documentary that other methods do not? My answer can be organized according to the double sense in which these *See It Now* programs are "rhetorical." First, I will summarize the principal strategies used in these particular programs. Then I will clarify the relationship of the programs to the historical context. Finally, I will consider television documentary at the intersection of history, aesthetics, and ideology.

## *See It Now* and the Rhetoric of Anti-McCarthyism

Each of the four *See It Now* documentary broadcasts examined in this book touched, in one fashion or another, upon elements of McCarthyism—the blacklist, the anonymous insinuations of Communist influence, the curtailing of civil rights, the fear of controversy, the right to face one's accusers, the abuse of congressional hearings, and the tactics of Senator McCarthy.

A traditional approach would read these case studies according to their standard classification as "reports" within the category of "television news documentaries" and with the accompanying associations of "objectivity" and "fairness." As I have noted, however, this classification and the assumptions it entails would not advance us very far in understanding these programs. In part, such traditional entry to the problem is itself complicated by the nature of the news documentary as discourse. In the second chapter, I discussed the contradiction at the heart of news documentary—the contradiction between reporting the facts, guided by journalistic standards of objectivity, and the finding of a larger "truth" behind those facts that justifies the historic social concerns of the genre. The very term "documentary" carries with it a perplexing equivocation: it is a guarantee of sorts that what is depicted is "authentic," yet at the same moment, it is a casting of this reality in symbolic terms so as to make it "mean." As Dai Vaughan has said about the study of documentary in general, it is "the way in which a 'slice of life' takes on the quality of being 'about' something."[6]

It has become clear in various ways, I suggest, that these four *See It Now* texts "play" upon and with this tension in the documentary form between "facts" and "artifice." In part my reading of these programs has been concerned with a rejection of both the commonsense assumption implied in the term "documentary" that documentaries are a transparent rendering of historical situation and the postmodern assumption that documentary is solely a "textual construction"—a chain of signifiers that is ultimately and finally only about other discursive representations. Instead, I suggest that documentary resides in the uneasy ground at the juncture of these two perspectives. So perhaps, then, the essential question to ask is this: "by what devices and strategies does a text make itself believable as a re-presentation of reality and at the same moment, hide its identity as a work of artifice?"[7] I believe that three such distinct but interrelated moments in the *See It Now* texts may be distilled from our four case studies. These are image, genre, and form.

*The Appeal of Photographic Depiction*

On one level, these *See It Now* programs exploit a commonsense readiness to assent to the ontological power of the photograph. Audiences "believe what they see" and concede a special measure of veracity to the photograph because they are likely inclined to grant its claim of indexical link to reality and consequently take the photograph as "actuality." But this persuasiveness of the natural image is "inflected" by the *See It Now* rhetors and so attains a second level of potential meaning. *See It Now* "writes" its connotative message over the denotated and uncoded image of reality. Alternatively, we might say that in these *See It Now* texts, depiction as argument occurs as conventional (or coded) meaning is layered over natural (or uncoded) meaning.

As we have seen, sometimes this connotation is carried on the verbal or linguistic plane of the text; at other times, the image itself is loaded with connotated meanings because of the rhetor's interventions on the visual level. The image provides evidence, but commentary, either on the verbal or visual channel, guides the viewer to those aspects of the denoted images most important to the thesis presented by the text.[8]

Such visual depiction can have significant impact. As in "An Argument in Indianapolis," depiction can prompt an audience to associate everything negative with those who represent McCarthyism and everything positive with those who speak against it—without an explicit verbal statement from the program makers. In that telecast, and others, sensibilities toward McCarthyism are addressed by the painting of an increasingly negative second-level message over the zero-degree photograph.

*The Suasory Power of Genre*

There is another level at which these *See It Now* programs draw upon the tension in the documentary text—by exploiting audience expectations (specifically generic conventions) and by taking advantage of the commonplace distinction between reportage and argument. In examining "A Report on Senator McCarthy," I argued that *See It Now* defies its generic heritage, drawing upon an initial assent to it as news report, but then coloring that expectation by ironically suggesting a different genre. The program exploits the psychology of the news report in such a way as to prompt a simultaneous recategorization both of its own genre and of Sen. Joseph R. McCarthy. In short, it presents an argument intended to shift an audience's sensibilities, but does so by ironically using the conventions of another and parallel generic category.

I suggest that this inherent intertextuality is even more striking in "Annie Lee Moss Before the McCarthy Committee," where the *See It Now* program exploits certain stock literary or filmic genres. In "Moss," the tension between material taken from the real world and a manner of realization that borrows from conventions of representation common to dramatistic forms is plainly drawn. As the documentary form becomes "indirect" and takes on the manner of more dramatic forms, it likely draws upon expectations and modes of understanding and valuing that are usually associated with these dramatistic texts.

## The Synthesis of the Dramatic and the Discursive

There is, in other words, a third level at which *See It Now* exploits the documentary tension between fact and argument. Discourses may present themselves as "reality" while hiding artifice in various ways. These documentaries may work by employing two modes of argumentative appeal in one discourse and may derive some potency from this combination of the dramatic and the discursive. That is, *See It Now* is not a single rhetorical form; instead, it represents a confluence of forms combining appeals usually associated with dramatic forms and those usually attributed to discursive argumentative discourses.[9]

Specifically, these documentaries work initially through dramatic form.[10] In each, a persona is created, and a conflict arises. The persona becomes the object for audience identification, allowing for the displacement of differences, and establishes the ground for identification and transcendence. And as I argued, the creation of persona functions synecdochically—representing an essence shared by all members of the audience.

But the dramatic action exists alongside an interdependent body of discursive argument, and while the persona both allows the development of basic shared premises and embodies the conclusion of the argument, an equal part of the power of *See It Now* comes from its argumentative structure: as demonstration, its form is deductive. Given the perspective developed by the rhetor in the creation of the persona, the discursive argument functions to develop the implications of the perspective. The argument of *See It Now* does not produce new conclusions; instead it seeks to explore the implications of the dramatic perspective shared by rhetor and audience. The documentary form is deductive and enthymematic insofar as it proceeds from premises supplied through the interaction of rhetor and audience. It is inductive and develops from the force of the example insofar as it promotes the single case as the synecdochic representative of a larger class. In *See It Now*, the messages in the dramatic action and the discursive argument serve to reinforce one another.

In drawing upon the shared conventions of image, genre, and form, then, these texts probably inflect the neutral and "objective facts" with value. By layering connotations, taken from shared knowledge and value systems, over the denotated natural image, by drawing upon the codes of reportage to lever itself into argument, and by combining dramatic stylization with discursive "argument," *See It Now* presents its perspective on McCarthyism. Comprising texts that are at once both reflexive and representative, both natural and conventional, *See It Now* depends upon the convergence of rhetorical action.

## The Effects of the Broadcasts

The consideration of effects takes us into the relationship between text and context, and a second sense in which these programs are "rhetorical" has to do with this connection between discourse and world. But a rhetorical approach does not limit what is meant by "effect" to the immediate or local. Instead, reflections upon this question seem to channel into three separate streams: the effects on the movement of McCarthyism, the effects on the medium and the industry, the effects upon the audience.

This book cannot answer the question of whether or not *See It Now* caused the downfall of McCarthyism. The beginning of Senator McCarthy's regular appearances on the program did indeed coincide with the beginning of the end of the senator's power, however. Joseph McCarthy was a very potent figure; he drew upon fears and suspicions that were deeply ingrained in the American postwar psyche, and to dislodge the senator and the movement he represented took the combined actions of a number of players.

Because the programs share characteristics of a persuasive campaign, the effects of these *See It Now* broadcasts have been the subject of an energetic popular debate. By far, the largest contingent of those who contend the programs were instrumental to McCarthy's fall are Murrow's biographers and contributors to the *See It Now* legend. To claim that the program "destroyed" McCarthy and McCarthyism has become nearly a ritual—a recurring anecdote in the steady mythologizing of the program and its makers. Some argue, for instance, that one reason for the impact of the program was Ed Murrow's role as spokesman. Murrow was a war hero, it is said, a symbol of victory and national purpose—one of the most popular television celebrities of the decade and its most respected journalist.[11] So, for example, Alexander Kendrick argues that the programs were instrumental in the shifting of the national mood against the senator—"public opinion was decided against McCarthy" and the ultimate Senate censure was "forced by public opinion" forged and motivated by Murrow and Friendly.[12] But contrary conclusions also predominate. James Baughman surveyed historical literature and found little consensus that the programs had any effect upon McCarthy or the movement.[13] And others contend that the one single factor most important in bringing McCarthy down was arguably the televised army hearings in the spring and summer of 1954.[14] Even Murrow himself at times seemed to desire a more realistic assessment of *See It Now*'s effect on history: he acknowledged that the program's criticism of McCarthyism was "late" and declared that he had said nothing that many others had not been saying for a long while.[15]

However, another, less dramatic point about these programs is that they may have had the very discernible "effect" of shifting the topic of debate about McCarthyism from the question of ends to the question of means. In part because these programs so graphically depicted the maneuvers of the McCarthyites and the victims of their methods, public opinion seemed to quicken against the tactics of McCarthyism. This view accounts for the effects of the program by arguing that such a shift would permit audiences to agree that the dismissal of those disloyal, the ferreting out of subversives, even the assumed existence of traitors and Communists within government was a worthy objective. But these audiences could at the same moment reserve judgment on McCarthyism's tactics for accomplishing these objectives and could even have rejected these methods as extreme or "un-American" in themselves. Thus, the programs, in visually depicting the consequences of McCarthyism upon individuals, could have opened a sort of middle ground encompassing the opinions of a wide cross section of its potential audience and permitting those so inclined to disagree with the methods of McCarthyism while not necessarily repudiating its purposes.

There has also been speculation about the role of *See It Now* in the history of the media and its effect upon the manner of news reporting. Media historian Erik Barnouw, for example, remarks that while *See It Now* may have played some minor role in the toppling of McCarthyism, its material effect was to help make television an indispensable medium to both viewers and sponsors.[16] *See It Now* seemed to reveal the power of the new visual medium to reach an audience that had been heretofore untapped. In part this was "proved" by the extraordinary reaction to these four programs. Never had such immediate response—letters, phone calls, telegrams—occurred as a result of a television broadcast. While some have admitted that Murrow and Friendly really did not "say" anything "new" in the McCarthyism debate, that they said it "on television" seemed to give it greater significance and effect. It appeared indisputable at the time that where the media press had, in a sense, "made" Joe McCarthy through its uncritical reporting of his various charges, they helped also, largely in these programs, to "unmake" him. Never again would the infant medium of television, and in particular its reach and potential influence, be underestimated.[17]

In another way, I suggest, these programs had an "effect" of a wholly different nature upon the industry. We have seen how the media—newspaper, radio, film, television—were a primary target of McCarthyite intimidation. The blacklist, the purges, and the "Hollywood Hearings" before the House Un-American Activities Committee were all indicative of a disposition to control or at least to influence the content and production of the media in the postwar decade. Given the powerful capacity for persuasion and propaganda granted to the media in those years, this will to influence is at least in part understandable. But the battle over McCarthyism, from the perspective of the industry, was likely also a confrontation over freedom of speech—over who would speak and what they would say—over who would control the products of a vast popular culture industry. In the case of television specifically, the joining of this libertarian issue came at a crucial time. The networks were newly formed, and though they had roots in radio broadcasting, they lacked the tradition of First Amendment rights used by newspapers to support their coverage of controversy. As a result the fledgling television was "ripe" for McCarthyism's pressure tactics.

I contend that *See It Now* performed a necessary commission for the industry: it used the powers of television to present a case against a movement that apparently aimed at the control and mastery of the medium. Indeed, as we have seen, a sizable portion of the motivation to cover McCarthyism on *See It Now* was an alarmed reaction to the continuing attacks upon the media, both print and broadcast. And by framing the issue, implicitly, as one of the McCarthyism movement's conformity versus the medium's "open access" and "plurality of views," the program may have contributed to a public revulsion at these continued intimidations of the public institutions of the media (institutions supposedly the "cornerstone" of a democratic society). To some audiences this apprehension in itself may well have prompted the final reaction against McCarthyism. In this way, in combination with the print press and with some radio commentators, Murrow and Friendly were on the leading edge of the tide that turned against McCarthyism. This was probably a turning point for the industry as well, imbuing it with a measure of credibility and goodwill that sustained it through the troubled years of expansion and quiz-show scandal that occurred shortly thereafter.

There was also a corresponding change in the nature of the news reporting in the years following McCarthyism. In his study of the senator and the press, Edwin Bayley argues that the print and broadcast press "learned" how to do investigative reporting as a result of covering the movement. Where prior to 1955, for the most part, the McCarthyites exploited "straight" reporting to get their version of charges out before the public, after that time, Bayley contends, there was a "gradual but fundamental change in American journalism." It may have been, Bayley says, the dangers of McCarthyism and the senator's adeptness at "using" the news media that "moved the guardians of objectivity to admit that the meaning of an event is as important as the facts of an event." This turn to interpretive reporting and redefinition of the principles of objectivity was, according to Bayley, one of the beneficial legacies of the years of McCarthyism.[18] "McCarthy's propaganda techniques had forced newspapers and wire services to reexamine their practices and to make greater use of interpretive reporting," Bayley says. "His effect on television was equally important, and his aggressive efforts to use the new medium for his own ends forced networks and stations into major policy decisions."[19]

There is, finally, a third broad area of deliberation about the potential effects of these programs. In this area, *See It Now*'s "effects" extend to the relationship between media texts and their readers or audiences. I suggest that even as the *See It Now* programs "defined" and shaped the genre of the television news documentary, they were simultaneously shaping and defining an audience—a public and its expectations. This point is in line with the commonplace that genres are more than convenient philosophical categories for grouping and organizing objects. Genres are instead, from the perspective of audiences, "pretextual" codifications of expectations and conventions that they bring to a discourse prior to reading or viewing it. Audiences may be expected to decode or interpret a text partly in line with their prior experience and assumptions about the work formed by their experience with texts of a similar or identical genre.[20] While, on the one hand, this conclusion establishes this study of *See It Now* as having considerable import (here, after all, is the urtext of an entire genre), on the other hand, I believe that this examination of *See It Now* might reveal what audiences "learned" from this program about how to "read" the documentary discourse, and so an understanding of this program gives a position to describe the codes of the genre of television documentary. Thus, perhaps the most significant effect of these *See It Now* broadcasts was in teaching an audience how to "read" the genre of documentary television, and how to apply the interpretations decoded there to exigencies in the world. These speculations, of course, take us to the interesting and complex problem of the ideological motifs within these four programs—the way they provided an organizing "template" for understanding the experience of McCarthyism in the decade after 1945.

## Ideological Motifs

"Ideology" itself has become highly "ideologized."[21] Nevertheless, the ideology embedded in textual practice may provide, when excavated, a perspective upon the assumptions and the social life of the culture that produced the text. Contemporary views hold that ideology may be revealed in discourse both in the way the text is formulated (what it explicitly says) and in what is taken for granted there (what is the "unspoken"). A rhetorical approach, engaging both these senses, permits us to dramatize social attitudes and ideology implicit in the text by reconstructing the understandings the textual "voice" and the reader reach by way of both the manifest content of the text and its formal structures. Such an approach, which emphasizes the struggles over potential meaning within texts, might give the best chance of understanding the workings of ideology as it is shaped in discursive form and content.

Reading *See It Now* in this fashion yields an outline of the social attitudes implicit in these texts as responses to McCarthyism. These programs share a central cluster of motifs: they comprise an emphasis upon the common man, the valuation of controversy, and a defense of the pluralistic society. Each of these has significant implications as an ideological response to McCarthyism.

The first motif, showing the effects of the movement upon the common man and focusing on the everyday citizen as its victim, is central to *See It Now*'s negative portrayal of McCarthyism. By featuring Milo Radulovich, the "good folks" of Indianapolis, Annie Lee Moss, even Reed Harris in "A Report on Senator McCarthy," *See It Now* reveals a particular "angle" on the issues. In this fashion, the programs depict what McCarthyism "means" in human terms, while the stylistics of visualization and Murrow's "tail pieces" point beyond the "immediate story," and all four texts seek to capture in the small event its much larger implications. Clearly, *See It Now* systematically elevates its private and individual stories from the realm of the specific and particular to the realm of the societal and the universal.

But the texts also reverse the valence of this representation, and the "common men" we see serve also as indexes of a complex ideology that articulates more generalized ideological themes in terms of a specific and intelligible representation. Grounding a political position opposed to McCarthyism in an "everyday" perspective on events, *See It Now* may present necessarily anti-McCarthy perspectives as apolitical and as part of a commonsense consensus. This provides a kind of political "cover" for the *See It Now* makers and, at the same time, embeds anti-McCarthyism in popular sentiments— in an audience that the text itself constructs.[22]

However, I suggest that there is another, perhaps less well recognized assumption of commonsense constructed beneath this appeal. This concentration on the common man represents in itself a perspective on the relationship between the public and its institutions. Hal Himmelstein has noted that this seems consistent with a basic operating frame of the myth of the individual as it appears in television news and current affairs programming. "[When] the individual meets the institution in confrontation," Himmelstein observes, "[and] when the individual is the common man, the likely outcome is that the individual will be wronged by the institution and rendered seemingly helpless, but will be saved through the intervention of the journalist as moral defender of the truth (thus demonstrating that democracy works; i.e., that a free press protects men from abuses of power)."[23]

This focus upon the common man thus reveals an implicit sense of the power of the television medium as represented by *See It Now* to function as the intermediary between common citizens and the McCarthyism movement. Furthermore, it suggests that one of the understandings reached in the form of the program relates to the medium, its role in American society, and a message about institutions in general. Shortly, when we turn to summarizing the supposed "partisanship" of the programs, I will return to this insight as an aid in explaining the way in which this message might well be the most important of the ideological assumptions within the *See It Now* discourse.

A second motif noted in these four programs is that of struggle. We are invited to read the *See It Now*-McCarthyism exchange as a conflict between two ways of organizing experience of the world. In its defense of the systematic exchange of ideas, *See It Now* epitomizes a relativist plurality holding that each viewpoint has its own partial and limited validity. Indeed, it is clear that the programs support the historic aspirations of liberalism: pluralism, diversity, localism, privacy, individualism, and freedom for the personal and idiosyncratic.[24] But McCarthyism is characterized in contrast—as the positivistic affirmation of the "straight facts." In McCarthyism, we find represented the perspective that suggests an orthodox faith in "valueless facts" and a distrust of "subjective" and human intentions as "hidden" or "disguised," "unknowable" and therefore suspect. But I suggest that the strategies of appeal of these *See It Now* texts succeed precisely because they define an alternative to McCarthyism by transcending its positivistic dogma. That is, the *See It Now* documentaries use an appeal to "facticity," just as McCarthyism does, but they prompt a negative reaction that runs against McCarthyism by the manner in which those "facts" infused with ideological value are presented.[25]

Along the same lines, the third motif is the celebration of controversy itself as a necessary and even therapeutic aspect of American society. This motif can be extracted directly from the content of some programs (e.g., "An Argument in Indianapolis") and is also evident in the controversial nature of each of these *See It Now* telecasts.

Furthermore, I believe that the style and format of the programs also work to sustain this motif of controversy and that the textuality of the programs themselves exemplifies this ideological understanding. For example, *See It Now* casts itself as the direct link between antagonists (the title "See It Now," the bank of monitors, the Indianapolis debate, Eisenhower's statement at the end of "Annie Lee Moss"), and in this way, part of the symbolism of *See It Now* involves the ability of the medium of television itself to appear to facilitate the open and free exchange of ideas. The medium is symbolically promoted as "connecting" its audience with those advocating different views and arguments; and the logomachy of an open society is perhaps the subject matter of these programs. In *See It Now*, the American tradition of open debate and the value of conflicting viewpoints is instantiated in the form of the television news documentary.

In a way, then, *See It Now* argues this ideological assumption against the assumptions of McCarthyism. Both the stories it covers and the way it purports to cover them allow *See It Now* to advocate quite clearly that controversy is a "good thing" and disagreement wholly "American"—a position clearly antithetical to McCarthyism. In short, the text "uses" the commonsense assumption of the open and live television form—the symbolism of the new medium with its transparency and its fabricated "lack" of mediation—as an antidote to McCarthyism's stifling of debate and exchange of ideas.[26]

In the end, I believe that this notion of ultimate nationalistic "unity"—a unity achieved by and through a pluralistic diversity—is part and parcel of the liberalism celebrated and instantiated in the form of *See It Now* itself. In the bank of monitors that call forth reporters, citizens, and events from around the nation, all seemingly controlled by Murrow and the program, the medium promotes itself as the very instrument of this national unity that is pulling together disparate elements. The ideological understanding embedded in the form of the text suggests that the nation is indeed a union, that democracy and individualism "work" but do so, paradoxically, only through the "neutral" intervention of the electronic medium.

Thus, I suggest, the members of an audience are offered the chance to find themselves—to construct themselves as "The People" by and through the only institution that apparently "works" in society—the institution of television. In the end, according to the commonsense view that See It Now proffers its viewers, television in general and the documentary series in particular prevail and warrant approbation as institutions totally in concert with a commonsense view of American democracy—simultaneously embodying and representing this view of unity from out of diversity.

## Partisanship and Ideological Effect

These ideological operations and cultural functions of the See It Now documentary programs bear a striking resemblance to what Stuart Hall has termed "the ideological effect" of the mass media. Hall argues that the media help individuals not merely to "know about the world" but more importantly "to make sense of it" by helping construct a "social knowledge," or social imagery, through which the world is perceived.[27] In so doing, the media reflect the plurality of modern social life, but most important for Hall, the mass media organize and "bring together" this plurality by simultaneously conferring coherence and a sort of integration as areas of consensus and consent begin to emerge. Thus, the media construct a "space" in which representative voices—majority and minority—are "heard" so that "all reasonable men" can agree to the views that emerge. This process of building "consensus" from the plurality of partial positions is the ideological effect of the media. "This [is] the great unifying and consolidating level of the media's ideological work," Hall argues, "the production of consensus, the construction of legitimacy—not so much the finished article itself, but the whole process of argument, exchange, debate, consultation, and speculation by which it emerges."[28]

This argument, of course, redirects simplistic considerations of the bias or impartiality of the news documentary. Thus, while See It Now is not partisan in relation to one side or the other in local political dispute, the broadcasters are certainly partisan in terms of the maintenance of a certain mode and type of institutionalized power—namely a sort of discursive democracy where positions may be set off in opposition to one another, where counterposed arguments lead ultimately to some sort of consensus, even if, as Hall suggests, the only consensus is that disagreement itself is a "good." Thus, *See It Now* is biased toward the state as a model of pluralistic parliamentary democracy.

Such, in my opinion, is the ideological message of these *See It Now* programs on McCarthyism. The fit between the tradition of American liberal pluralism and its institutionalization in parliamentary democracy is hand and glove with the formal demands of the news documentary, which requires a variety of perspectives, the reduction of positions to dialectical opposites, the conferring of "consensus" upon the partial and fragmentary viewpoints. The national common sense of a society united by free speech and the forging of consensus from diversity is represented metaphorically within the field of the *See It Now* documentary—where the institution of unity is the medium itself. *See It Now*'s argumentative and ideological tactics tamed McCarthyism by framing it within the pious principles of traditional Americanism, and once framed in this way, McCarthyism, within the dominant American ideology of liberal pluralism, is deviant.

One way to further explain this ideological effect is to borrow the notion of hegemony. As a term, "hegemony" refers to the ideological domination of the thought, the common sense, the life ways, and the everyday assumptions of individuals within a society. According to this view, liberal society's hegemony develops by domesticating opposition, absorbing it into forms compatible with core ideological structures. Thus, social conflicts are brought into the cultural system and framed in compatibility with dominant systems of meaning.[29]

By framing McCarthyism as a challenge to plurality and diversity, the *See It Now* discourse reinforces what Todd Gitlin has identified as one of the central rhythms of American political history.[30] The programs meet McCarthyism's partial challenge to liberal pluralism by adapting—balancing here, adjusting there, framing, excluding, absorbing. In short, the *See It Now* discourse may well perform the vital function of reducing the excesses of McCarthyism, its tactics and its means, to a debate over the value of free speech and consensus. McCarthyism then appears as a threat to American freedoms, a challenge to the pluralism that defines the society and, coincidentally, the genre of television news documentary as well.[31] I believe that this is not an insignificant point. The myth of plurality and its presentation is absolutely necessary for the media; in fact, the legitimacy of the medium rests on its claim to present "all reasonable" views, and so it is essential to the ideology conveyed by the institution of television.[32] It seems, then, reasonable to conclude that *See It Now* was destined to address McCarthyism not just for ideological reasons but as well for explicit reasons relating to the medium itself. The media as an institution must maximize their audience, their profits, their legitimacy, and their status, and so they must take on and deal in some fashion with all challenges to the dominant social order. *See It Now*'s hegemonic strategy was to tame, to contain, to neutralize the ideology of the McCarthyism movement by relocating it to the idiosyncratic and by reframing it as a manifestation of a dangerous conformity that runs counter to the American mythos. This conformity threatens liberal pluralism and simultaneously the television documentary, which exemplifies the same ideology in its form and its content.

## Beyond *See It Now*

By concentrating upon the specific and particularized dynamic of four *See It Now* programs on McCarthyism, this book has remained closely bound to their specific situation and textuality. But now, I believe, we are in position to extend conclusions about the discourse of nonfiction beyond the four programs and to reflect upon these case studies as they illuminate the documentary itself.

In concluding the previous chapter, I spoke of documentary as a discursive category that combines expectations and stylistic forms drawn from several realms, whose structural elements, organization, and textual demands upon a reader sometimes approach those commonly attributed to discourses more imaginary or fictional. I suggest that this prospect, more than any other, promotes a reconceptualization of documentary even as it highlights the interaction of rhetoric and poetics. To begin with, it invites us to consider what might be the "proper" relationship of these two grand discursive domains.

In the history of the rhetorical tradition, one view widely circulated is that rhetoric as originally conceived was persuasive "oratory," not a persuasive "art." Accordingly, the realm of art was poetics, not rhetoric, and evidence for this orthodox division is often found in the fact that Aristotle wrote two separate works dealing with discourse—the *Rhetoric* and the *Poetics*. It is contended, in short, that Aristotle viewed the pleasures of art as categorically different and ultimately separate from the persuasion of rhetoric.[33] Starting with this distinction, tradition holds that the key difference between poetics and rhetoric is the purpose with which they engage audiences (for "appreciation" or to "encourage action") and the sorts of subject matters characteristic of each ("timeless values" or "immediate historical exigency").[34]

But it is clear from the preceding case studies that such division has limited use for the understanding of the rhetoric of television documentary. Instead, it has become evident, as we moved from the operation of synecdoche in the Radulovich program to questions of depiction in the Indianapolis one, from the blurring of genres of reportage and argument in the McCarthy program to the parallel blurring between the dramatic and the nonfictional in "Annie Lee Moss," that documentary as a discursive form is, par excellence, the blending of conventions. These texts operate as both persuasion and art. I suggest that this dual function supports a conception of documentary as a symbolic form that unites the argumentative and the aesthetic functions of discourse, a form that performs "bimodally": rhetoric and poetic, historical and aesthetic, are mutually dependent. This power of discourse to "make" experience "mean" is in one sense the "documentary idea." And in his recent book *Representing Reality*, Bill Nichols captures the essence of this paradoxical blending of discursive forms when he describes documentary as "a fiction (un)like any other."[35]

A sort of triangulation might help in speculating about this blending as it contributes to a contemporary assessment of documentary. There are, I propose, three dominant intertextual relationships important for our understanding of documentary discourse: documentary and history, documentary and fiction, and documentary and ideology.[36] Each of these relationships contributes to a sense of how the documentary account both is and is not historical reality, both is and is not fiction, and how it engages social structures. Moreover, I will argue that the documentary encourages the activation of these three intertextual relationships as a way of attempting a local "persuasive" task—that is, its potential for public argument depends upon this tripartite relationship. As will become clear, the three intertextual relationships are themselves inextricably bound—they build upon each other and reinforce each other—it is their constant dynamic that is the heart of the symbolic action of the documentary. And though I do not think any of these relationships is more important than the others, and my ordering of them suggests no priority, for purposes of explanation I will discuss them one at a time.

Documentary stands in a peculiar, even a unique, relationship to the "real" and to conventions of interpretation. The genre claims to provide its audience with a way to grasp the world; such has been the driving impetus behind documentary since its inception. First, common sense suggests that documentary is shackled to "brute facts," and because it is constructed from series of photographic images, documentary necessarily indexes events that are verifiable independent of the imagination.[37] This realization is part and parcel of the largely technological factors that necessarily lie at the root of the documentary enterprise. Precisely this technological capacity to record the visual and/or aural elements of a particular piece of the world provides the primary evidential quality sought by documentary accounts.[38] The documentary is "referential"—a "document" of the profilmic historical event. Thus, in semiotic terms, the image is index, and typically, viewers grant a certain presumptive power to the force of witness it provides.

More than anything else, certainly, this indexical relationship to the historical event is the defining moment for the documentary. This status as discourse "tied" to the world of experience undergirds the definition of documentary as "fact" and as a "document" of the real. Indeed, in a sense, the remaining intertextual relationships in some way depend upon this one. As a piece of discourse whose historical concern has been to shift perspectives on some situation in the world, the documentary typically demands assent to the "reality" of the historical before it encourages the reading of the symbolic or the ideological over the "real." In the terms used earlier in this book, the denoted image, the "objective" image, "grounds" the connotated, "inflected" image that is the channel of ideology and argument.

But upon reflection, this seemingly genial relationship itself is problematic and complex, especially when we begin to examine the way the documentary text interacts with the conventions that viewers likely hold prior to reading. First, the documentary discourse secures the assent of the viewer to the historical, in part, not so much by presenting a "record" of events, as by observing the expected conventions of such a recording. Viewers have expectations about the form that the documentary discourse will take and about stylistic features of those forms. They have, in short, some considerable experience and prior exposure to what John Caughie has termed the "documentary look." Caughie argues that documentary has a severely mediated style that is clearly "marked" but has a prior association with truth and neutrality. This appearance of objectivity is marked, Caughie says, by a certain textual style, and this style in part accounts for such documentary clichés as the predominance of the hand-held camera, the cramped shot, natural lighting, and inaudible sound.[39] Thus, this coded "documentary look" establishes the notion of unproblematic "fact" conveyed via the denoted image and subsequently guarantees its validity.

I suggest that Caughie's insight supports a more troubling and intriguing point: as Caughie implies, and as we specifically demonstrated in the case study of "A Report on Senator McCarthy," the notion of denotation itself remains but a perspective—and as such may function as an element in argument to legitimate suasive discourse however open it may be to ironic reversal. In the opening pages of *S/Z*, Roland Barthes defends this idea that denotation, even though an "effect," is taken as "true."

Structurally, the existence of two supposedly different systems—connotation and denotation—enables the text to operate like a game, each system referring to the other according to the requirements of a certain illusion. Ideologically, finally, this game has the advantage of affording the classic text a certain innocence: of the two systems, denotative and connotative, one turns back on itself and indicates its own existence: the system of denotation; denotation is not the first meaning, but pretends to be so; under this illusion, it is ultimately no more than the last of the connotations (the one which seems both to establish and to close the reading), the superior myth by which the text pretends to return to the nature of language, to language as nature.[40]

This conclusion suggests that as denotation is the "last of the connotations," the documentary activates conventions that prepare us to expect a privileged status for the indexical link between sign and referent and thus to prompt a new perspective on an historical situation. Denotation, then—an assumption of the factual representation of the historical event—bolsters the power of the documentary. But even these conventions are ways of managing the meaning of the "real" and depend for their understanding on viewers' prior experience with symbolic forms. Thus, even at what must at first appear to be its most material relationship—that of text and history—it seems now clear that documentary is complex: it is involved even at the most simple level in the symbolic restructuring and discursive remaking of the world and with the ideology of representation.

In addition to the denoted or indexical or technological dimension of documentary, there is a corresponding aesthetic dimension. That is, documentary must necessarily be organized according to compositional principles, and it must be structured through one and the same discursive and symbolic process of construction and selection that all discourse uses.[41] If we acknowledge a unity of formal and symbolic processes in the discourses of rhetoric and those of poetic, this acknowledgment adds weight to the argument that the divide between rhetorical documentaries and aesthetic texts might be attenuated. In order to describe the functions of this aestheticizing of the natural, I contend that the documentary discourse has not so much a single referent (the historical event) as it has a "split reference" and indeed that, as a form, documentary exploits the difference between its dual referents. This point, I believe, requires some explanation.

To clarify how documentary discourse has a "split reference," it may be enough to consider the nature of language itself.[42] A heuristic distinction may be made between poetic language on the one side and ordinary language on the other. Poetic language systems, or fictional texts, may be considered as "closed" systems. That is, they are for the most part self-referential. While they may offer events, characters, and motivations that resemble those in the real world, poetic language seeks verification in itself, and its plausibility rests on those elements within the system. "Poetic truth" is a function of internal consistency. We may think of poetic language as centripetal—as spiraling in on itself.[43]

Ordinary language stands in contrast. A crude distinction might consider ordinary language as a thoroughly referential language. That is, it "names" things in the world and is concerned with actions and events. We assume that ordinary language (unless it is the speech of the mad) may be largely verified by events, situations, and activities in the world of shared experience. Its plausibility rests on elements outside its own system. We attribute its verification to the "world"; its truth we take as a function of experience. Ordinary language is centrifugal—it spirals outward to the world.

Documentary discourse exploits this essential difference between poetic and ordinary systems of signification. As the documentary structures an account of the world in forms such as narrative, character, synecdoche, contrast, and parallelism, the account invites a reading that acquires the status of a closed and centripetal fiction. For example, "Annie Lee Moss Before the McCarthy Committee" fashions a narrative of the hearing and has the expected features of such narrative—recurring characters, consistency, temporal development, and closure. Thus, a portion of the charge of this text is its apparent status as a self-contained drama suggesting a resolution paralleling those that a reader expects from dramatic narratives. And such documentary discourse effects an aesthetic unity: it spirals in upon itself.

But because of the split reference, documentaries such as "Annie Lee Moss" also point outward to the world. That is, as the aesthetic structure is recognized by the audience, the documentary is able to suggest associations between the symbolic and the social situation, with the result that the discourse reads a social situation in categories drawn from the world of fiction. In sum, an audience is invited to think of the documentary in terms of archetypal symbolic frames, and so the documentary layers a signification drawn from conventions of "story" or "drama" over the nonfiction film footage. Indeed, we may say that documentary imposes an order on the real that is a function of alternation between conventions of the nonfiction "reality" and a symbolic reading that promises a resolution paralleling that of other stories.

Thus the documentary text represents an intersection of two sorts of signifying codes: the one, based on assent to the indexical relation of image and world, an acknowledgment of the ontological potency of the observational text. The other, based on the mythic and dramatic, drawn from a cultural stock of characters and soliciting a reading of the text as melodrama, as the acting out of an allegory or parable. For instance, a reading of "The Case of Milo Radulovich" made it clear that the central figure of the lieutenant took on a positive charge by nature of a carefully calculated and developed equivalence between him (a historical person) and the conventionalized dramatic figure of the "bashful hero" (a fictional persona).

Thus to account partly for the persuasive potency of the documentary program is to look for the relationship between the historical and the fictional. As the documentary account encodes the historical situation in structures borrowed at least in part from the symbolic or imaginative, reading is likely suspended between intertextual relations. I am claiming more here than that the imagery of the symbolic account is embellishment; often it is far more. Instead, a dramatic structure both describes and redescribes the setting and the people involved and lets the confused, tangled, and perhaps unclear historical situation come to be seen in terms of the better-known, the clearer, the more elaborated dramatic form drawn from the reader's prior experiences with other texts. A truth beyond the real is figured as a reader is invited to "see" the situation through the associations called up from the original dramatic presentations. And so the documentary text "opens" and spins out "centrifugally" to the situation. That is, the documentary's use of symbolism drawn from the world of the imaginary might well serve as a template, for the situation both orients the audience's view of the situation and adjusts audience attitudes toward it. In this way documentary remains a discursive form that maintains its integrity through its centripetal dramatic model and, at the same time, maps itself onto a situation in the world.

The useful heuristic of the split reference suggests two distinct but closely related conclusions. First, it suggests that the documentary reading is clearly dependent upon prior experience not only with the genre of documentary but also with the practice of other discourses. It is well known that response to a text is partly a function of generic expectations and that knowledge of antecedent genres creates expectations in rhetors, viewers, and critics alike. Genre has come to be considered a means of constructing both the audience and the reading subject, and its work is partly to influence the meanings of a program that are preferred by, or are offered to, particular audiences. Some have argued that the idea of genre performs this function by preferring some intertextual relations and their associated meanings over others.[44] But perhaps to a degree greater than in verbal discourses, in the analysis of documentary texts, intertextuality becomes crucial.

A second, related point seems more radical and of greater critical significance. We may account for part of the exploitation of the form we have described by examining the collusion of the intertextuality of history with the intertextuality of fiction. It may be that a part of the split reference of the documentary text might have to do with the veracity of the documentary account. That is, veracity becomes a function of the visual elements and the intertextual relationship of the fictional and the historical.

In this book, I have paid progressively more attention to the way in which the documentary genre is situated at the intersection of the dramatic and the argumentative. I noted that these texts are an interesting mix of aesthetic reflexivity and worldly referentiality. But we may speculate that, in the documentary genre as much as in any other form of public discourse, the way an audience responds to the "real" is a function of audience reactions to conventions more appropriate to the "dramatic." As Nichols puts this point, the impression of authenticity is likely based more upon the reality of representation than upon the representation of reality.[45] In the documentary the nonfictional becomes charged with the energy of a dramatic reading by the stylistics of its presentation.[46] Certain kinds of shots characteristic in the "documentary look" in fact take on the "look" of conventions that we have learned to read from dramatic programs. We have seen some of these in the *See It Now* series: traveling shots, certain panning shots, intercutting, and, in the "Moss" program, even eye-line match edits. It is probable, then, that in the documentary text, as it uses more and more dramatic devices, and as it fabricates itself as a combination of dramatic form and nonfictional material, its veracity becomes a function of its artistry. It may be that audiences are encouraged to judge a situation in the world partly on the basis of the pleasing aesthetic reflexivity of the text rather than on the basis of its often controversial referential "argument." Once again, the documentary apparently operates on two levels, with two references at the same time: veracity combines the "fictional" form and the nonfictional material, and any viewer is likely to read the documentary discourse with reference at least partly to expectation of the form drawn from discourses of the imaginary.

As a tightly wrought discourse, the documentary throws into contrast the tension between its reflexive and referential dimensions. The documentary, like other successful rhetorical performances, simultaneously closes in on itself and opens out to the world. Documentary in particular and the visual text in general have the potential to speak to difficult questions of the relation of discourses both to the world they seek to influence and to the world of aesthetics from which they draw their tactics and techniques. Indeed, to fully understand documentary texts is to take into account both the centripetal/textual and the centrifugal/sociological energy of their rhetorical performance. Simultaneously reflexive and referential, *See It Now* manifests both a consciously fabricated aesthetic unity and a partisan perspective on an area of experience in the world.

## Documentary as Ideology

There is no doubt that the relationship between documentary and history interacts in several different ways with the relationship between documentary and aesthetics. The final relationship, that between documentary and ideology, is also closely bound up with these prior relationships and especially with that of aesthetics.

In *The Political Unconscious*, Fredric Jameson suggests that the critic ought look at the formal processes of discourse as a sort of "sedimented content" and as carrying ideological messages quite apart from the manifest content.[47] This code, Jameson argues, is an index of a prevailing larger ideological unity of the social system. Thus, the ideological assumptions and the common sense that the text speaks may be read not in the said of the text but in its manner of saying. In short, Jameson points the way to a concept of the ideology of the form.

Certainly the television documentary, with its generic heritage drawn from the news report, is committed to notions of "objectivity" and "impartiality." Like some other institutions, journalism and current affairs support the status quo by appearing to be above and beyond politics. But we may speculate that the very form of the typical television documentary—its invocation of impartiality and objectivity—constitutes an essential part of television's ideological work.[48] Part of the problem in grappling with this idea has been that the argument about the possibility or impossibility of this "objectivity" has centered nearly exclusively upon content or upon the widening of access that might lead to an even greater plurality and diversity of sources and perspectives on social issues. In this process, the aesthetics and the form of television documentary have been nearly overlooked as contributing to the reproduction of ideology.[49] What I want to consider, then, is how aesthetic style and form must be interrogated not just as a technique but rather as a moral outlook or a social perspective—in brief, how we may describe the ideology of the documentary form.[50]

Some work done by Sol Worth and others at the Annenberg School of Communications has established the ideological significance of visual and aesthetic style. Worth's studies extend the conclusions of Edward Sapir and Benjamin Whorf, that the grammar of language incorporates a worldview, into the field of visual communication. In a cunningly simple design, Worth carefully chose distinct and differentiated social groups and asked them to make films. What emerged was that each group—American Indians, middle-class suburb kids, and ghetto kids—used an identifiably different film language, a language quite clear to other members of the group but not at all clear to outsiders. In short, Worth established that visual style is not neutral.[51]

Building on this conclusion, we may infer that, in order to sustain its ideological status as "impartial," the television documentary must claim to "reflect" the world, not to "argue" for a view of what "might" be, but to present a case study—observation—of things, as they "are." It seems therefore essential that, to sustain this ideology, the paradigm television documentary must adopt an aesthetic code that claims to do the same. This style is what Nicholas Garnham calls the style of "naturalism."[52] Naturalism involves "a scrupulous fidelity to here and now; to immediate and apparent . . . , an aesthetic which seeks to minimize the mediation through consciousness of the real, in perception and representation."[53] Naturalism sees the act of the documentary re-presentation as essentially passive and neutral. It stresses the recording function of the visual rather than its manipulative or illusion-creating function—it emphasizes its link with the denotated image and the historical event.[54]

This style, according to Garnham, has ideological consequences: the aesthetic of naturalism rules out progress. "If things are as they are . . . you can only go on adding slice of life to slice of life, all equal, all essentially the same. . . . But of course, naturalism is not neutral, it supports the status quo by allowing people to believe that things are as they are."[55]

In this way, Garnham demonstrates that the ideological message of documentary may be precisely in the way that it naturalizes events and conflicts. Furthermore, his conclusion suggests that the place to study the relationship between documentary and ideology is, paradoxically, to study the site where the documentary account aestheticizes the historical event. For the way in which the symbolic is layered over the historical reveals the ideology of the documentary text.

Some contend that the television documentary is an essentially conservative discursive form and that, insofar as it instantiates its content in the form of naturalism, it also presents itself as nonideological and aligns with a similar apparently nonideological class-transcendent public and national interest.[56] While further study might bear out this observation, I believe we are warranted in concluding at least tentatively that the television documentary discourse necessarily reinforces the status quo by the politics of rhetorical action and its intertextuality with "conservative" discourse forms. The content of the form—its rhetorical action—found through careful attention to the discrete text, may serve as the index *not* to the intentions of the authors, *not* to the responses of ideal audiences, but to the ideological assumptions encoded in the form itself.

## Afterword

My rhetorical perspective on documentary discourse invites the conclusion that such discourse constitutes viewers as subjects by positioning them within a matrix of at least three other discourses: the historical, the symbolic, and the ideological. Documentary uses the stylistic and aesthetic conventions of symbolic discourses to frame and at the same time to ground the story in specific places/people. This intertextuality is not merely generic (in that it suggests that all documentaries refer to each other), however, but is also more broadly cultural: documentary as discourse refers to all other discourses and their knowledges.[57] It may well be that a reader's final recovery of any particular documentary is in large measure determined by which of these discursive relationships are privileged.

But in saying this, I am not saying that the documentary text is read like a "fictional" discourse. On the contrary, the reader is constantly pulled back by the "stickiness of the indexical image" to the notion that the documentary depicts real people, in real situations, in a "real world" that we "know." This difference in the imaginary and the indexical separates the documentary discourse from the "fictional." As Bill Nichols has said, the ground of documentary resides in the relation between character and social agent; a person acts as an agent in history, not in a narrative, no matter how much we give meaning to the former by way of the latter.[58]

But it is also this ambiguity of reading levels—these "leaky" intertextual relationships—that allows the documentary to keep its potential for success as a discrete, exigent, persuasive argument. More precisely, the form solicits reaction to the people and events we "meet" as historical personae, as symbolic characters, and as representatives of ideology. These permeable reading levels account well for the potential persuasive potency of the documentary argument. Documentary can be read on any of its levels while simultaneously retaining the documentary premise that the images framing the exigence are ultimately tied to the "real." Thus, the documentary discourse may mobilize response to a historical exigence by giving a viewer the opportunity to read the exigence across three distinct yet tightly connected intertextual relationships, and reaction on even one of these levels prepares the viewer for action in the world.

Finally, and ultimately then, it is clear that the documentary moves back and forth between the world of our experience and the symbolic restructuring of it. Documentary justifies itself as a category of discourse on the grounds of its ability to present reality not for the purposes of entertainment or diversion but for argument and action. As an action, it seeks to cast the shared experience of our times into a symbolic form so that we might discuss, debate, decide, and conduct our public business. To those ends, and with those tools, documentary may well be the master rhetorical form of our time. It exists at the place where ideology and art meet: its concern is the politics of representation.

# Notes

## Introduction

1. In the most comprehensive communication analysis to date of the programs, Michael Murray concludes that they were "instrumental" in undermining the power of Senator McCarthy. See Michael D. Murray, "*See It Now* Versus McCarthyism: Dimensions of Documentary Persuasion" (Ph.D. diss., University of Missouri—Columbia, 1974), 163–70; hereafter cited as Murray, "Dimensions." But in his survey of the historical accounts of the era and the program, James Baughman notes that few historians consider the impact of the programs on the historical situation and even the few who do do not claim that the programs were in any sense important or contributing to McCarthy's downfall. See James L. Baughman, "'See It Now' and Television's Golden Age, 1951–1958," *Journal of Popular Culture* 15 (1981): 106–15.

2. Todd Gitlin, "Prime Time Ideology: The Hegemonic Process in Television Entertainment," *Social Problems* 26 (1979): 251.

3. Stuart Hall, "Signification, Representation, Ideology: Althusser and the Post-Structuralist Debates," *Critical Studies in Mass Communication* 2 (1985): 97.

4. Clifford Geertz, "Ideology as a Cultural System," in *Interpretation of Cultures* (New York: Harper, 1973), 213.

5. Stuart Hall, "The Rediscovery of 'Ideology': The Return of the Repressed in Media Studies," in *Culture, Society, and the Media,* ed. Michael Gurevitch et al. (London: Methuen, 1982), 56–90.

6. Geertz, "Ideology as a Cultural System," 219.

7. James R. Andrews, *A Choice of Worlds: The Practice and Criticism of Public Discourse* (New York: Harper and Row, 1973).

8. Bill Nichols, *Representing Reality: Issues and Concepts in Documentary* (Bloomington: Indiana University Press, 1991), x.

# Chapter 1: McCarthyism, the Red Scare, and the Television Industry

1. Robert C. Goldston, *The American Nightmare: Senator Joseph R. McCarthy and the Politics of Hate* (Indianapolis, Ind.: Bobbs-Merrill, 1973), 5.

2. Joseph R. McCarthy is quoted in ibid., 70; McCarthy's actual words on the occasion are the subject of widespread debate, as there is no transcription of the speech, and the senator revised his number of "known Communists" at least three times over the next ten days.

3. "Truman Accuses Brownell of Lying; Sees Office Debased in White Case; Says GOP Embraces McCarthyism," *New York Times*, 17 November 1953, p. A1.

4. Several historians have made this point. See, for example, Thomas Reeves, *The Life and Times of Joe McCarthy: A Biography* (New York: Stein and Day, 1982), 207.

5. There are, of course, other perspectives that attempt to explain McCarthyism as "status resentment" or as a distinctly revolutionary social movement. I am persuaded by the argument that McCarthyism is best considered within the framework of "politics as usual." See Michael Paul Rogin, *The Intellectuals and McCarthy: The Radical Specter* (Cambridge: Massachusetts Institute of Technology Press, 1967), and Nathan Polsby, "Towards an Explanation of McCarthyism," *Political Studies* 8 (1960): 250–71; other views include Seymour Martin Lipset, "Three Decades of the Radical Right," in *The Radical Right*, ed. Daniel Bell (Garden City, N.Y.: Anchor-Doubleday, 1964), 373–446; Richard Hofstadter, "The Pseudo-Conservative Revolt," in *The Radical Right*, ed. Bell, 75–96; Peter Viereck, "The Revolt Against the Elite," in *The Radical Right*, ed. Bell, 161–84; Talcott Parsons, "Social Strains in America (1955)," in *The Radical Right*, ed. Bell, 209–29; Allen J. Matusow, ed., *Joseph R. McCarthy* (Englewood Cliffs, N.J.: Prentice-Hall, 1970).

6. Erik Barnouw, *Tube of Plenty: The Evolution of American Television* (New York: Oxford University Press, 1975), 121.

7. Ibid., 130.

8. Edwin R. Bayley, *Joe McCarthy and the Press* (Madison: University of Wisconsin Press, 1981), 41, 68, 86.

9. Ibid., 47.

10. Ibid., 177.

11. Ibid.

12. Barnouw, *Tube of Plenty*, 151.

13. Bayley, *McCarthy and the Press*, 184.

14. Ibid., 180.

15. Ibid., 212.

16. David Oshinsky agrees that the *See It Now* programs on Mc-Carthyism are defenses against an expected McCarthyite "attack"; see Oshinsky, *A Conspiracy So Immense: The World of Joe McCarthy* (New York: Free Press, 1983), 398.

17. For a readable account of this link, see Melvin L. De Fleur and Sandra Ball-Rokeach, *Theories of Mass Communication*, 4th ed. (New York: Longman, 1982), 143–65.

18. Erik Barnouw has suggested that McCarthyism's attacks on the Voice of America were part and parcel of other "un-American activities" investigations and a symptom of a general uneasiness over the ideological conflict between democracy and communism; see Erik Barnouw, *Documentary: A History of the Non-Fiction Film* (New York: Oxford University Press, 1982), 221–23.

19. Bayley, *McCarthy and the Press*, 212.

20. "'See It Now': Television Premiere," writ. Edward R. Murrow and Fred W. Friendly, *See It Now,* 18 November 1951, dir. Don Hewitt, prods. Edward R. Murrow and Fred W. Friendly, transcript, Edward R. Murrow Papers, Edwin Ginn Library, Fletcher School of Law and Diplomacy, Tufts University, Medford, Mass., 3. Also Fred W. Friendly, *Due to Circumstances Beyond Our Control . . .* (New York: Random House, 1967), xiii.

21. Quoted in Murray R. Yaeger, "The Evolution of 'See It Now,'" *Journal of Broadcasting* 1 (1957): 337.

22. An excellent and concise summary of the history of the series may be found in Daniel J. Leab, "'See It Now': A Legend Reassessed," in *American History/American Television: Interpreting the Video Past*, ed. John O'Connor (New York: Frederick Ungar Publishing, 1983), 1–32.

23. Michael J. Arlen, John Crosby, Newton M. Minow, and Michael Novak, quoted in ibid., 1.

24. A. William Bluem, *Documentary in American Television* (New York: Hastings House, 1970), 99–100.

25. Gary P. Gates, *Air Time: The Inside Story of CBS News* (New York: Harper and Row, 1978), 107; Charles M. Hammond, Jr., *The Image Decade: Television Documentary, 1965–1975* (New York: Hastings House, 1981), 12.

26. Raymond L. Carroll, "Factual Television in America: An Analysis of Network Television Documentary Programs, 1948–1975" (Ph.D. diss., University of Wisconsin—Madison, 1978), 103; Fred Freed, "The Rise and Fall of the Television Documentary," *Television Quarterly* 10 (1972): 57.

27. Alexander Kendrick, *Prime Time: The Life of Edward R. Murrow* (Boston: Little, Brown, 1969), 339.

28. Ibid., 112–13.

29. Ibid., 4.

30. Carroll, "Factual Television," 101.

31. Michael D. Murray, "Television's Desperate Moment: A Conversation with Fred Friendly," *Journalism History* 1 (1974): 71. Also see Barnouw, *Tube of Plenty*, 181–82.

32. Friendly, *Due to Circumstances*, 3.

33. Kendrick, *Prime Time*, 342.

34. Prior to "The Case of Milo Radulovich," *See It Now* was not known for its controversial stories. It featured mostly interviews and what has come to be called "soft news" and "features." As Merron argues, "few of the hundreds of *See It Now*s provoked controversy." See Jeff Merron, "Edward R. Murrow's Contributions to Television Journalism, 1951–55: A Study of 'See It Now' and 'Person to Person'" (M.A. thesis, University of Wisconsin—Madison, 1985), 120.

35. Leab, "Legend Reassessed," 7.

36. Gilbert Seldes, *The Public Arts* (New York: Simon and Schuster, 1956), 217.

37. Erik Barnouw, *The Image Empire: A History of Broadcasting in the United States from 1953* (New York: Oxford University Press, 1970), 46.

38. A. M. Sperber, *Murrow: His Life and Times* (New York: Freundlich Books, 1986), 390–91 (also mentioned in Yaeger, "Evolution," 341).

39. Ibid., 370.

40. Reeves, *Life and Times of Joe McCarthy*, 398.

41. Leab, "Legend Reassessed," 9.

42. Ibid., 9.

43. Christopher H. Sterling and John M. Kitross, *Stay Tuned: A Concise History of American Broadcasting*, 2d ed. (Belmont, Calif.: Wadsworth, 1990), 657–58.

44. Barnouw, *Image Empire*, 54.

# Chapter 2: Documentary Television and *See It Now*

1. Quoted in William Stott, *Documentary Expression and Thirties America* (New York: Oxford University Press, 1973), 5.

2. *The American Heritage Dictionary of the English Language* (New York: American Heritage, 1969).

3. Nichols, *Representing Reality*, x.

4. Ibid., x. The terms "evidence from" and "discourse about" the world, as descriptions of the division in documentary theorizing, are borrowed from Nichols.

5. Barnouw, *Documentary*, 83–182.

6. Ibid., 85.

7. For more on Grierson and the beginnings of documentary, see Paul Swann, *The British Documentary Film Movement, 1926–1946* (Cambridge: Cambridge University Press, 1989).

8. John Grierson, "First Principles of Documentary," in *Grierson on Documentary*, ed. Forsyth Hardy (New York: Praeger, 1966), 257.

9. For a discussion of the influences upon the television documentary by documentary filmmakers, albeit from more of an historical perspective, see Bluem, *Documentary in American Television*, 32–59.

10. Ibid., 51.

11. Stott, *Documentary Expression*, 21.

12. Henry Luce, quoted in Barnouw, *Documentary,* 121.

13. Ibid., 121–22, 131.

14. Bluem, *Documentary in American Television,* 51.

15. Ibid., 52.

16. David H. Culbert, *News for Everyman: Radio and Foreign Affairs in Thirties America* (Westport, Conn.: Greenwood Press, 1976), 187.

17. For an historical perspective, in more detail, of the development of radio documentary and its influence, see Bluem, *Documentary in American Television,* 60–72.

18. Ibid., 100.

19. Ibid., 14.

20. Stott, *Documentary Expression,* 14, 21.

21. Bluem, *Documentary in American Television,* 90.

22. Ibid., 90.

23. Ibid., 141–44.

24. Ibid., 90.

25. Ibid., 98.

26. Ibid., 13.

27. Ibid.

# Chapter 3: *See It Now,* Documentary Persuasion, and Rhetorical Analysis

1. David Morley and Roger Silverstone, "Domestic Communication—Technologies and Meanings," *Media, Culture, and Society* 12 (1990): 31–55.

2. Ibid., 47.

3. Thomas W. Benson, "The Rhetorical Structure of Frederick Wiseman's 'High School,'" *Communication Monographs* 47 (1980): 233–61; Benson and Carolyn Anderson, "The Cultural World of Frederick Wiseman's 'Model,'" *Journal of Film and Video* 36 (1984): 30–40; Benson, "The Rhetorical Structure of Frederick Wiseman's 'Primate,'" *Quarterly Journal of Speech* 71 (1985): 204–17; Benson and Anderson, "Standing on Ceremony: Believing as Seeing in Frederick Wiseman's 'Canal Zone'" (Public Address Division, Speech Communication Association Convention, Chicago, November 1986); Benson and Anderson, *Reality Fictions: The Films of Frederick Wiseman* (Carbondale: Southern Illinois University Press, 1989).

4. Benson, "The Rhetorical Structure of Frederick Wiseman's 'High School,'" 234, 254.

5. Martin J. Medhurst and Thomas W. Benson, "'The City': The Rhetoric of Rhythm," *Communication Monographs* 48 (1981): 54–72.

6. Ibid., 58.

7. This idea is more explicitly developed in Kenneth Burke, *A Rhetoric of Motives* (1950; reprint, Berkeley: University of California Press, 1969), 55–58; and Burke's *Counter-Statement,* 2d ed. (1931; reprint, Berkeley: University of California Press, 1968), 29–44, 123–212.

8. Benson, "The Rhetorical Structure of Frederick Wiseman's 'High School,'" 235.

9. Ibid., 234.

10. But what is missing in Benson's early work is a sense of the social dimension of the documentary text—a way to connect the structures and reactions that the text solicits of its audience with the social, cultural, and political systems that give rise to it. This shortcoming may be attributed partly to the texts Benson typically chooses—Wiseman documentaries are not produced as intentional responses to specific events in the public domain and instead address more general subject matter than that on which these *See It Now* broadcasts focus. This deficiency seems to be corrected in the later work of Benson and his sometime coauthor Carolyn Anderson. In later essays, they seek a specifically cultural meaning to the Wiseman films, sometimes to the detriment of the text itself. What is needed is a critique to unify the two sides. See Benson, "The Rhetorical Structure of Frederick Wiseman's 'Primate'"; Benson and Anderson, "Standing on Ceremony: Believing as Seeing in Frederick Wiseman's 'Canal Zone'"; Benson and Anderson, "The Ultimate Technology: Frederick Wiseman's 'Missile,'" in *Communication and the Culture of Technology*, ed. M. J. Medhurst, R. Gonzalez, and T. R. Peterson (Pullman: Washington State University Press, 1990), 257–83.

11. Michael C. Leff, "Interpretation and the Art of the Rhetorical Critic," *Western Journal of Speech Communication* 44 (1980): 348.

12. Leff defines the general outline of the enterprise of textual criticism in "Textual Criticism: The Legacy of G. P. Mohrmann," *Quarterly Journal of Speech* 72 (1986): 377–89. See also Edwin Black, "A Note on Theory and Practice in Rhetorical Criticism," *Western Journal of Speech Communication* 44 (1980): 331–36; Stephen Lucas, "The Renaissance of American Public Address: Text and Context in Rhetorical Criticism," *Quarterly Journal of Speech* 74 (1988): 243–62.

13. Leff, "Textual," 378, 380. Other critics have also contributed to the restatement of textual criticism. One of the most notable is Lawrence W. Rosenfield's "The Experience of Criticism," *Quarterly Journal of Speech* 60 (1974): 489–96; also G. P. Mohrmann, "Elegy in a Critical Graveyard," *Western Journal of Speech Communication* 44 (Fall 1980): 265–74.

14. See Stuart Hall, "Introduction to Media Studies at the Centre," in *Culture, Media, Language*, ed. S. Hall, D. Hobson, A. Lowe, and P. Willis (London: Hutchinson, 1980), 117–21. In this view, the text is seen not as a transparent bearer of meaning but as a "message" composed of a number of variables that is "read" by the viewer not just genetically or physiologically but historically and linguistically. The viewer actively makes meaning from the text, and indeed, viewing demands a cognitive and creative response. The argument that follows draws upon Hall's assumptions as well as those of Richard B. Gregg, "The Criticism of Symbolic Inducement: A Critical-Theoretical Connection," in *Speech Communication in the Twentieth Century*, ed. Thomas Benson (Carbondale: Southern Illinois University Press, 1985), 41–62, and Carole Berger, "Viewing as Action: Film and Reader Response Criticism," *Literature-Film Quarterly* 6 (1978): 144–51.

15. Berger, 144.

16. Wolfgang Iser, "The Reading Process: A Phenomenological Approach," in *Reader-Response Criticism: From Formalism to Post-Structuralism*, ed. Jane P. Tompkins (Baltimore, Md.: Johns Hopkins University Press, 1980), 57.

17. Terry Eagleton, *Literary Theory: An Introduction* (Minneapolis: University of Minnesota Press, 1983), 81.

18. It should be noted, however, that I shall be functioning on two distinct levels: on one, as an individual reader responding to the text, on the other, as a rhetorical critic analyzing and interpreting these responses. For a similar approach, see Susan Suleiman, "Ideological Dissent from Works of Fiction: Toward a Rhetoric of 'Roman à Thèse,'" *Neophilologus* 60 (1976): 165.

19. Edwin Black, "The Second Persona," *Quarterly Journal of Speech* 56 (1970): 109–19.

20. Jean-Paul Sartre, "For Whom Does One Write?" *What Is Literature?* trans. Bernard Frechtman (1949; reprint, New York: Harper and Row, 1965), 64.

21. For a parallel discussion, see Walter J. Ong, "The Writer's Audience Is Always a Fiction," *PMLA* 90 (1975): 9–21.

22. Wolfgang Iser, *The Implied Reader: Patterns of Communication in Prose Fiction* (Baltimore, Md.: Johns Hopkins University Press, 1974).

23. See Ong, "Writer's Audience," 11; Eagleton, *Literary Theory*, 84.

24. William Gibson, "Authors, Speakers, Readers, and Mock Readers," in *Reader-Response Criticism*, ed. Tompkins, 3.

25. I mean by this more than the simpleminded notion that the visual may be decoded as a sort of "language" in which each style and manner of image corresponds to a particular semantic meaning. I mean, specifically, that each sequence must be examined for its sense in its specific context; see David Bordwell and Kristin Thompson, *Film Art: An Introduction*, 2d ed. (New York: Addison-Wesley, 1979).

26. Michael Osborn, "Rhetorical Depiction," in *Form, Genre, and the Study of Political Discourse*, ed. Herbert W. Simons and Aram A. Aghazarian (Columbia: University of South Carolina Press, 1987), 79.

27. Roland Barthes, "The Photographic Message," in *Image-Music-Text*, trans. Stephen Heath (New York: Hill and Wang, 1978), 16.

28. Roland Barthes, "Rhetoric of the Image," in *Image-Music-Text*, 36.

29. Ibid., 45.

30. Barthes, "Photographic Message," 19.

31. Barthes, "Rhetoric of the Image," 36.

32. Bordwell and Thompson, *Film Art*, vi.

33. Barthes, "Rhetoric of the Image," 46.

34. Kathleen H. Jamieson, "Generic Constraints and the Rhetorical Situation," *Philosophy and Rhetoric* 6 (1973): 167.

35. Ibid., 163.

36. Kathleen H. Jamieson, "Antecedent Genre as Rhetorical Constraint," *Quarterly Journal of Speech* 61 (1975): 414.

37. Rick Altman, *The American Film Musical* (Bloomington: Indiana University Press, 1987).

38. Stephen Neale, *Genre* (London: British Film Institute, 1980), 20.

39. Ronald Primeau, *The Rhetoric of Television* (New York: Longman, 1979), 96.

40. Suggested by Charlotte Brunsdon and David Morley, *Everyday Television: "Nationwide"* (London: British Film Institute, 1978), 22.

41. On the other hand, many of these same reflexive devices were used in other television programs of the time, and many more were prominent conventions of live radio news programs in both the 1930s and 1940s. See Culbert, *News for Everyman*, 187, 192.

42. "Now" appears six times: we "stand by now" and wait for Murrow to speak to us "now."

43. We are invited to "see" something factual ("it") and to do so "now." *See It Now* continually evokes the sense that it is indeed a live program, but only Murrow's pieces were done live, because *See It Now* lacked the technology to broadcast live. Nevertheless, the program plays upon the special power of "now"; see Yaeger, "Analysis of 'See It Now,'" 165–74, for more on the program's production.

44. Murrow was, of course, one of the most highly respected news commentators of his era; his reputation rested on his radio broadcasts during the Second World War. Also, at this time, Murrow appeared nightly on CBS radio with a news summary and commentary program; he also hosted the program *Person to Person*, whose audience was several times as large as that of *See It Now*; and he introduced the radio series *This I Believe*, which featured prominent individuals giving their philosophy of life. Murrow was, in a word, a trusted and respected media figure whose ethos helped determine the impact of *See It Now*. Inasmuch as others have devoted much attention to Murrow's ethos, I will accept their conclusions and will focus on other sources of the series' power. See Merron, "Contributions"; Kendrick, *Prime Time*, 20–42. Sarah Kozloff makes some suggestions about the special power that such a narration may have in "Humanizing the Voice of God: Narration in 'The Naked City,'" *Cinema Journal* 23 (1984): 41–53.

45. Culbert, *News for Everyman*, 179–200; Bayley, *McCarthy and the Press*, 195–96.

46. The way the opening sequence works in relation to the rest of the text strikingly resembles the rhetorical figure of metonymy. Kenneth Burke calls metonymy the trope of reduction and says that the "basic strategy in metonymy is to convey some incorporeal or intangible state in terms of the corporeal or tangible." See "Four Master Tropes," in *Grammar of Motives*, 2d ed. (Berkeley: University of California Press, 1969), 508. Our repositioning before the monitors in the control room hints at a whole galaxy of attitudes implicit in the text. In a way, then, we may see the opening sequence of *See It Now* as a metonymy for the strategies in the rest of the text.

## Chapter 4: A Little Picture of an Enormous Problem: "The Case of Milo Radulovich, A0589839"

1. "The Case of Milo Radulovich, A0589839," writ. Edward R. Murrow and Fred W. Friendly, *See It Now*, 20 October 1953, dir. Don Hewitt, prods.

Edward R. Murrow and Fred W. Friendly. All quotations come from Edward R. Murrow and Fred W. Friendly, transcript, Edward R. Murrow Papers, Edwin Ginn Library, Fletcher School of Law and Diplomacy, Tufts University, Medford, Mass.

2. Kendrick, *Prime Time*, 369. For discussions of the era, see Eric F. Goldman, *The Crucial Decade: America, 1945–1955* (New York: Knopf, 1956); see also David Caute, *The Great Fear: The Anti-Communist Purge Under Truman and Eisenhower* (New York: Simon and Schuster, 1978); and chapter 1 above.

3. Friendly, *Due to Circumstances*, 11.

4. Kendrick, *Prime Time*, 37. See also Leab, "Legend Reassessed," 11; Barnouw, *Tube of Plenty*, 175; Sperber, *Murrow*, 418.

5. Yeager, "Analysis," 83–179; Barnouw, *Image Empire*, 46–56; Leab, "Legend Reassessed," 9–16; Murray, "Dimensions," 26–49.

6. Fred W. Friendly, quoted in Murray, "Television's Desperate Moment," 69.

7. John Corner, *Documentary and the Mass Media* (Baltimore, Md.: Edward Arnold, 1986), xiv.

8. Georg Lukacs, "Art and Objective Truth" and "Narrate or Describe?" in *Writer and Critic*, trans. A. Kahn (New York: Grosset and Dunlap, 1970), 25–60, 110–48; Richard Collins, "Seeing Is Believing: The Ideology of Naturalism," in *Documentary and the Mass Media*, ed. Corner, 125–40.

9. Bill Nichols, "The Voice of Documentary," in *Movies and Methods II* (Berkeley: University of California Press, 1985), 262.

10. James A. Wood, "An Application of Rhetorical Theory to Filmic Persuasion" (Ph.D. diss., Cornell University, 1967), 139–43; see also Lawrence Behrens, "The Argument in Film: Applying Rhetorical Theory to Film Criticism," *Journal of University Film and Video Associations* 31 (1979): 3–11; John Harrington, *The Rhetoric of Film* (New York: Holt, Rinehart and Winston, 1973); Roger Silverstone, *The Message of Television: Myth and Narrative in Contemporary Culture* (London: Heinemann, 1981).

11. Corner, *Documentary and the Mass Media*, xi.

12. Burke, "Four Master Tropes," 503–5.

13. Reeves, *Life and Times of Joe McCarthy*, 509.

14. Ibid., 516.

15. This account follows that given in Caute, *The Great Fear*, 274–76.

16. Caute says that during the decade 1947–56, there were 2,700 "security dismissals" and roughly 12,000 "voluntary resignations" within the government; see *The Great Fear*, 276.

17. Reeves, *Life and Times of Joe McCarthy*, 494.

18. Friendly reports that they began collecting film clips on Senator McCarthy and began recording his public statements and hearings in the spring of 1953 but without specific plans to use the material; see *Due to Circumstances*, 4.

19. The following is based on Friendly, *Due to Circumstances*, 5–22. Other sources are Kendrick, *Prime Time*, 35–39; Sperber, *Murrow*, 416–20; Barnouw, *Image Empire*, 46–56, and *Tube of Plenty*, 179–84; Murray, "Dimensions," 34–38.

20. Until this time, the format of *See It Now* was generally limited

to brief ten-minute segments on selected topics. See Barnouw, *Image Empire*, 56.

21. Friendly, *Due to Circumstances*, 10.

22. Murray, "Dimensions," 37; Friendly, *Due to Circumstances*, 11; Kendrick, *Prime Time*, 38.

23. *New York Times*, 20 October 1953, p. B21. Friendly reports that the advertisement cost them $1,500; see *Due to Circumstances*, 11.

24. Friendly, *Due to Circumstances*, 10–12; Friendly is quoted in Murray, "Dimensions," 38.

25. Friendly, *Due to Circumstances*, 13.

26. Barnouw, *Image Empire*, 48.

27. The events that make up the *See It Now* world are drawn from the "news." As a current affairs program, *See It Now* involves the selection and translation of items from the "news." See Brunsdon and Morley, *Everyday Television*, 1–35.

28. With Murrow's turn to the monitors, he joins with us in watching the Radulovich story as it comes into the "control room," and in the presentation of the story over the "live monitor," the text refers to the codes of "live" television. The transition reveals a text that is extremely self-conscious: not only do we watch "together" with Murrow, but are included in a medium that brings us the world, and we are being shown how this medium of television supposedly "works" to show us that world.

29. One of the interesting features of interviews is that we are never able to stop reading the interview on two levels simultaneously. We hear the words the interviewee is saying, but at the same time we are continually constructing an ethical judgment of the person on the basis of the way in which the words are spoken. For example, we learn in this sequence about the specific allegations that are lodged against Milo Radulovich. But we also are encouraged to come to an understanding about Radulovich himself. In the way that he speaks, we are encouraged to read back from the things he says to form an opinion of Milo himself.

30. Aristotle, *Rhetoric and Poetics*, trans. W. Rhys Roberts and Ingram Bywater (New York: Random House, 1954), 242, 238–39.

31. Ibid., 100.

32. H. D. F. Kitto, *Greek Tragedy: A Literary Study* (London: Methuen, 1939).

33. Donald J. Conacher, "Some Dramatic Uses of the Chorus in Greek Tragedy," *University of Toronto Quarterly* 44 (1975): 82.

34. Albert Weiner, "The Function of the Tragic Greek Chorus," *Theatre Journal* 32 (1980): 209.

35. Conacher, "Some Dramatic Uses," 88.

36. Weiner, "Function of the Tragic Greek Chorus," 211.

37. Perhaps she is "subversive"; certainly she is "suspect." Margaret Radulovich Fishman did indeed engage in activities that, by the definition of the day, would be considered provocative. The charges include going to meetings of the Communist front and picketing in support of jailed Communist leaders. See Murray, "Dimensions," 28.

38. It is interesting that in one way, the whole of the text is organized

spatially. Murrow's comments suggest a sort of movement in space rather than any overt logical or argumentative movement. The camera work and the editing also serve the same end.

39. Yaeger suggests that this questioning of Nancy Radulovich by the *See It Now* reporter may have been especially meaningful for the "women in the audience." Indeed, Yaeger may be correct; the emphatic power of the use of the pronoun "we" in the wife's remarks would seem to show that she thinks that both she and Milo are equally involved. See Yaeger, "Analysis of 'See It Now,'" 110.

40. This signification may have to do with the manner of Murrow's delivery. For the most part, Murrow looks down and reads; but at points in the transcript that may be taken as significant, he looks up at the camera. By the mere raising of an eyebrow, Murrow seems to emphasize certain portions of the transcript he reads.

41. Note again that the Air Force is reduced to the status of a passive and impersonal bureaucracy by the use of the third-person pronoun.

42. This quotation seems to be based on similar ones in religious and secular literature, and though it retains a distinctly religious tone, there is no direct source. The most direct biblical reference is Exodus 20:5–7: "For I the Lord thy God am a jealous God, visiting the iniquity of the fathers upon the children unto the third and fourth generation of them that hate me." Secular fragments include: "The Gods visit the sins of the fathers upon the children," Euripides, *Fragments*, No. 970. And "This is thy eld'st son's son, / Infortunate in nothing but in thee. / Thy sins are visited in this poor child." Shakespeare, *King John*, II, i, 177.

43. CBS management, however, was curiously silent after the telecast. Friendly remembers that there was no interference but no feedback either. It was, rather, the CBS affiliates who seemed uneasy about having been given a distinctly controversial program with no warning. Friendly, *Due to Circumstances*, 17.

44. Ibid., 15.

45. "Eyes of Conscience: 'See It Now,'" *Newsweek*, 7 December 1953, p. 66. Yaeger reports that some 12,000 additional letters and telegrams were directed to Secretary of the Air Force Talbott. Yaeger, "Analysis of 'See It Now,'" 239. See also Murray, "Dimensions," 43.

46. Rating figures are from the A. C. Neilsen Company, reported in Yaeger, "Analysis of 'See It Now,'" 172. Coverage refers to the number of television homes able to receive the program in percentage of total U.S. television homes. In other words, 54 percent of those who owned television receivers could have seen the telecast had they wished; for the remaining 46 percent, the local outlet was broadcasting some other program in this time slot. Total television homes for 1953 were approximately 20,400,000, as reported in *Television Factbook*, quoted in Christopher H. Sterling and John M. Kitross, *Stay Tuned: A Concise History of American Broadcasting*, 2d ed. (Belmont, Calif.: Wadsworth, 1990), 535.

47. Jack Gould, "Video Journalism: Treatment of Radulovich Case History by 'See It Now' Is Fine Reporting," *New York Times*, 25 October 1953, p. B13.

48. Robert Kass, *Catholic World*, October 1953, p. 227.

49. Harriet Van Horne, "'See It Now' Review," *New York World Telegram and Sun*, 21 October 1953, p. 27.

50. Sperber, *Murrow*, 418.

51. Gould, "Video Journalism."

52. Sperber, *Murrow*, 20; Bayley, *McCarthy and the Press*, 1; Murrow and Friendly became targets for McCarthy's supporters: the two were held up as examples of the left-wing bias of the national broadcast media.

53. See Barnouw, *Image Empire*, 9–13; Bayley, *McCarthy and the Press*, 212.

54. Kass, *Catholic World*, 227.

55. "Edward R. Murrow, or the 'See' Around Us," *Variety*, 6 January 1954, p. 196. See also "The Hue (Tint) and the Cry (Content): TV's Hope for a Brighter Tomorrow," *Variety*, 6 January 1954, p. 89.

56. "The Case of Lieutenant Radulovich," *Variety*, 28 October 1953, p. 37.

57. Friendly, *Due to Circumstances*, 15.

58. Ibid., 3–4. See also Barnouw, *Image Empire*, 48.

59. Kendrick, *Prime Time*, 369; Seldes, *Public Arts*, 217.

60. Friendly, *Due to Circumstances*, 22. The program was broadcast in March 1954; see chapter 6 below.

61. Burke, "Four Master Tropes," 503.

62. Richard Lanham, *A Handlist of Rhetorical Terms* (Berkeley: University of California Press, 1968), 97.

63. Arthur Quinn, *Figures of Speech* (Salt Lake City, Utah: Gibbs Smith, 1982), 58.

64. Burke, "Four Master Tropes," 503, 508 (emphasis added).

65. Russell Merritt, "The Bashful Hero in American Film of the Nineteen Forties," *Quarterly Journal of Speech* 61 (1975): 129–39.

66. Stuart Hall, "The Determination of News Photographs," in *The Manufacture of News*, ed. Stanley Cohen and Jock Young (Beverly Hills, Calif.: Sage, 1973), 176–90.

67. Brunsdon and Morley, *Everyday Television*, 71–92.

68. The term comes from A. C. H. Smith, *Paper Voices: The Popular Press and Social Change, 1935–65* (Totowa, N.J.: Rowman and Littlefield, 1975), 38.

69. See Culbert, *News for Everyman*; Laurence Rudner, "Born to a New Craft: Edward R. Murrow, 1938–1940," *Journal of Popular Culture* 15 (1981): 106–15.

70. Brunsdon and Morley, *Everyday Television*, 6–9.

71. Ibid., 13–40.

72. André Bazin, "Ontology of the Photographic Image," *What Is Cinema?* vol. 1, trans. Hugh Gray (Berkeley: University of California Press, 1967), 3–16.

73. Bill Nichols, "Questions of Magnitude," in *Documentary and the Mass Media*, ed. John Corner (Baltimore, Md.: Edward Arnold, 1986), 107–25.

74. Barthes, "The Rhetoric of the Image," 32–51.

75. Osborn, "Rhetorical Depiction," 99.

# Chapter 5: Depiction and the Defense of Plurality: "An Argument in Indianapolis"

1. "On Television," *New York Times*, 24 November 1953, p. 41.
2. "An Argument in Indianapolis," writ. Edward R. Murrow and Fred Friendly, *See It Now*, 24 November 1953, dir. Don Hewitt, prods. Edward R. Murrow and Fred W. Friendly. All quotations come from Edward R. Murrow and Fred W. Friendly, transcript, Edward R. Murrow Papers, Edwin Ginn Library, Fletcher School of Law and Diplomacy, Tufts University, Medford, Mass.
3. Joe Wershba, quoted in Sperber, *Murrow*, 420.
4. Friendly says that, "as much as any other single factor, the Radulovich program encouraged us to attempt the McCarthy broadcast"; *Due to Circumstances*, 22.
5. Yaeger, "Analysis of 'See It Now,'" 179.
6. Ibid., 185.
7. This was the first time that the device was used in a *See It Now* program, and the producers considered it "most effective"; Friendly, *Due to Circumstances*, 18. Others called the technique "a highly effective use of the television medium" and said that it allowed "the antagonists to speak for themselves." See Kendrick, *Prime Time*, 39.
8. Seldes, *Public Arts*, 217–19.
9. Joseph Keeley, *The Left-Leaning Antenna: Political Bias in Television* (New Rochelle, N.Y.: Arlington House, 1971), 36.
10. Osborn, "Rhetorical Depiction," 81.
11. "Civil Liberties, Unlimited," *Indianapolis Times*, 19 November 1953, p. 22; "Murrow to Televise Civil Rights Dispute: Top News Analyst to Present City Story to U.S.," *Indianapolis Times*, 20 November 1953, p. 1; both quoted in Murray, "Dimensions," 55. The two coproducers had first attended to the local newspapers after an earlier campaign by zealous Indianapolis anti-Communists. In that dispute, the attempted banning of a book by the Indiana School Book Commission had made the national newswires. Murrow devoted part of his radio commentary of November 13 to a denunciation of the actions of the commission, and the commentary was reprinted on the front page of the *Indianapolis Times* the following day. "Indiana Censor Fears Little Red Riding Hood," *New York Times*, 14 November 1953, pp. A1ff.; "Once upon a Time, Madam, There Just Were No Communists," *Indianapolis Times*, 14 November 1953, p. 1. See Murray, "Dimensions," 49–56.
12. Alan Reitman is quoted in Sperber, *Murrow*, 421–22.
13. The following account is based on Joseph Wershba, "Murrow Versus McCarthy: 'See It Now,'" *New York Times Magazine*, 4 March 1979, pp. 30–36. The account is also mentioned in Friendly, *Due to Circumstances*, 20; Kendrick, *Prime Time*, 42–44; Murray, "Dimensions," 46–48; Sperber, *Murrow*, 414–16.
14. Wershba would later interpret the incident as a contrived warning by McCarthy indicating that, since the Radulovich broadcast, Murrow had become a more vulnerable subject and that perhaps one more action by Murrow would lead to a full-scale attack. As for the Moscow seminar, it was

canceled by the Soviet government before the educators ever arrived. Wershba, "Murrow Versus McCarthy," 35.

15. This may have been a serious miscalculation by the McCarthyites for a number of reasons. At this time, Murrow was near the height of his popularity; he had won a 1953 Emmy as the year's television personality. Furthermore, in October 1953, he began to host the program *Person to Person*, which garnered several times the audience *See It Now* achieved. Murrow became a kind of cultural folk hero, the subject of New Yorker cartoons, and "to Murrow" came into the vernacular as a verb meaning "to engage in social chitchat." Now Murrow was on television two nights a week, had his nightly radio broadcast, and was heard on the *This I Believe* radio series. Whatever else might be said, most historians believe that this exposure gave Murrow such a broad basis of popular esteem and what television calls "acceptance" that, in the coming conflict with Joe McCarthy, he carried ethical appeal and enjoyed an advantage over the senator. Kendrick, *Prime Time*, 35, 43–46, 355, 364–67; Gates, *Air Time*, 30; Wershba, "Murrow Versus McCarthy," 34; Friendly, *Due to Circumstances*, 45; Merron, "Contributions," 108–29.

16. Murray, "Dimensions," 55–56.

17. Friendly, *Due to Circumstances*, 18–19; also Sperber, *Murrow*, 420.

18. Initially, Talbott held a press conference early in the day to make his formal announcement. The *See It Now* statement was filmed before the press conference. Elie Abel, "Talbott Voids Ouster of Reservist Whose Kin Allegedly Had Red Ties," *New York Times*, 25 November 1953, p. A1.

19. Curiously, only one study of this program has noted that the Talbott section might affect an audience watching on that night. The rest treat the Talbott statement as belonging to the Radulovich broadcast rather than as the opening for "An Argument in Indianapolis." See Murray, "Dimensions," 45–46, 48–49; Murray, "Indianapolis," 12–20; Kendrick, *Prime Time*, 38–39; Leab, "Legend Reassessed," 19–20; the lone exception to the rule is Sperber, *Murrow*, 420–23.

20. This illusion is a careful fabrication: after all, the standard procedure that was followed in all cases of security and loyalty board issues was that they were subject to a final review by the Air Force secretary. Murrow said as much in the conclusion to the Radulovich broadcast. Yet this detail has conveniently been omitted from the story here.

21. These concerns—the position and ethos of Murrow and his function as narrator within the *See It Now* text—are more fully and carefully described in chapter 3 above.

22. A noteworthy exception of course occurs in the "chorus" sequence of "The Case of Milo Radulovich," in which we are situated "in" the town of Dexter, Michigan, in an effort to shorten the distance and hence our response to the comments of the townspeople. See chapter 4 above.

23. The following discussion follows closely the categories of film style discussed in Bordwell and Thompson, *Film Art*, 78–85.

24. Murray claims the difference in lighting merely reflected the *See It Now* camera crew's hurried "setup" of lights and microphones at the Legion meeting. See Murray, "Dimensions," 56.

25. The Smith Act or Alien Registration Act, passed in 1940, prohibited "teaching or advocating the overthrow of the government of the United States by force or violence." It was supplemented in 1950 by the Subversive Activities Control Act or the McCarran Act, which required that all Communist organizations register and submit information regarding activities to the Department of Justice; see Franklin S. Haiman, *Freedom of Speech: Issues and Cases* (New York: Random House, 1967), 49.

26. Friendly, *Due to Circumstances*, 18.

27. "Eyes of Conscience," *Newsweek*, 7 December 1953, p. 65.

28. Ibid., 66.

29. Sperber, *Murrow*, 423.

30. "Eyes of Conscience," 67.

31. Yaeger, "Analysis," 173; "The Hue (Tint) and the Cry (Content): TV's Hope for a Brighter Tomorrow," *Variety*, 6 January 1954, p. 89. See also Kendrick, *Prime Time*, 39.

32. Some agree and consider "An Argument in Indianapolis" patently biased. Most of those objections expressed bewilderment at the thought of encapsulating the two lengthy meetings into a total of less than ten minutes for the telecast version. For this reason, the Legion claimed the film was unfairly edited. See "Midwinter Conference to Be Held in January," *Hoosier Legionnaire*, December 1953, p. 6, quoted in Murray, "Dimensions," 75; also "Murrow: The Man, the Myth, and the McCarthy Fighter," *Look*, 24 August 1954, p. 27. An editorial in the *Indianapolis Times* also accused the program of bias; see "ACLU Aimed at Jenner?" *Indianapolis Times*, 30 November 1953, p. A10; all are quoted in Murray, "Dimensions," 75.

33. See "Eyes of Conscience," 65. One national Legion official went so far as to charge that the entire dispute was contrived by Murrow and the ACLU as a "calculated propaganda campaign" and based this odd charge on a brief statement in which reporter Wershba spoke "flippantly" about the Legion's executive meeting. See "Official of Legion Charges Murrow Aids 'Propaganda,'" *Indianapolis Times*, 21 November 1953, p. 2, quoted in Murray, "Dimensions," 75.

34. Osborn, "Rhetorical Depiction," 80.

35. Ibid., 79.

36. Ibid., 100.

37. Ibid., 99.

38. Marcus Tullius Cicero, *De Inventione*, trans. H. M. Hubbell, Loeb Classical Library (Cambridge, Mass.: Harvard University Press, 1976), 185.

39. Ibid., 73, 61.

40. Chaim Perelman and L. Olbrechts-Tyteca, *The New Rhetoric*, trans. John Wilkinson (Notre Dame, Ind.: Notre Dame University Press, 1969), 295. This point was recognized in the classical rhetorics: Aristotle, for instance, recommended that rhetors make the obvious connection between actions and attributes: "For the wrongs a man does to others will correspond to the bad quality or qualities that he himself possesses" (*Rhetoric*, 64); furthermore, Aristotle noted, one could determine from the ends pursued by an individual both the person's intention and the person's character (see *Rhetoric*, 209).

41. Perelman and Olbrechts-Tyteca, *New Rhetoric*, 334.
42. Ibid., 295.
43. Osborn, "Rhetorical Depiction," 98–99.
44. Hall, "Determinations of News Photographs," 188. See also Bazin, "Ontology," 13–24; Barthes, "The Photographic Message," 16–19, and "The Rhetoric of the Image," 32–51.
45. Barthes, "The Photographic Message," 19–20.
46. Barthes surmises that "denotation . . . is powerless to alter opinions: no photograph has ever convinced or refuted anyone (but the photograph can 'confirm')"; see "Photographic Message," 30. See also Hall, "Determinations of News Photographs," 185.
47. By "linguistic message" Barthes, in his example, means the printed text that appears in the still photograph. In considering the film text, I am enlarging the category to include the spoken, verbal remarks of the participants.
48. Barthes, "Photographic Message," 19–20.
49. Hall, "Determinations of News Photographs," 176.
50. Barthes, "Photographic Message," 19–20.
51. Kenneth Burke's method of "cluster agon analysis" furnishes a vocabulary to explain the system of equations found in the connotative message of the photographic image. In Burke's suggestive terminology, every text contains a set of "implicit equations" or "associational clusters." See *Philosophy of Literary Form* (Berkeley: University of California Press, 1973), 20, 69.
52. Michael Osborn, "Archetypal Metaphor in Rhetoric: The Light-Dark Family," *Quarterly Journal of Speech* 53 (1967): 115–26.
53. Murray, "Dimensions," 49–77, especially 67–74.
54. Ibid., 70–73. Murray, in turn, draws upon James Rorty and Moshe Decter, *McCarthy and the Communists* (Boston: Beacon Press, 1954), 51–85, for his list of shared methods. In all, Rorty and Decter identified ten typical McCarthy tactics in the third chapter of their book.
55. This "partisanship" Stuart Hall has characterized as a bias toward the maintenance of the "mode of institutionalized power," the ideology of parliamentary democracy itself. In Hall's view, the disagreements within a society are managed, even celebrated, as "disagreement" but are never allowed within the media to question the structure of the society itself. See Stuart Hall, "Culture, Media, and the Ideological Effect," in *Mass Communication and Society*, ed. Michael Curran et al. (Beverly Hills, Calif.: Sage, 1977), 315–48; and "The 'Unity' of Current Affairs Television," *Popular Television and Film*, ed. Tony Bennett (London: British Film Institute, 1981), 93–115.
56. Suggested in Brunsdon and Morley, *Everyday Television*, 81.
57. These symbolic motifs of the medium are developed in chapter 3, and I expand upon them in my conclusion.
58. Suggested in Barthes, "Photographic Message," 19–20.
59. In the autumn of 1953, the country was treated to one of the most sensational spectacles of the McCarthy era: the current Republican attorney general, Herbert Brownell, accused a Democratic former president of

deliberately hiding and promoting Harry Dexter White, an alleged "Red" spy. Truman denied the charges in a nationwide address; accusing the new administration of fully embracing "McCarthyism" "for political advantage," Truman urged Americans to fight "this evil at every level of our national life." See "Truman Accuses Brownell of Lying; Sees Office Debased in White Case; Says GOP Embraces McCarthyism," *New York Times*, 17 November 1953, p. A1; the next day, Senator McCarthy demanded equal time from the Federal Communications Commission to answer "unprecedented" charges and this "personal attack upon me." FCC officials and the networks quickly complied and granted the senator a full half hour. The senator's reply was scheduled for Tuesday, November 24, directly following *See It Now.* See "McCarthy Bars [*sic*] NBC Time," *New York Times*, 19 November 1953, p. A15; also Reeves, *Life and Times of Joe McCarthy*, 528.

60. "Text of McCarthy Speech to Nation," *New York Times*, 25 November 1953, p. A5; also "McCarthy Accuses Truman in Reply; Says Ex-President Gave Aid to Suspected Red Agents," *New York Times*, 25 November 1953, p. A1; James Reston, "Eisenhower Staff Interprets McCarthy Speech as Attack," *New York Times*, 26 November 1953, p. A1; Reeves, *Life and Times of Joe McCarthy*, 528–29.

61. Friendly, *Due to Circumstances*, 21–22.

# Chapter 6: Argument and the News Documentary: "A Report on Senator Joseph R. McCarthy"

1. "A Report on Senator McCarthy," writ. Edward R. Murrow and Fred W. Friendly, *See It Now*, 9 March 1954, dir. Don Hewitt, prods. Edward R. Murrow and Fred W. Friendly. All quotations come from Edward R. Murrow and Fred W. Friendly, transcript, Edward R. Murrow Papers, Edwin Ginn Library, Fletcher School of Law and Diplomacy, Tufts University, Medford, Mass.

2. Seldes, *The Public Arts*, 226; John Crosby, *New York Herald Tribune*, quoted in Reeves, *Life and Times of Joe McCarthy*, 565.

3. Kendrick, *Prime Time*, 4; see also Barnouw, *The Image Empire*, 53–55; Leab, "Legend Reassessed," 1–3, 25–26.

4. Barnouw, *The Image Empire*, 51.

5. Leab, "Legend Reassessed," 17.

6. Bluem, *Documentary in American Television*, 97.

7. Seldes, *The Public Arts*, 219–22.

8. Bluem, *Documentary in American Television*, 97–98.

9. John Cogley, "The Murrow Show," *Commonweal*, 26 March 1954, p. 618.

10. Michael Murray concludes that the program was "unfair" and "not objective"; see Murray, "The Persuasive Dimensions of 'See It Now's' Report on Senator Joseph R. McCarthy," *Today's Speech* 22 (1975): 18 (hereafter cited as "Report"); on the basis of his interviews, Murray Yaeger submits that the program was not objective because "it was Murrow's intent to show only one side of the situation." Yaeger, "Analysis of 'See It

Now,'" 101; a noteworthy exception to this trend is Robert L. Ivie, "Diffusing Cold War Demagoguery: Murrow Versus McCarthy on 'See It Now,'" in *Cold War Rhetoric*, ed. Martin Medhurst, Robert L. Ivie, Philip Wander, and Robert L. Scott (Westport, Conn.: Greenwood Press, 1990), 81–102; Ivie investigates the metaphoric patterns used by *See It Now* and accounts for the partial appeal of the program in the way that negative archetypal patterns are linked to Senator McCarthy and more positive ones to Murrow.

11. For a review of the traditional distinction between reportage and argument, see Robert A. Hackett, "Decline of a Paradigm? Bias and Objectivity in News Media Studies," *Critical Studies in Mass Communication* 1 (1984): 229–59.

12. Discussed in chapter 1 above.

13. "Radio, TV Take the Stage in New McCarthy Tempest," *Broadcasting/Telecasting*, 46 (15 March 1954): 31.

14. This account follows the description in Reeves, *Life and Times of Joe McCarthy*, 535–59; see also Bayley, *McCarthy and the Press*, 187–92; John E. O'Connor, "Edward R. Murrow's 'Report on Senator McCarthy': Image as Artifact," *Film and History* 16 (1986): 55–72.

15. Quoted in Reeves, *Life and Times of Joe McCarthy*, 544.

16. Ibid., 547.

17. Adlai Stevenson, "Democratic Address to the Nation," *New York Times*, 7 March 1954, p. A18.

18. *New York Times*, 9 March 1954, p. A7.

19. Friendly, *Due to Circumstances*, 28–30. See also Kendrick, *Prime Time*, 46–71; Barnouw, *Image Empire*, 46–56; Oshinsky, *Conspiracy*, 398.

20. See chapter 4 above.

21. Unlike other *See It Now* projects, which were largely written by Friendly and approved by Murrow, this broadcast was apparently dictated word for word entirely by Murrow. See Wershba, "Murrow Versus McCarthy," 36.

22. Friendly, *Due to Circumstances*, 30.

23. Wershba, "Murrow Versus McCarthy," 35.

24. Ibid.

25. Kendrick, *Prime Time*, 51.

26. As work continued on the program, the senior executives at CBS apparently took no part. Indeed, the autonomy enjoyed by Murrow and Friendly has been the source of much speculation. Clearly, both were answerable to senior executives, but because of Murrow's wartime friendship with Chairman of the Board William S. Paley, and Murrow's membership on the CBS board of directors, it seems reasonable to suppose that they were aware of *See It Now*'s intentions; see Murray, "Dimensions," 108. For instance, while Friendly (*Due to Circumstances*, 35) says he never knew of management's direct knowledge of their intention to do the McCarthy program, Paley telephoned Murrow and pledged support prior to the broadcast. Kendrick (*Prime Time*, 49) maintains that Paley was aware and "heartily approving" of the McCarthy program, that Murrow visited him the day before the broadcast, and that Paley's only recommendation was that McCarthy be given equal time to reply. Wershba ("Murrow Versus

McCarthy,'" 36) agrees. He says that no program ever got on the air without the knowledge of some members of senior management. Murrow's latest biographer, A. M. Sperber, also mentions confusion over what CBS executives knew; see Sperber, *Murrow,* 435–36.

27. *New York Times,* 9 March 1954, p. A34.

28. The reminiscence of the evening of the broadcast is found in Friendly, *Due to Circumstances,* 36–37.

29. Gaye Tuchman, "Objectivity as Strategic Ritual: An Examination of Newsmen's Notions of Objectivity," *American Journal of Sociology* 77 (1972): 664.

30. Ernst H. Gombrich, *Art and Illusion* (New York: Pantheon Books, 1960), 41–51, 363–91.

31. Erving Goffman reminds us that as soon as we accept representational conventions as fact, then reality becomes vulnerable to manipulation. *Frame Analysis* (New York: Harper and Row, 1974), 450.

32. Tuchman, "Objectivity," 674–76.

33. Ibid., 669.

34. Of course, slow motion or instant replays are used often in contemporary television. But they are always labeled as such and usually both by the commentator and by on-screen graphics.

35. Gaye Tuchman, *Making News: A Study of the Construction of Reality* (New York: Free Press, 1978), 110.

36. Tuchman, "Objectivity," 665.

37. See chapter 3 above; see also Tuchman, *Making News,* 107–10.

38. Aristotle, *Rhetoric,* trans. Ingram Bywater (New York: Modern Library, 1954), 96; Quintilian, *Institutio Oratoria,* vol. 3, trans. H. E. Butler (Cambridge, Mass.: Harvard University Press, 1958), 333.

39. Perelman and Olbrechts-Tyteca, *The New Rhetoric,* 205–7.

40. Emphasized in William R. Brown, "Will Rogers: Ironist as Persuader," *Communication Monographs* 39 (1972): 183.

41. Quintilian, vol. 3, p. 333.

42. Wayne C. Booth, *A Rhetoric of Irony* (Chicago: University of Chicago Press, 1974), 47–86, 175.

43. This seeming incongruency has been noted by other analysts though nowhere characterized as "ironic." See, for instance, O'Connor, "Edward R. Murrow's 'Report on Senator McCarthy,'" 59.

44. Others have commented similarly on this point; see ibid., 60–61.

45. Likewise noted in ibid., 61.

46. Booth calls such a form "stable irony." See Booth, *Rhetoric of Irony,* 1–26.

47. Ibid., 29.

48. Goffman, *Frame Analysis,* 40–82.

49. Wil A. Linkugel has tentatively suggested some features of rhetorical accusation or what he calls an "anti-ethos rhetoric." Linkugel places the burden upon the maker of an accusation to appear to treat the accused "fairly" and to prove the attack justified. Linkugel thus proposes that accusatory rhetors themselves are on trial and as a result draw upon the sharp contrast between abstract notions of good and evil and use them to

play on the patriotic feelings of the audience. Linkugel has also briefly noted that irony is a strategy in accusatory rhetoric. See Linkugel and Susan S. Huxman, "Political Fallout of the New Deal: Accusations and Apologies from a General, a Senator, and a Priest" (paper presented at the Speech Communication Association Conference, Chicago, Illinois, 1986). Except for mention in studies of apologia and in Halford R. Ryan's concept of accusation and defense as "speech set," little else has been written about accusation as a rhetorical genre. See Ryan's "Kategoria and Apologia: On Their Rhetorical Criticism as a Speech Set," *Quarterly Journal of Speech* 68 (1982): 254–61, and a companion piece, "Baldwin Versus Edward VIII: A Case Study in Kategoria and Apologia," *Southern Speech Communication Journal* 49 (1984): 125–34.

50. Booth, *Rhetoric of Irony*, 12.

51. The *Chicago Tribune* was one of the most conservative of newspapers and one of McCarthy's staunchest backers. At the time, this irony could hardly have been lost on some in the audience. Bayley, *McCarthy and the Press*, 36, 46.

52. E. D. Hirsch, Jr. makes a similar argument and claims that all interpretation must pivot around the expectations and requirements of genres or "types." See *Validity in Interpretation* (New Haven: Yale University Press, 1967), 68–126.

53. Linkugel and Huxman, "Political Fallout of the New Deal," n.p.

54. For discussions of victimage and, especially, mortification as elements of dramatism and as rhetorical strategies, see Kenneth Burke, *Permanence and Change*, 3d ed. (Berkeley: University of California Press, 1984), 274–94; *Rhetoric of Motives*, 13–15, 252–66; *Rhetoric of Religion* (Berkeley: University of California Press, 1979), 208–12. See also William H. Rueckert, *Kenneth Burke and the Drama of Human Relations*, 2d ed. (Berkeley: University of California Press, 1982), 128–62.

55. Campbell and Jamieson define enactment as a type of argument in which the speaker "incarnates the argument, is the proof of what is said." Karlyn Kohrs Campbell and Kathleen Jamieson, "Form and Genre in Rhetorical Criticism: An Introduction," in *Form and Genre: Shaping Rhetorical Action* (Falls Church, Va.: Speech Communication Association, 1978), 9.

56. "The Scorched Air: Murrow Versus Senator McCarthy," *Newsweek*, 22 March 1954, p. 88. Ratings from the A. C. Neilsen Company, quoted in Yaeger, "Analysis," 174. "Coverage" refers to the number of television homes able to receive the program in percentage of total U.S. television homes. Total television homes in 1954 were approximately 26,000,000; reported in *Television Factbook*, quoted in Sterling and Kitross, *Stay Tuned*, 535.

57. Friendly, *Due to Circumstances*, 42.

58. Bayley, *McCarthy and the Press*, 195. See also the *New York Times*, 11 March 1954, p. A12; similar figures quoted in Reeves, *Life and Times of Joe McCarthy*, 563; Yaeger, "Analysis," 173–74; Murray, "Dimensions," 120.

59. Reeves, *Life and Times of Joe McCarthy*, 564. Wershba reports that even today the CBS archives contain twenty-two boxes, each holding 750–

1,000 communications; eighteen marked "favorable" and the remaining four "unfavorable." See Wershba, "Murrow Versus McCarthy," 37.

60. Reeves characterizes the response as "ecstatic" (*Life and Times of Joe McCarthy*, 565); see also O'Connor, "Edward R. Murrow's 'Report on Senator McCarthy,'" 68.

61. "TV in Controversy," *Newsweek*, 22 March 1954, p. 50.

62. John Crosby, "McCarthy and the Networks," *New York Herald Tribune*, 11 March 1954, p. A18. See also *Variety*, 17 March 1954, p. 34; "The Baited Trap," *Time*, 29 March 1954, p. 77; Jack Gould, "Murrow Versus McCarthy," *New York Times*, 11 March 1954, p. B38; and "TV and McCarthy: Network's Decision and Murrow Show Represent Advance for Medium," *New York Times*, 14 March 1954, p. X13; "When Television Came of Age," *St. Louis Post Dispatch*, 21 March 1954, p. E2.

63. Murray, "Dimensions," 110; Yaeger, "Analysis," 174.

64. *Variety*, 17 March 1954, p. 34.

65. Jack Gould, "Murrow Versus McCarthy," *New York Times*, 11 March 1954, p. B38; and "TV and McCarthy: Network's Decision and Murrow Show Represent Advance for Medium," *New York Times*, 14 March 1954, p. X13.

66. Gould, "Murrow Versus McCarthy," B38.

67. Crosby, *New York Herald Tribune*, 11 March 1954, p. A18.

68. "When Television Came of Age," *St. Louis Post Dispatch*, 21 March 1954, p. E2.

69. "Murrow Wins the Nation's Applause," *Broadcasting and Telecasting* 46 (15 March 1954): 33. This latter point was later emphatically denied by CBS.

70. Bayley, *McCarthy and the Press*, 195.

71. Sperber, *Murrow*, 446.

72. Reeves, *Life and Times of Joe McCarthy*, 561.

73. Barry Gray, "Television," *New York Post*, 11 March 1954, p. B6. See also Murray, "Dimensions," 160–61; Murray, "Report," 18; Kendrick, *Prime Time*, 54–55. James Baughman reviewed accounts of the telecast and could find no historian explicitly claiming that the broadcast was a factor in McCarthy's eventual censure. Baughman, "See It Now," 106–15.

74. Edwin Bayley reaches the same conclusion. He called Murrow's final statement: "a relatively mild editorial statement, hardly critical of McCarthy; it was almost defensive, a justification for making such a program. It was not nearly as strong as the editorials that had appeared regularly in some newspapers for four years. In some ways, the most remarkable thing about the program was that it was so late. Even the conservative Republican newspapers had begun to turn on McCarthy as it became apparent that he was willing to fight Eisenhower in the same way that he had fought Truman. But television had been so cowed by the Red-baiters, the blacklisters, and the fearful sponsors that Murrow's cautious courage seemed heroic"; see Bayley, *McCarthy and the Press*, 193.

75. Gould, "Scorched Air," 89.

76. This argument is made most cogently, albeit polemically, in Richard H. Rovere, *Senator Joe McCarthy* (New York: Harcourt, 1959), 167–70.

77. Goffman, *Frame Analysis*, 40–83.

78. Brown, "Will Rogers," 183–84.

79. It would be possible to argue that the pull between objectivity and accusation and their unity via irony is a result of the conditions of the industry itself. Facing the Fairness Doctrine, so this argument goes, would force *See It Now* to conform or to at least appear to conform to those fairness standards. Thus the institution of broadcasting and the situations of its historical conditions are of prime importance.

80. Booth, *Rhetoric of Irony*, 81.

81. Quintilian, vol. 3, pp. 471–73. See also vol. 3, pp. 349–51; vol. 2, p. 475; vol. 3, p. 333.

82. Burke, "Four Master Tropes," 503–17.

83. Ibid., 514.

84. See Bell, *The End of Ideology*; Hofstadter, "The Pseudo-Conservative Revolt," 75–96; Parsons, "Social Strains in America (1955)," 209–30; Viereck, "The Revolt Against the Elite," 161–84.

85. Edwin Black, "Ideological Justifications," *Quarterly Journal of Speech* 70 (1984): 150.

86. Kathleen Jamieson, "Generic Constraints and the Rhetorical Situation," *Philosophy and Rhetoric* 6 (1973): 167, 163; and "Antecedent Genre as Rhetorical Constraint," *Quarterly Journal of Speech* 61 (1975): 414; Kathleen Hall Jamieson and Karlyn Kohrs Campbell, "Rhetorical Hybrids: Fusions of Generic Elements," *Quarterly Journal of Speech* 68 (1982): 146–57.

# Chapter 7: Naturalism and Television Documentary: "Annie Lee Moss Before the McCarthy Committee"

1. "Annie Lee Moss Before the McCarthy Committee," writ. Edward R. Murrow and Fred W. Friendly, *See It Now*, 16 March 1954, dir. Don Hewitt, prods. Edward R. Murrow and Fred W. Friendly. All quotations come from Edward R. Murrow and Fred W. Friendly, transcript, Edward R. Murrow Papers, Edwin Ginn Library, Fletcher School of Law and Diplomacy, Tufts University, Medford, Mass.

2. Friendly, *Due to Circumstances*, 50.

3. *Time*, 29 March 1954, p. 77.

4. Max Wylie, *Clear Channels: Television and the American People* (New York: Funk and Wagnalls, 1955), 56.

5. Edward R. Murrow and Fred W. Friendly, eds., *See It Now* (New York: Simon and Schuster, 1955), 54.

6. Roy Cohn, however, disagreed. He said the broadcast made Mrs. Moss a heroine by stressing the theme "that a poor, innocent Negro woman can, through mistaken identity, be wrongfully accused of Communist ties." Cohn argued that such a conclusion was unjust and misrepresented the facts of the hearing. Furthermore, Cohn contended that the Annie Lee Moss who testified that March day was indeed the same Annie Lee Moss who was listed on Communist party roles. See Roy Cohn, *McCarthy* (New York: New American Library, 1968), 122–24.

7. Marya Mannes, "The People Versus McCarthy," *Reporter*, 27 April 1954, p. 26.

8. Seldes, *Public Arts*, 223.

9. John Harrington, *The Rhetoric of Film* (New York: Holt, Rinehart and Winston, 1973), 89. Harrington argues that the narrator is always the camera in one sense—that is, the camera substitutes for the narrator. In contrast, Annette Kuhn argues in "Camera I" that the camera substitutes for the spectator and so defines a place within the film for the spectator. See "Camera I," *Screen* 19, 2 (1978): 71–83.

10. Bill Nichols, *Ideology and the Image* (Bloomington, Ind.: Indiana University Press, 1981), 182. What Nichols means by "address" is the "pattern of sound/image relationship that specifies somewhat different "places" or attitudes for the viewer.

11. Nichols, *Representing Reality*, 36.

12. Ibid., 37.

13. Ibid., 41.

14. Nichols, *Ideology and Image*, 183.

15. Nichols, *Representing Reality*, 42.

16. Nichols, *Ideology and Image*, 208.

17. Other analysts of documentary persuasion have acknowledged a similar bifurcation within the genre. Like Nichols, William Stott identified two kinds of documentary persuasion, which he called direct and indirect. In the first, facts are put before the audience as forcefully as possible; and in the indirect, the text substitutes another person in the place of the auditor, and we come to our realization by participating or by observing the effects upon another in a sort of vicarious participation. See Stott, *Documentary Expression*, 26, 33. Likewise, James Wood, one of the earliest analysts of visual persuasion within the rhetorical tradition, identified two types of filmic persuasion. Wood labeled the two modes, "argumentation" ("the use of a 'predigested' combination of speech and visuals which interweave assertion, evidence and emotional amplification") and "discovery," which Wood describes as "the vicarious exploration of life, a facsimile of experience . . . , a subtle way of making the viewer conclude something based on his own experience." See Wood, "Application of Rhetorical Theory to Filmic Persuasion," 270.

18. John Fiske, *Television Culture* (New York: Methuen, 1987), 108.

19. Roland Barthes, *S/Z*, trans. Richard Miller (New York: Hill and Wang, 1974), 18–21.

20. See chapter 6 above.

21. W. H. Lawrence, "McCarthy Asserts He Has New 'Red' to Link to Army," *New York Times*, 23 February 1954, p. A1.

22. Murray, "Dimensions," 128–29.

23. The Markward testimony on February 24, 1954, was the first meeting of the McCarthy subcommittee to be attended by its Democratic members since July 1953. The Democrats ended their boycott of McCarthy's often sensational hearings.

24. W. H. Lawrence, "McCarthy Says Red Decodes Secrets, But Army Denies It," *New York Times*, 24 February 1954, p. A1.

25. Reeves, *Life and Times of Joe McCarthy*, 548.

26. McCarthy is quoted in ibid., 550.

27. "Cohn Scored When Woman Denies McCarthy's Charges," *New York Times*, 11 March 1954, p. A1.

28. For a summary of the national events leading up to March 11, 1954, see chapter 6 above.

29. McCarthy is quoted in Sperber, *Murrow*, 443.

30. "Senator Attacks, Claims Murrow Tainted," *New York Times*, 12 March 1954, p. A11.

31. Kendrick, *Prime Time*, 57.

32. "Turn of Tide?" *New York Times*, 14 March 1954, p. D1.

33. Reeves, *Life and Times of Joe McCarthy*, 575.

34. Sperber, *Murrow*, 447.

35. "Turn of Tide?" D1.

36. "Murrow Defends His '35 Role," *New York Times*, 13 March 1954, p. A8.

37. Sperber, *Murrow*, 444.

38. "Turn of Tide?" D1.

39. Murray, "Dimensions," 130.

40. Friendly, *Due to Circumstances*, 45.

41. Ibid., 47.

42. Ibid., 51.

43. An exception is "A Report on Senator McCarthy"; see chapter 4 above.

44. See chapter 4 above.

45. That an audience might assent to this invitation to side with Mrs. Moss is not surprising. The tactics that *See It Now* uses to develop the motif of innocence around Moss have a long history in the teaching of oratory. The ancient Greek logographers developed the quite sophisticated strategy of adapting the style of language and choice of imagery to suit the character of the speaker for whom he wrote. So, if one was a farmer, for instance, the logographer would craft an oration suited to the audience's expectations of the style and character of a farmer—using images and examples from farm life and affecting a simple and bucolic character. The aim, of course, is to avoid any contradiction between the portrayal of the character of the speaker and his language. And when used in specific situations, this strategy, *ethopoeia*, fosters a powerful and seemingly artless sort of proof by character. Ethopoeia as a rhetorical strategy was highly developed by the students of Antiphon, especially the orator and logographer Lysias.

46. McCarthy's "rather important appointment" is, of course, his appearance on Fulton Lewis's radio program later that evening. Some analysts have attributed the senator's obviously distracted demeanor during the Moss testimony to the events of the previous week and to the forthcoming national radio broadcast.

47. Sergei Eisenstein, "Montage of Attractions, An Essay," trans. Jay Leyda, in *The Film Sense* (New York: Harcourt, 1975), 217–29.

48. The section is from Eisenhower's address before the National B'nai B'rith, which was telecast live on all television and radio networks. The meeting was originally designed as an opportunity for Eisenhower to speak

out against Senator McCarthy. But with characteristic caution, the president never mentioned the senator by name. Most considered his speech a disappointment. See Barnouw, *Image Empire*, 13.

49. "Coverage" refers to the percentage of television homes able to receive the broadcast over local stations; the numbers of viewers are Neilsen television estimates; reported in Yaeger, "Analysis," 176. The total number of television homes for 1954 was approximately 26,000,000, reported in *Television Factbook*, quoted in Sterling and Kitross, *Stay Tuned*, 535.

50. Kendrick, *Prime Time*, 60; see also Reeves, *Life and Times of Joe McCarthy*, 569.

51. Television's power to take over events was initially described in Kurt Lang and Gladys Engel Lang, *Politics and Television* (Chicago: Quadrangle Books, 1968), 297.

52. Reeves, *Life and Times of Joe McCarthy*, 534.

53. John Crosby, "The Aroma of Decency," *New York Herald Tribune*, 19 March 1954, p. A19; Murray, "Dimensions," 138.

54. Reeves, *Life and Times of Joe McCarthy*, 534, 569.

55. Kendrick, *Prime Time*, 36.

56. Quoted in Murray, "Desperate Moment," 71.

57. Friendly, *Due to Circumstances*, 51.

58. Hall et al., "The 'Unity' of Current Affairs Television," 102.

59. See also chapter 3 above.

60. Collins, "Seeing Is Believing," 125–40.

61. Nichols, *Ideology and the Image*, 241.

62. Jeanne Allen, "Self-Reflexivity in Documentary," *Cine-Tracts* 1 (1977): 37.

63. Lang and Lang, *Politics and Television*, 34.

64. Ibid., 148.

65. See chapter 4 above.

66. Used in a slightly different fashion in Barthes, "Rhetoric of the Image," 43–45.

67. Wood hints at this point in his dissertation, though Wood does not base his distinction upon the place that the text constructs for its viewers. See Wood, "Application of Rhetorical Theory to Filmic Persuasion," chap. 1.

68. In the progression of the *See It Now* series, the first programs use the "private" space and correspond more to a narrative form. It might be that it is necessary in order for the campaign against McCarthyism to succeed that narrative precede argument, that the victims be shown before the victimizer is refuted.

69. Barnouw, *Documentary*, 113–39; see also Stott, *Documentary Expression*.

70. Bluem, *Documentary in American Television*, 104.

71. Stott, *Documentary Expression*, 46–67. Likewise, this strategy of revealing a wide canvas by focusing upon the small detail is a feature that many analysts have noted in the oeuvre of Murrow himself, some taking this as one of Murrow's lasting contributions to broadcast journalism: to capture the larger meaning of events by concentrating on smaller details of human expression. See Rudner, "Born to a New Craft," 98.

72. Brunsdon and Morley, *Everyday Television*, 10.

73. Ibid., 34. See also the discussion of depiction in chapter 3 and the source of pathos in such depiction, found in chapter 2 above.

74. Nichols, *Ideology and the Image*, 264.

75. Ibid., 183. The term "diegesis" comes from the Greek for "narrative" and refers to the creation of a fictional reality verisimilar to the world.

76. Suggested by Charles Affron, "Reading the Fiction of Non-fiction: William Wyler's 'Memphis Belle,'" *Quarterly Review of Film Studies* 7 (1982): 54.

77. Peter J. Rabinowitz, *Before Reading: Narrative Conventions and the Politics of Interpretation* (Ithaca, N.Y.: Cornell University Press, 1987), 19.

78. See Paul H. Weaver, "Newspaper News and Television News," in *Television as a Social Force: New Approaches to TV Criticism*, ed. Douglass Cater and Richard Adler (New York: Praeger, 1975), 84.

79. Ibid., 83–84.

80. Todd Gitlin, *The Whole World Is Watching* (Berkeley: University of California Press, 1980), 146.

81. Himmelstein, *Television Myth*, ix–xvi.

82. James Novak, "Television Shapes the Soul," in *Television as a Social Force: New Approaches to TV Criticism*, ed. Douglass Cater and Richard Adler (New York: Praeger, 1975), 14.

83. The comedic as it develops within this text has an important and overlooked appeal. The charges against Annie Lee Moss are clearly not to be taken seriously, as they are the result of a series of miscalculations and fumbles. The text invites our seriocomic response for persuasive effect. Once we are able to join together in laughing at the wild accusations and innuendos of the Communist hunters, then we have both defused their "power" over our imagination and have also "come together" in a common bond. This bonding and satirizing effect of the laughter and comedy in the text undercuts McCarthyism as well. While deadly serious and corrosive of our state of affairs, McCarthyism, insofar as we are made to laugh at its representatives, is shown to be neither omnipotent nor invincible.

84. Affron, "Reading the Fiction of Non-fiction," 54.

85. E. Ann Kaplan, "Theory and Practice of the Realist Documentary Form in 'Harlan County, U.S.A.,'" in *"Show Us Life": Toward a History and Aesthetics of the Committed Documentary*, ed. Thomas Waugh (Metuchen, N.J.: Scarecrow Press, 1984), 218.

86. Murray, "Dimensions," 162–71.

87. Hal Himmelstein, *Television Myth and the American Mind* (New York: Praeger, 1984), 224.

88. Suggested in William G. Kirkwood, "Story-Telling and Self-Confrontation: Parables as Communication Strategies," *Quarterly Journal of Speech* 69 (1983): 68.

89. *See It Now* presented other telecasts dealing with aspects of "The Great Fear" spread over the next year and a half. On April 6, 1954, less than a month after "Annie Lee Moss," Senator McCarthy took up *See It Now*'s offer for reply and appeared in a filmed speech. Describing Murrow as "a symbol, the leader and the cleverest of the jackal pack which is always

found at the throat of anyone who dares to expose individual Communists and traitors," McCarthy quoted the *Daily Worker* citing *See It Now* among its "Best Bets" listing for TV and implicated Murrow as a "glib" supporter of those who condoned subversion. He attacked Murrow's statement from the "Report" about giving comfort to the enemy; he said that, if this were the case, he, McCarthy ought not to be in the Senate. "If on the other hand Mr. Murrow is giving comfort to our enemies, he ought not to be brought into the homes of millions of Americans by the Columbia Broadcasting System." On *See It Now* a week later, Murrow responded with a short rebuttal. Saying he needed "no lectures from the junior senator from Wisconsin as to the dangers of Communism," Murrow asked his audience, "Who has helped the Communist cause and who has served his country better, Senator McCarthy or I? I would like to be remembered by the answer to that question." The direct exchange between *See It Now* and the senator went no further—after the March 11 report McCarthy was embroiled with the army and was on the defensive. Several other telecasts that dealt with McCarthyism followed. Preceding Murrow's rebuttal, on April 13, 1954, *See It Now* broadcast "Communism: Internal and External," featuring two long interviews, the "external" situation described by the commander of the North Atlantic Treaty Organization in Europe, the "internal" by the archbishop of Chicago. Eric Barnouw says that *See It Now* offered a subsequent telecast on McCarthyism—"to many viewers the greatest of the programs." It developed from McCarthy's "Reply," in which McCarthy had, as usual, shifted to new, sensational charges about the hydrogen bomb. Soon after, physicist Robert Oppenheimer had been stripped of his security clearance. On January 4, 1955, *See It Now* offered "A Conversation with Dr. J. Robert Oppenheimer," a long filmed interview made at the Institute for Advanced Study in Princeton, New Jersey. Oppenheimer did not refer to the security ruling but discussed on a philosophic plane the implications of increasing government control over research and its bearing on the freedom of the human mind and the future of men on earth. See Barnouw, *The Image Empire*, 53.

# Conclusion: Documentary as Rhetoric? Fiction? Ideology?

1. Bill Nichols, "Documentary Theory and Practice," *Screen* 17, 4 (1976): 34–48.
2. Waugh, *"Show Us Life,"* xxi.
3. Corner, *Documentary and the Mass Media*, vii.
4. Roger Silverstone, "The Right to Speak: On a Poetic for Television Documentary," *Media, Culture, and Society* 5 (1983): 145.
5. Eagleton, *Literary Theory*, 206.
6. Dai Vaughan, "The Space Between Shots," *Screen* 15, 1 (1974): 80.
7. A similar question is posed in Silverstone, "The Right to Speak," 145.
8. Nichols, *Representing Reality*, 154.

9. William Stott suggests that radio did the same thing: presenting the facts firsthand and also using the commentator. The facts and the observer reinforced each other's credibility: if one was believed, it was hard not to believe the other; if listeners accepted a report, they accepted the observer's tone as well. Given Murrow's and Friendly's background in radio, this result is not so surprising; Stott, *Documentary Expression*, 84.

10. The following is parallel to the speculations found in Kauffman, "The Reflexive Form in Rhetoric," 233–40.

11. Bayley, *McCarthy and the Press*, 195.

12. See Kendrick, *Prime Time*, 35; see also Murray, "Dimensions," 162–71.

13. Baughman, "'See It Now' and Television's Golden Age," 106–15; see also my introduction above.

14. Bayley, *McCarthy and the Press*, 202. See also chapter 6 above.

15. Ibid., 195.

16. Barnouw, *Documentary*, 225; see also chapter 2 above.

17. Bayley, *McCarthy and the Press*, 195.

18. Ibid., 85.

19. Ibid., 176.

20. Peter J. Rabinowitz, *Before Reading: Narrative Conventions and the Politics of Interpretation* (Ithaca, N.Y.: Cornell University Press, 1987), 24.

21. Geertz, "Ideology as a Cultural System," 193.

22. This argument is developed in considerable detail in chapter 4.

23. Himmelstein, *Television Myth and the American Mind*, 217.

24. For discussion of pluralism as a political philosophy, see Robert P. Wolff, *The Poverty of Liberalism* (Boston: Beacon Press, 1968), especially chapter 1; see also Bernard Crick, *In Defence of Politics*, 2d ed. (Chicago: University of Chicago Press, 1972).

25. This point is developed in chapter 6 above.

26. This notion is developed along slightly different lines in chapter 4 above.

27. Hall, "Culture, Media, and the 'Ideological Effect,'" 340–41.

28. Ibid., 342.

29. Gitlin, "Prime Time Ideology," 251–52, 263–64.

30. Todd Gitlin, *The Whole World Is Watching*, 291–92.

31. Ibid., 52.

32. Ibid.

33. Martin Medhurst and Thomas Benson, *Rhetorical Dimensions in Media* (Dubuque, Iowa: Kendall-Hunt, 1984), xi.

34. While this division is nowadays certainly blurring, it remains active in the margins of discussion about the rhetorical dimensions of art and the media; see ibid., xi–xix.

35. Nichols, *Representing Reality*, 105–98.

36. In what follows, the intertextual relationships are suggested in the argument advanced by Bill Nichols, "Questions of Magnitude," 107–22. Also, see Nichols, "History, Myth, and Narrative in Documentary," *Film Quarterly* 41 (Fall 1987): 9–20. However, I develop my line of explication taking a different perspective.

37. While I do not want to imply here that the documentary text presents an "innocent" and "objective" image of the real, it does seem clear that the documentary text has its grounding in ontology of the photographic image. See Bazin, "Ontology of the Photographic Image," 9–14.

38. Corner, *Documentary and the Mass Media*, viii.

39. John Caughie, "Progressive Television and Documentary Drama," in *Popular Television and Film*, ed. Tony Bennett, Susan Boyd-Bowman, Colin Mercer, and Janet Woollacott (London: British Film Institute, 1981), 343.

40. Barthes, *S/Z*, 9; see also Nichols, *Representing Reality*, 127.

41. Corner, *Documentary and the Mass Media*, x.

42. The differences between poetic language and ordinary language that I sketch in this section are grounded in a traditional approach whose distinctions are helpful to my discussion. Certainly, these distinctions imply theoretical issues considerably more complex than I suggest here. Nevertheless, the documentary does indeed unarguably fit into certain classes of discourse that have observable features (e.g., closure, consistency, and referentiality).

43. Murray Krieger, "Mediation, Language, and Vision in the Reading of Literature," in *Interpretation: Theory and Practice*, ed. C. S. Singleton (Baltimore, Md.: Johns Hopkins University Press, 1969), 267–79.

44. Fiske, *Television Culture*, 114.

45. Nichols, *Representing Reality*, 185.

46. Affron, "Reading the Fiction of Non-fiction," 55.

47. Fredric Jameson, *The Political Unconscious: Narrative as a Socially Symbolic Act* (Ithaca, N.Y.: Cornell University Press, 1981), 39–99.

48. Hackett, "Decline of a Paradigm?" 252.

49. Nicholas Garnham, "TV Documentary and Ideology," *Screen* 13, 2 (1972): 110.

50. Nichols, *Representing Reality*, 80.

51. Sol Worth, *Studying Visual Communication* (Philadelphia: University of Pennsylvania Press, 1981), 185–204; this idea is also developed in Garnham, "TV Documentary and Ideology," 111.

52. Garnham, "TV Documentary and Ideology," 111.

53. Collins, "Seeing Is Believing," 128.

54. Garnham, "TV Documentary and Ideology," 111.

55. Ibid.

56. Hackett, "Decline of a Paradigm?" 249.

57. Fiske, *Television Culture*, 116.

58. Nichols, "Questions of Magnitude," 121.

# Bibliography

## Primary Works

"An Argument in Indianapolis." Produced/written by Edward R. Murrow and Fred W. Friendly. Edward R. Murrow Papers, Edwin Ginn Library, Fletcher School of Law and Diplomacy, Tufts University, Medford, Massachusetts. Originally broadcast on the CBS Television Network, 24 November 1953.

"Annie Lee Moss Before the McCarthy Committee." Produced/written by Edward R. Murrow and Fred W. Friendly. Edward R. Murrow Papers, Edwin Ginn Library, Fletcher School of Law and Diplomacy, Tufts University, Medford, Massachusetts. Originally broadcast on the CBS Television Network, 16 March 1954.

"The Case of Milo Radulovich, A0589839." Produced/written by Edward R. Murrow and Fred W. Friendly. Edward R. Murrow Papers, Edwin Ginn Library, Fletcher School of Law and Diplomacy, Tufts University, Medford, Massachusetts. Originally broadcast on the CBS Television Network, 20 October 1953.

"A Report on Senator Joseph R. McCarthy." Produced/written by Edward R. Murrow and Fred W. Friendly. Edward R. Murrow Papers, Edwin Ginn Library, Fletcher School of Law and Diplomacy, Tufts University, Medford, Massachusetts. Originally broadcast on the CBS Television Network, 9 March 1954.

# Secondary Works

Adams, John G. *Without Precedent: The Story of the Death of Mc-Carthyism.* New York: W. W. Norton, 1983.

Adams, John W. "Representation and Context in the Ethnographic Film." *Film Criticism* 4 (1979): 89–100.

Affron, Charles. "Reading the Fiction of Non-fiction: William Wyler's 'Memphis Belle.'" *Quarterly Review of Film Studies* 7 (1982): 53–59.

Aiken, Henry D., ed. *The Age of Ideology.* New York: Mentor, New American Library, 1956.

Allen, Jeanne. "Self-Reflexivity in Documentary." *Cine-Tracts* 1 (1977): 37–43.

Altheide, David. *Creating Reality: How TV News Distorts Events.* Beverly Hills, Calif.: Sage, 1976.

Altman, Rick. *The American Film Musical.* Bloomington: Indiana University Press, 1987.

Andrews, James R. *A Choice of Worlds: The Practice and Criticism of Public Discourse.* New York: Harper and Row, 1973.

Aristotle. *Poetics.* Translated by Ingram Bywater. New York: Modern Library, 1954.

Aristotle. *Rhetoric.* Translated by W. Rhys Roberts. New York: Modern Library, 1954.

Bantz, Charles R. "Television News: Reality and Research." *Western Speech Communication Journal* 39 (1975): 123–30.

Barnouw, Erik. *Documentary: A History of the Non-Fiction Film.* New York: Oxford University Press, 1982.

———. *The Image Empire: A History of Broadcasting in the United States from 1953.* New York: Oxford University Press, 1970.

———. *Tube of Plenty: The Evolution of American Television.* New York: Oxford University Press, 1975.

Barsam, Richard M. *Nonfiction Film: A Critical History.* New York: E. P. Dutton, 1973.

———. *Non-Fiction Film Theory and Criticism.* New York: E. P. Dutton, 1976.

Barthes, Roland. "The Photographic Message." In *Image-Music-Text,* translated by Stephen Heath. New York: Hill and Wang, 1978.

———. "The Rhetoric of the Image." In *Image-Music-Text,* translated by Stephen Heath. New York: Hill and Wang, 1978.

———. *S/Z.* Translated by Richard Miller. New York: Hill and Wang, 1974.

Baughman, James L. "'See It Now' and Television's Golden Age, 1951–1958." *Journal of Popular Culture* 15 (1981): 106–15.

———. "The Strange Birth of 'CBS Reports' Revisited." *Historical Journal of Film, Radio, and TV* 2 (1982): 27–38.

Bayley, Edwin R. *Joe McCarthy and the Press.* Madison: University of Wisconsin Press, 1981.

Bazin, André. "Ontology of the Photographic Image." In *What Is Cinema?* translated by Hugh Gray. 2 vols. Berkeley: University of California Press, 1967.

Behrens, Lawrence. "The Argument in Film: Applying Rhetorical Theory to Film Criticism." *Journal of University Film and Video Associations* 31 (1979): 3–11.

Belfrage, Cedric. *The American Inquisition, 1945–60*. Indianapolis, Ind.: Bobbs-Merrill, 1973.

Bell, Daniel. *The End of Ideology: On the Exhaustion of Political Ideas in the Fifties*. Rev. ed. New York: Free Press, 1962.

———, ed. *The Radical Right*. 2d ed. Garden City, N.Y.: Anchor-Doubleday, 1964.

Benson, Thomas. "'Joe': An Essay in the Rhetorical Criticism of Film." *Journal of Popular Culture* 8 (1974): 610–18.

———. "The Rhetorical Structure of Frederick Wiseman's 'High School.'" *Communication Monographs* 47 (1980): 233–61.

———. "The Rhetorical Structure of Frederick Wiseman's 'Primate.'" *Quarterly Journal of Speech* 71 (1985): 204–17.

———, ed. *Speech Communication in the Twentieth Century*. Carbondale: Southern Illinois University Press, 1985.

Benson, Thomas, and Carolyn Anderson. "The Cultural World of Frederick Wiseman's 'Model.'" *Journal of Film and Video* 36 (1984): 30–40.

———. *Reality Fictions: The Films of Frederick Wiseman*. Carbondale: Southern Illinois University Press, 1989.

———. "Standing on Ceremony: Believing as Seeing in Frederick Wiseman's 'Canal Zone.'" Public Address Division, Speech Communication Association Convention, Chicago, November 1986.

———. "The Ultimate Technology: Frederick Wiseman's 'Missile.'" In *Communication and the Culture of Technology*, edited by Martin J. Medhurst, R. Gonzalez, and T. R. Peterson. Pullman: Washington State University Press, 1990.

Berg, David M. "Rhetoric, Reality, and the Mass Media." *Quarterly Journal of Speech* 58 (1972): 255–63.

Berger, Carole. "Viewing as Action: Film and Reader Response Criticism." *Literature-Film Quarterly* 6 (1978): 144–51.

Bernstein, Matthew. "Visual Style and Spatial Articulations in 'Berlin, Symphony of a City.'" *Journal of Film and Video* 36 (1984): 5–12.

Bilksi, Theodore J., Jr. "A Descriptive Study: Edward R. Murrow's Contribution to Electronic Journalism." Ph.D. diss., Case Western Reserve University, 1971.

Bitzer, Lloyd, and Edwin Black, eds. *The Prospect of Rhetoric*. Englewood Cliffs, N.J.: Prentice-Hall, 1971.

Black, Edwin. "Ideological Justifications." *Quarterly Journal of Speech* 70 (1984): 144–50.

———. "A Note on Theory and Practice in Rhetorical Criticism." *Western Journal of Speech Communication* 44 (1980): 331–36.

———. "The Second Persona." *Quarterly Journal of Speech* 56 (1970): 109–19.

Bluem, A. William. *Documentary in American Television*. New York: Hastings House, 1965.

Blumenberg, Richard M. "Documentary Films and the Problem of Truth." *Journal of University Film and Video Associations* 29 (1977): 19–22.

Bohn, Thomas W., and Lawrence W. Lichty. "'The March of Time': News as Drama." *Journal of Popular Film* 2 (1973): 373–87.

Booth, Wayne C. *The Rhetoric of Fiction*. Chicago: University of Chicago Press, 1961.

―――. *A Rhetoric of Irony*. Chicago: University of Chicago Press, 1974.

Bordwell, David, and Kristin Thompson. *Film Art: An Introduction*. 2d ed. New York: Addison-Wesley, 1979.

Bormann, Ernest G. "Rhetorical Criticism and Significant Form: A Humanistic Approach." In *Form and Genre*, edited by Karlyn Kohrs Campbell and Kathleen Jamieson. Falls Church, Va.: Speech Communication Association, 1978.

Breen, Myles. "Rhetorical Criticism and the Media: The State of the Art." *Central States Speech Journal* 27 (1976): 15–21.

Brown, William R. "Will Rogers: Ironist as Persuader." *Communication Monographs* 34 (1972): 183–92.

Brunsdon, Charlotte, and David Morley. *Everyday Television: "Nationwide."* London: British Film Institute, 1978.

Bryant, Donald C. "Rhetoric: Its Functions and Scope." *Quarterly Journal of Speech* 39 (1953): 401–24.

Burke, Kenneth. *Counter-Statement*. 2d ed. Berkeley: University of California Press, 1968.

―――. *Grammar of Motives*. 2d ed. Berkeley: University of California Press, 1969.

―――. *Permanence and Change*. 3d ed. Berkeley: University of California Press, 1984.

―――. *The Philosophy of Literary Form*. 3d ed. Berkeley: University of California Press, 1973.

―――. *A Rhetoric of Motives*. 2d ed. Berkeley: University of California Press, 1969.

―――. *The Rhetoric of Religion*. Berkeley: University of California Press, 1970.

Campbell, Karlyn Kohrs, and Kathleen Jamieson, eds. *Form and Genre: Shaping Rhetorical Action*. Falls Church, Va.: Speech Communication Association, 1978.

Carroll, Raymond L. "Factual Television in America: An Analysis of Network Television Documentary Programs, 1948–1975." Ph.D. diss., University of Wisconsin—Madison, 1978.

Cater, Douglass, and Richard Adler, eds. *Television as a Social Force: New Approaches to TV Criticism*. New York: Praeger, 1975.

Caughie, John. "Progressive Television and Documentary Drama." In *Popular Television and Film*, edited by Tony Bennett, Susan Boyd-Bowman, Colin Mercer, and Janet Woollacott. London: British Film Institute, 1981.

Caute, David. *The Great Fear: The Anti-Communist Purge Under Truman and Eisenhower*. New York: Simon and Schuster, 1978.

Chapel, Gage William. "Television Criticism: A Rhetorical Perspective." *Western Journal of Speech Communications* 39 (1975): 81–91.

Cicero, Marcus Tullius. *De Inventione.* Translated by H. M. Hubbell. Loeb Classical Library. Cambridge, Mass.: Harvard University Press, 1976.

————. *De Oratore.* Translated by E. W. Sutton and H. Rackham. Loeb Classical Library. Cambridge, Mass.: Harvard University Press, 1979.

Cohn, Roy L. *McCarthy.* New York: New American Library, 1968.

Collins, Richard. "Seeing Is Believing." In *Documentary and Mass Media,* edited by John Corner. Baltimore, Md.: Edward Arnold, 1986.

Conacher, Donald J. "Some Dramatic Uses of the Chorus in Greek Tragedy." *University of Toronto Quarterly* 44 (1975): 81–95.

Cook, Fred J. *Nightmare Decade: The Life and Times of Senator Joe McCarthy.* New York: Random House, 1971.

Corner, John, ed. *Documentary and the Mass Media.* Baltimore, Md.: Edward Arnold, 1986.

Crick, Bernard. *In Defence of Politics.* 2d ed. Chicago: University of Chicago Press, 1972.

Culbert, David H. *News for Everyman: Radio and Foreign Affairs in Thirties America.* Westport, Conn.: Greenwood Press, 1976.

————. "'Why We Fight': Social Engineering for a Democratic Society at War." In *Film and Radio Propaganda in World War II,* edited by K. R. M. Short. London: Croom Helm, 1983.

Davis, Leslie K. "Controversy and the Network Documentary." *Communication Quarterly* 26 (1978): 45–52.

De Fleur, Melvin L., and Sandra Ball-Rokeach. *Theories of Mass Communication.* 4th ed. New York: Longman, 1982.

Eagleton, Terry. *Literary Theory: An Introduction.* Minneapolis: University of Minnesota Press, 1983.

Eisenstein, Sergei. "Montage of Attractions: An Essay." Translated by Jay Leyda. In *The Film Sense.* New York: Harcourt, 1975.

Epstein, Edward Jay. "The Selection of Reality." *New Yorker,* 3 March 1973, pp. 41ff.

Fish, Stanley E. "Literature in the Reader: Affective Stylistics." *New Literary History* 2 (1970): 123–62.

Fisher, Walter R. "Genre: Concepts and Applications in Rhetorical Criticism." *Western Journal of Speech Communication* 44 (1980): 288–99.

Fiske, John. *Television Culture.* New York: Methuen, 1987.

Flannery, Gerald V. "Documentary as Essay." *Southern Speech Communication Journal* 34 (1968): 146–53.

Freed, Fred. "The Rise and Fall of the Television Documentary." *Television Quarterly* 10 (1972): 57–68.

Fried, Richard. *Men Against McCarthy.* New York: Columbia University Press, 1976.

Friendly, Fred W. *Due to Circumstances Beyond Our Control . . .* New York: Random House, 1967.

Garnham, Nicholas. "TV Documentary and Ideology." *Screen* 13 (1972): 109–15.

Gates, Gary P. *Air Time: The Inside Story of CBS News.* New York: Harper and Row, 1978.

Geertz, Clifford. "Ideology as a Cultural System." In *The Interpretation of Cultures*. New York: Harper, 1973.

Gibson, William. "Authors, Speakers, Readers, and Mock Readers." In *Reader-Response Criticism: From Formalism to Post-Structuralism*, edited by Jane P. Tompkins. Baltimore, Md.: Johns Hopkins University Press, 1980.

Gitlin, Todd. "Prime Time Ideology: The Hegemonic Process in Television Entertainment." *Social Problems* 26 (1979): 251–66.

———. "Spotlights and Shadows: Television and the Culture of Politics." *College English* 38 (1977): 789–801.

———. *The Whole World Is Watching*. Berkeley: University of California Press, 1980.

Goffman, Erving. *Frame Analysis*. New York: Harper and Row, 1974.

Goldman, Eric F. *The Crucial Decade: America, 1945–1955*. New York: Alfred Knopf, 1956.

Goldston, Robert C. *The American Nightmare: Senator Joseph R. McCarthy and the Politics of Hate*. Indianapolis, Ind.: Bobbs-Merrill, 1973.

Gombrich, Ernst H. *Art and Illusion*. New York: Pantheon Books, 1960.

Gregg, Richard B. "The Criticism of Symbolic Inducement: A Critical-Theoretical Connection." In *Speech Communication in the Twentieth Century*, edited by Thomas Benson. Carbondale: Southern Illinois University Press, 1985.

———. "Rhetoric of Political Newscasting." *Central States Speech Journal* 28 (1977): 221–37.

Grierson, John. *Grierson on Documentary*. Edited by Forsyth Hardy. New York: Praeger, 1966.

Griffith, Robert. *The Politics of Fear: Joseph R. McCarthy and the Senate*. Lexington: University of Kentucky Press, 1970.

Gronbeck, Bruce. "Celluloid Rhetoric: On Genres of Documentary." In *Form and Genre*, edited by Karlyn Kohrs Campbell and Kathleen Jamieson. Falls Church, Va.: Speech Communication Association, 1978.

Hackett, Robert A. "Decline of a Paradigm? Bias and Objectivity in News Media Studies." *Critical Studies in Mass Communication* 1 (1984): 229–59.

Haiman, Franklin S. *Freedom of Speech: Issues and Cases*. New York: Random House, 1967.

Hall, Stuart. "Culture, Media, and the Ideological Effect." In *Mass Communication and Society*, edited by Michael Curran et al. Beverly Hills, Calif.: Sage, 1977.

———. "The Determination of News Photographs." In *The Manufacture of News*, edited by Stanley Cohen and Jock Young. Beverly Hills, Calif.: Sage, 1973.

———. "Encoding and Decoding in the Television Discourse." In *Culture, Media, Language*, edited by S. Hall, D. Hobson, A. Lowe, and P. Willis. London: Hutchinson, 1980.

———. "Introduction to Media Studies at the Center." In *Culture, Media, Language*, edited by S. Hall, D. Hobson, A. Lowe, and P. Willis. London: Hutchinson, 1980.

———. "The Rediscovery of 'Ideology': The Return of the Repressed in Media Studies." In *Culture, Society, and the Media*, edited by Michael Gurevitch et al. London: Methuen, 1982.

———. "Signification, Representation, Ideology: Althusser and the Post-Structuralist Debates." *Critical Studies in Mass Communication* 2 (1985): 91–114.

Hall, Stuart, Ian Connell, and Lidia Curti. "The 'Unity' of Current Affairs Television." In *Popular Television and Film*, edited by Tony Bennett. London: British Film Institute, 1981.

Hammond, Charles M., Jr. *The Image Decade: Television Documentary, 1965–1975*. New York: Hastings House, 1981.

Harrell, Jackson, and Wil A. Linkugel. "On Rhetorical Genre: An Organizing Principle." *Philosophy and Rhetoric* 11 (1978): 262–81.

Harrington, John. *The Rhetoric of Film*. New York: Holt, Rinehart and Winston, 1973.

Head, Sydney W., and Christopher H. Sterling. *Broadcasting in America*. 4th ed. Boston: Houghton Mifflin, 1982.

Hendrix, Jerry, and James Wood. "The Rhetoric of Film: Toward a Critical Methodology." *Southern Speech Communication Journal* 39 (1973): 105–22.

Himmelstein, Hal. *Television Myth and the American Mind*. New York: Praeger, 1984.

Hirsch, E. D. *Validity in Interpretation*. New Haven: Yale University Press, 1967.

Hofstadter, Richard. "The Pseudo-Conservative Revolt." In *The Radical Right*, edited by Daniel Bell. Garden City, N.Y.: Anchor-Doubleday, 1964.

Iser, Wolfgang. *The Implied Reader: Patterns of Communication in Prose Fiction*. Baltimore, Md.: Johns Hopkins University Press, 1974.

———. "The Reading Process: A Phenomenological Approach." In *Reader-Response Criticism: From Formalism to Post-Structuralism*, edited by Jane P. Tompkins. Baltimore, Md.: Johns Hopkins University Press, 1980.

Ivie, Robert L. "Diffusing Cold War Demagoguery: Murrow Versus McCarthy on 'See It Now.'" In *Cold War Rhetoric*, edited by Martin Medhurst, Robert L. Ivie, Philip Wander, and Robert L. Scott. Westport, Conn.: Greenwood Press, 1990.

Jameson, Fredric. *The Political Unconscious: Narrative as a Socially Symbolic Act*. Ithaca, N.Y.: Cornell University Press, 1981.

Jamieson, Kathleen H. "Antecedent Genre as Rhetorical Constraint." *Quarterly Journal of Speech* 61 (1975): 406–15.

———. "Generic Constraints and the Rhetorical Situation." *Philosophy and Rhetoric* 6 (1973): 162–70.

Jamieson, Kathleen Hall, and Karlyn Kohrs Campbell. "Rhetorical Hybrids: Fusions of Generic Elements." *Quarterly Journal of Speech* 68 (1982): 146–57.

Kahn, Frank J. *Documents of American Broadcasting*. New York: Appleton-Century-Crofts, 1968.

Kaplan, E. Ann. "Theory and Practice of the Realist Documentary Form in 'Harlan County, U.S.A.'" In *"Show Us Life": Toward a History and Aes-*

*thetics of the Committed Documentary,* edited by Thomas Waugh. Metuchen, N.J.: Scarecrow Press, 1984.

———, ed. *Regarding Television: Critical Approaches—An Anthology.* Frederick, Md.: American Film Institute, University Publications of America, 1983.

Kauffman, Charles. "Poetic as Argument." *Quarterly Journal of Speech* 67 (1981): 407–15.

———. "The Reflexive Form in Rhetoric." In *Rhetoric 78: Proceedings of Theory of Rhetoric: An Interdisciplinary Conference,* edited by Robert L. Brown, Jr., and Martin Steinmann, Jr. Minneapolis: University of Minnesota, Center for Advanced Studies, 1979.

Keeley, Joseph. *The Left-Leaning Antenna: Political Bias in Television.* New Rochelle, N.Y.: Arlington House, 1971.

Kendrick, Alexander. *Prime Time: The Life of Edward R. Murrow.* Boston: Little, Brown, 1969.

Kirkwood, William G. "Story-Telling and Self-Confrontation: Parables as Communication Strategies." *Quarterly Journal of Speech* 69 (1983): 58–74.

Kitto, H. D. F. *Greek Tragedy: A Literary Study.* London: Methuen, 1939.

Kozloff, Sarah. "Humanizing the Voice of God: Narration in 'The Naked City.'" *Cinema Journal* 23 (1984): 41–53.

Krieger, Murray. "Mediation, Language, and Vision in the Reading of Literature." In *Interpretation: Theory and Practice,* edited by C. S. Singleton. Baltimore, Md.: Johns Hopkins University Press, 1969.

Kuhn, Annette. "The Camera I." *Screen* 19, 2 (1978): 71–83.

Lang, Kurt, and Gladys Engel Lang. *Politics and Television.* Chicago: Quadrangle Books, 1968.

Lanham, Richard. *A Handlist of Rhetorical Terms.* Berkeley: University of California Press, 1968.

Larson, Charles U. "Media Metaphors: Two Models for Rhetorically Criticizing the Political Television Spot Advertisement." *Central States Speech Journal* 33 (1982): 533–46.

Leab, Daniel J. "'See It Now': A Legend Reassessed." In *American History/American Television,* edited by John E. O'Connor. New York: Frederick Ungar, 1983.

Leff, Michael C. "Interpretation and the Art of the Rhetorical Critic." *Western Journal of Speech Communication* 44 (1980): 337–49.

———. "Textual Criticism: The Legacy of G. P. Mohrmann." *Quarterly Journal of Speech* 72 (1986): 377–89.

Linkugel, Wil A., and Susan S. Huxman. "Political Fallout of the New Deal: Accusations and Apologies from a General, a Senator, and a Priest." Paper presented at the Speech Communication Association Conference, Chicago, November 1986.

Linton, James M. "The Moral Dimension in Documentary." *Journal of University Film and Video Associations* 28 (1976): 17–22.

Lipset, Seymour Martin. "Three Decades of the Radical Right." In *The Radical Right,* edited by Daniel Bell. Garden City, N.Y.: Anchor-Doubleday, 1964.

Longinus. *On the Sublime.* Translated by W. Hamilton Frye. Loeb Classical Library. Cambridge, Mass.: Harvard University Press, 1932.

Lucas, Stephen. "The Renaissance of American Public Address: Text and Context in Rhetorical Criticism." *Quarterly Journal of Speech* 74 (1988): 243–62.

Lukacs, Georg. "Art and Objective Truth." In *Writer and Critic,* translated by A. Kahn. New York: Grosset and Dunlap, 1970.

———. "Narrate or Describe?" In *Writer and Critic,* translated by A. Kahn. New York: Grosset and Dunlap, 1970.

Matusow, Allen J., ed. *Joseph R. McCarthy.* Englewood Cliffs, N.J.: Prentice-Hall, 1970.

Medhurst, Martin J., and Thomas Benson. "'The City': The Rhetoric of Rhythm." *Communication Monographs* 48 (1981): 54–72.

———, eds. *Rhetorical Dimensions in Media.* Dubuque, Iowa: Kendall-Hunt, 1984.

Merritt, Russell. "The Bashful Hero in American Film of the Nineteen Forties." *Quarterly Journal of Speech* 61 (1975): 129–39.

Merron, Jeff. "Edward R. Murrow's Contributions to Television Journalism, 1951–55: A Study of 'See It Now' and 'Person to Person.'" Department of Journalism and Mass Communications, University of Wisconsin—Madison, 1985. Photocopy.

Metz, Robert. *CBS: Reflections in a Bloodshot Eye.* Chicago: Playboy Press, 1975.

Mohrmann, G. P. "Elegy in a Critical Graveyard." *Western Journal of Speech Communication* 44 (1980): 265–74.

Morley, David, and Roger Silverstone. "Domestic Communication—Technologies and Meanings." *Media, Culture, and Society* 12 (1990): 31–55.

Murray, Michael D. "The Persuasive Dimensions of See It Now's 'Report on Senator Joseph R. McCarthy.'" *Today's Speech* 22 (1975): 13–20.

———. "'See It Now' Versus McCarthyism: Dimensions of Documentary Persuasion." Ph.D. diss., University of Missouri—Columbia, 1974.

———. "Television's Desperate Moment: A Conversation with Fred Friendly." *Journalism History* 1 (1974): 68–71.

———. "To Hire a Hall: 'An Argument in Indianapolis.'" *Central States Speech Journal* 26 (1975): 12–20.

Murrow, Edward R., rptr. *Person to Person.* Prods. John A. Aaron and Jesse Zousmer. CBS. 12 March 1954. Museum of Broadcasting, New York, General Collection. T77:0 333. VHS videocassette. 30 min.

Murrow, Edward R., and Fred W. Friendly. *'See It Now': A Selection in Text and Pictures.* New York: Simon and Schuster, 1955.

Neale, Stephen. *Genre.* London: British Film Institute, 1980.

Newcomb, Horace M. "American Television Criticism, 1970–1985." *Critical Studies in Mass Communication* 3 (1986): 217–28.

Nichols, Bill. "Documentary Theory and Practice." *Screen* 17, 4 (1976–77): 34–48.

———. *Ideology and the Image.* Bloomington: Indiana University Press, 1981.

———. "Questions of Magnitude." In *Documentary and the Mass Media,* edited by John Corner. Baltimore, Md.: Edward Arnold, 1986.

———. *Representing Reality: Issues and Concepts in Documentary.* Bloomington: Indiana University Press, 1991.

———. "The Voice of Documentary." In *Movies and Methods II.* Berkeley: University of California Press, 1985.

Novak, James. "Television Shapes the Soul." In *Television: The Critical View,* edited by Horace Newcomb. 3d ed. New York: Oxford University Press, 1982.

O'Connor, John E., ed. *American History/American Television: Interpreting the Video Past.* New York: Frederick Ungar, 1983.

———. "Edward R. Murrow's 'Report on Senator McCarthy': Image as Artifact." *Film and History* 16 (1986): 55–72.

Ong, Walter J., S.J. "The Writer's Audience Is Always a Fiction." *PMLA* 90 (1975): 9–21.

Osborn, Michael M. "Archetypal Metaphor in Rhetoric: The Light-Dark Family." *Quarterly Journal of Speech* 53 (1967): 115–26.

———. "Rhetorical Depiction." In *Form, Genre, and the Study of Political Discourse,* edited by Herbert W. Simons and Aram A. Aghazarian. Columbia: University of South Carolina Press, 1987.

Oshinsky, David. *A Conspiracy So Immense: The World of Joe McCarthy.* New York: Free Press, 1983.

Parsons, Talcott. "Social Strains in America (1955)." In *The Radical Right,* edited by Daniel Bell. Garden City, N.Y.: Anchor-Doubleday, 1964.

Perelman, Chaim, and L. Olbrechts-Tyteca. *The New Rhetoric.* Translated by John Wilkinson. Notre Dame, Ind.: University of Notre Dame Press, 1969.

Polsby, Nathan. "Towards an Explanation of McCarthyism." *Political Studies* 8 (1960): 250–71.

Primeau, Ronald. *The Rhetoric of Television.* New York: Longman, 1979.

Quinn, Arthur. *Figures of Speech.* Salt Lake City, Utah: Gibbs Smith, 1982.

Quintilian. *Institutio Oratoria.* Translated by H. E. Butler. 2 vols. Loeb Classical Library. Cambridge, Mass.: Harvard University Press, 1958.

Rabinowitz, Peter J. *Before Reading: Narrative Conventions and the Politics of Interpretation.* Ithaca, N.Y.: Cornell University Press, 1987.

Reeves, Thomas. *The Life and Times of Joe McCarthy: A Biography.* New York: Stein and Day, 1982.

Reynolds, O. T. "Reporter as Orator: Edward R. Murrow." *American Public Address.* Edited by Loren Reid. Columbia: University of Missouri Press, 1961.

Robinson, Michael J. "American Political Legitimacy in an Era of Electronic Journalism: Reflections on the Evening News." In *Television as a Social Force,* edited by Douglass Cater and Richard Adler. New York: Praeger, 1975.

Rogers, Jimmie, and Theodore Clevenger, Jr. "'The Selling of the Pentagon': Was CBS the Fulbright Propaganda Machine?" *Quarterly Journal of Speech* 57 (1971): 266–73.

Rogin, Michael Paul. *The Intellectuals and McCarthy: The Radical Specter.* Cambridge: Massachusetts Institute of Technology Press, 1967.

Rosenfield, Lawrence W. "The Experience of Criticism." *Quarterly Journal of Speech* 60 (1974): 489–96.

Rovere, Richard H. *Senator Joe McCarthy.* New York: Harcourt, 1959.

Rudner, Laurence. "Born to a New Craft: Edward R. Murrow, 1938–1940." *Journal of Popular Culture* 15 (1981): 106–15.

Rueckert, William H. *Kenneth Burke and the Drama of Human Relations.* 2d ed. Berkeley: University of California Press, 1982.

Ryan, Halford R. "Baldwin Versus Edward VIII: A Case Study in Kategoria and Apologia." *Southern Speech Communication Journal* 49 (1984): 125–34.

————. "Kategoria and Apologia: On Their Rhetorical Criticism as a Speech Set." *Quarterly Journal of Speech* 68 (1982): 254–61.

Sartre, Jean-Paul. "For Whom Does One Write?" In *What Is Literature?* translated by Bernard Frechtman. 1949. Reprint. New York: Harper and Row, 1965.

Schudson, Michael. *Discovering the News.* New York: Basic Books, 1978.

Seldes, Gilbert. "Murrow, McCarthy, and the Empty [Fairness] Formula: Giving Equal Time for Reply." *Saturday Review of Literature,* 24 April 1954, pp. 26–27.

————. *The Public Arts.* New York: Simon and Schuster, 1956.

Silverstone, Roger. *The Message of Television: Myth and Narrative in Contemporary Culture.* London: Heinemann, 1981.

————. "The Right to Speak: On a Poetic for Television Documentary." *Media, Culture, and Society* 5 (1983): 137–54.

Sloan, Thomas O., et al. "The Report of the Committee on the Advancement and Refinement of Rhetorical Criticism." In *The Prospect of Rhetoric,* edited by Lloyd Bitzer and Edwin Black. Englewood Cliffs, N.J.: Prentice-Hall, 1971.

Smith, A. C. H. *Paper Voices: The Popular Press and Social Change, 1935–65.* Totowa, N.J.: Rowman and Littlefield, 1975.

Smith, Craig R. "Television News as Rhetoric." *Western Journal of Speech Communication* 41 (1977): 147–59.

Sperber, A. M. *Murrow: His Life and Times.* New York: Freundlich Books, 1986.

Sterling, Christopher H., and John M. Kitross. *Stay Tuned: A Concise History of American Broadcasting.* 2d ed. Belmont, Calif.: Wadsworth, 1990.

Stewart, Charles, G. P. Mohrmann, and Donovan Ochs, eds. *Explorations in Rhetorical Criticism.* University Park: Pennsylvania State University Press, 1973.

Stott, William. *Documentary Expression and Thirties America.* New York: Oxford University Press, 1973.

Suleiman, Susan. "Ideological Dissent from Works of Fiction: Toward a Rhetoric of the 'Roman à Thèse.'" *Neophilologus* 60 (1976): 162–77.

Swann, Paul. *The British Documentary Film Movement, 1926–1946.* Cambridge: Cambridge University Press, 1989.

Tompkins, Jane P., ed. *Reader-Response Criticism: From Formalism to Post-Structuralism.* Baltimore, Md.: Johns Hopkins University Press, 1980.

Tompkins, Philip K. "In Cold Fact." *Esquire,* June 1966, pp. 125ff.

———. "Rhetorical Criticism of Non-Oratorical Works." *Quarterly Journal of Speech* 60 (1969): 432–39.

Tuchman, Gaye. *Making News: A Study of the Construction of Reality.* New York: Free Press, 1978.

———. "Objectivity as Strategic Ritual: An Examination of Newsmen's Notions of Objectivity." *American Journal of Sociology* 77 (1972): 660–79.

Vaughan, Dai. "The Space Between Shots." *Screen* 15, 1 (1974): 78–83.

———. *Television Documentary Usage.* London: British Film Institute, 1976.

Viereck, Peter. "The Revolt Against the Elite." In *The Radical Right*, edited by Daniel Bell. Garden City, N.Y.: Anchor-Doubleday, 1964.

Waugh, Thomas, ed. *"Show Us Life": Toward a History and Aesthetics of the Committed Documentary.* Metuchen, N.J.: Scarecrow Press, 1984.

Weaver, Paul H. "Newspaper News and Television News." In *Television as a Social Force*, edited by Douglass Cater and Richard Adler. New York: Praeger, 1975.

Weiner, Albert. "The Function of the Tragic Greek Chorus." *Theatre Journal* 32 (1980): 205–12.

Wershba, Joseph. "Murrow Versus McCarthy: 'See It Now.'" *New York Times Magazine*, 4 March 1979, pp. 31–38.

Wolfe, Charles. "Modes of Discourse in Thirties Social Documentary: The Shifting 'I' of Native Land." *Journal of Film and Video* 36 (1984): 13–20.

Wolff, Robert P. *The Poverty of Liberalism.* Boston: Beacon Press, 1968.

Wood, James A. "An Application of Rhetorical Theory to Filmic Persuasion." Ph.D. diss., Cornell University, 1967.

Worth, Sol. *Studying Visual Communication.* Philadelphia: University of Pennsylvania Press, 1981.

Wylie, Max. *Clear Channels: Television and the American People.* New York: Funk and Wagnalls, 1955.

Yaeger, Murray R. "An Analysis of Edward R. Murrow's 'See It Now' Television Program." Ph.D. diss., University of Iowa, 1956.

———. "The Evolution of 'See It Now.'" *Journal of Broadcasting* 1 (1957): 337–44.

# Index

Affron, Charles, 171
Altman, Rick, 46
"Annie Lee Moss Before the McCarthy
Committee," 3, 23; planning for, 142;
objectivity of, 143; reactions to, 143,
162; visual stylistics of, 143, 159, 161;
documentary address in, 144–45;
argument in, 146; production of, 146–
50; depiction in, 156–57, 158; and
due process of law, 159; effects of,
163, 167; and news, 164; intertextuality in, 164–73; and access to
reality, 164–67, 173; and conventional
plotline, 167–71, 173–74; rhetorical
action in, 167; as proletarian documentary, 167–68; relation to fictional
discourse, 169–71; and context of
preceding telecasts, 171–72, 173;
genre exploitation, 178
"Argument in Indianapolis, An," 3, 23;
neutrality of, 85–86, 100, 215
(nn. 32, 33); production of, 86–87, 213
(n. 11); as reflexive text, 89–90, 195–
96; theme of controversy and conformity in, 90–91, 95, 101, 109, 186;
depiction of groups in, 92–95, 97–
100, 107, 178; "debate" section, 95–
97; visual stylistics of, 97–99,

104–06; 107, response to, 101–03;
ethos and image in, 103–04; dramatic
conflict in, 107–08; as microcosm of
McCarthyism movement, 108–09; as
defense of television medium, 109;
American ideology in, 109–10; as
anti-McCarthyism, 110; as part of
campaign against McCarthyism, 172
Audience, 35; active, 38–39, 42; ideal,
40–41, 42, 58, 69, 77, 80, 93–94, 137,
165, 171, 185, 187; and rhetoric, 41;
position in the text, 49. *See also*,
Subjectivity

Barnouw, Erik, 23, 112, 181
Barthes, Roland, 43, 105–06, 146, 167,
192
Baughman, James, 181
Bayley, Edwin, 16, 19, 183
Benson, Thomas W., 36–37, 40; and
social dimensions of criticism, 206
(n. 10)
Bias. *See* Objectivity
Black, Edwin, 40–41, 139
Bluem, A. William, 30–32, 112–13, 168
Booth, Wayne, 127, 137
Bordwell, David, 45
Burke, Kenneth, 78, 81, 133, 139

Capra, Frank, 28
"Case of Milo Radulovich, The," 2, 23, 55–82; and guilt by association, 56; as symbolic of McCarthyism abuses, 56; production of, 59–61; particular or universal, 56, 78; links to public realm, 62, 72–73; as everyman, 63–66; visual stylistics of, 66–70; chorus of citizens in, 66–70, 75, 81; modeling of audience, 68–70; "end-piece" of, 73–74; response to, 75–77; as editorial, 76; as turning point for television documentary, 76; bias of, 76; as portraying common man, 79; as ideological argument, 79, 81; "bashful hero" in, 79, 194; enactment in, 133; as part of campaign against McCarthyism, 172
Caughie, John, 191
Chambers, Whittaker, 13
Cluster analysis, 106, 216 (n. 51)
Cohn, Roy, 130, 141, 147–49, 222 (n. 6)
Columbia Broadcasting System (CBS): reaction to blacklist, 16; and "Radulovich" program, 60, 76, 211 (n. 43); and "McCarthy" program, 117, 218 (n. 26); reaction to "Moss" program, 163
Common man, 66, 68; as theme, 79, 168; myth, 168
Commonsense, 185
Communism: as enemy, 12; domestic, 12–13; foreign, 13
Crosby, John, 134, 163

Depiction, 43, 57, 81–82, 86, 93, 103–07; defined, 43; and demonstration, 103; as persuasion, 103–05; and character, 104; as argument, 178. See also "Argument in Indianapolis"
Documentary: as argument, 6, 26, 32, 33, 46, 136; as constructed, 6, 26, 81; and television, 7, 30–33; and politics, 24; defined, 25–26; history of, 25–29; two meanings of, 26, 29, 30; bifurcation of form, 30, 82, 223 (n. 17); and typical subject matter, 31; expectations of objectivity in, 31, 118–19, 120, 137; and verbal emphasis, 32; paradox in, 32–33; as evidence, 33, 46, 81, 105, 135, 177, 178, 179; as open text, 39; history in, 81–82; ideology in, 81–82; as deno-

tative or connotative, 105–07; epistemological form of, 110; formal expectations of, 120, 137; as confrontational, 136; as ironic, 140–41; address in, 144–45, 150, 165–66; argument in indirect address, 145–46, 173; conventions of referentiality, 164–67, 191; related to fiction film, 169–71; as blending of discursive forms, 177, 190, 194–96; as ideological in form, 186; expectations of form, 191; and history, 191–92; aesthetics, 193–96; as fiction, 193–96; visual stylistics, 195; and ideology, 196–98; as master rhetorical form, 199
Documentary idea, 29, 33, 190
Doerfer, John C., 17

Eisenhower, Dwight D., 98, 111, 115, 121, 123, 128, 150, 161; administration, 13, 17, 59; and Federal Communications Commission, 17; and Army (McCarthy), 148–49
Eisenstein, Sergei, 159
Enactment, 93–94, 220 (n. 55). See also "Case of Milo Radulovich"
Equal time provision, 17, 18, 19
Ethos, 103; and depiction, 103–04, 210 (n. 29)

Federal Communications Commission, 17
Film style, 97–98
Form, 47, 179–80; synthesis of dramatic and discursive, 179; as ideology, 197
Freed, Fred, 21
Freedom of speech, 19, 182, 185, 188–89
Friendly, Fred W.: inspiration for See It Now, 20; and founding of documentary television, 21, 30; and Hear It Now, 29; enters debate over McCarthyism, 59; and "Radulovich" broadcast, planning of, 59–61; and reaction to "Radulovich" broadcast, 75–76, 77; as target of McCarthyites, 76; and planning of "Argument" broadcast, 86–87; and reaction to "Argument" broadcast, 101; called "eyes of conscience," 102; and planning of "McCarthy" broadcast, 111, 116–67; and reaction to "McCarthy" broadcast, 135; and

and defense of television, 109–10, 151; and ideology of pluralism, 139; rhetorical action in, 180; effects on McCarthyism, 180–84, 188; on making television important, 181; effects on medium of television, 181–82; effects on industry, 182; effects on news reporting, 183; effects on genre, 183; effects on audience, 183–84; ideological motifs in, 184; common man theme in, 184; as McCarthyism, 184–87; and role of television in society, 185; ideological struggle within, 185; pluralism, celebration of, 185; as developing "unity," 186–87; ideological response to ideological effect of, 187–88, 197; as hegemonic, 188; and controversy, 204 (n. 34); and other programs on McCarthyism, 226 (n. 89)

Seldes, Gilbert, 113, 143
Semiotics, 44, 81–82
Silverstone, Roger, 34–35, 175
Social knowledge, 44, 120, 185, 187. *See also* Commonsense
Social truth, 5, 35, 105
Split reference, of documentary discourse, 193–95, 229 (n. 42)
Stevens, Robert T., 115, 121, 128, 146, 149
Stevenson, Adlai, 18, 115, 130, 141, 148
Stott, William, 27, 30, 168
Subjectivity, 153, 167, 183, 198. *See also* Audience

Symington, Stuart, 155–57, 160
Synecdoche, 57, 77–81, 109, 179, 184; defined, 78; rhetorical functions of, 78–81; as describing documentary rhetoric, 82

Talbott, Harold, 74, 83, 88, 101
Television industry: blacklisting, 15–16; investigations of industry, 17; and control over, 19; and advertisers, 19; response to McCarthy, 114–26
Textual criticism, 38, 42. *See also* Rhetorical analysis
Truman, Harry S., 13, 14, 58, 59, 98, 111; administration, 13
Tuchman, Gaye, 120–22

Vaughan, Dai, 177
Verisimilitude, 165, 169
Voice of America, 18, 23, 130

Wershba, Joe, 60, 70, 72, 84, 87, 89, 94, 116, 150
White, Harry Dexter, 13, 216 (n. 59)
*Why We Fight* series, 28
Wood, James A., 57
Worth, Sol, 197

Yaeger, Murray, 85

Zwicker, Ralph, 115, 126, 148

# About the Series

STUDIES IN RHETORIC AND COMMUNICATION
*General Editors:*
E. Culpepper Clark, Raymie E. McKerrow, and David Zarefsky

The University of Alabama Press has established this series to publish major new works in the general area of rhetoric and communication, including books treating the symbolic manifestations of political discourse, argument as social knowledge, the impact of machine technology on patterns of communication behavior, and other topics related to the nature or impact of symbolic communication. We actively solicit studies involving historical, critical, or theoretical analyses of human discourse.

# About the Author

Thomas Rosteck is Assistant Professor in the Department of Communication, the University of Arkansas, Fayetteville. He received his bachelor's degree from Washington University, St. Louis, his master's from Brown University, Providence, and his doctorate from the University of Wisconsin, Madison. He has received several awards for papers and essays including the Aubrey Fisher Article Award of the *Western Journal of Speech Communication* and, from the Speech Communication Association, the Donald C. Eckroyd Emerging Scholar Award and the Debut Paper Award.